A Flight Through Life

An Aviator's Memoir

A Flight Through Life

An Aviator's Memoir

Albert J. DeGroote

Dedication

To all the fighter pilots who ushered in the jet age and laid it all on the line through the cold war and various shooting wars like Korea, Vietnam and the Gulf. The guys on the ground didn't have to worry very much about being attacked from above because you owned the skies.

To Marion and "the boys" who encouraged me to do this – especially Dave who worked tirelessly on the fringes.

Churchill said: "Writing a book is an adventure. To begin with it is a toy and an amusement. Then it becomes a mistress, then it becomes a master, then it becomes a tyrant. The last phase is that just as you are about to be reconciled to your servitude, you kill the monster and fling him to the public."

Dave kept me from killing the monster prematurely.

AJD

Contents

A Flight Through Life

This is an autobiography. I never thought I would write such a document and am wondering already whether I'll ever finish it. I've asked myself a number of questions about the project, beginning with the big one-why? Why should I spend the time and effort to do this? My first thought was that autobiographies are, in general, self conscious attempts to wish away one's past mistakes or, worse, pompous attempts at self-aggrandizement. I don't think I'll get involved in either of these traps because I know that at the end of the day my life just isn't very important and all the self-aggrandizement in the world won't wish away all the mistakes I've made over the years. So, that being said I can try, right at the start, to answer the question: Why?

I think the primary reason I've decided to do this is simple-- grandkids. My own kids might also factor into the decision but they're much closer to the story and might be bored. But I firmly believe that my grandkids, as they get older, will become more and more interested in the past, especially the family's past. I base this on my own life experience. As a young man I was thoroughly bored with family histories and thought that people who researched family trees qualified for their specialty by swinging from the vines attached to those trees. That's all changed now that I've reached, shall we call it, "The autumn of my years"?

I've decided that it would be fascinating to have some of the past exposed. My parents were born in France, and I know absolutely nothing about their ancestry. Did my grandparents and their grandparents fight in the many European wars, or did they live peaceful lives as peasants or tradesmen? Did someone from my family help to storm the Bastille or fight with Napoleon? I'll never know, and at this advanced age I feel that I've missed something of life.

Aviation and the US Air Force have made my life, probably, more diverse and maybe more interesting than it might have been had I chosen some other line of work. Also, since flying can fascinate, there might be some interest from people other than family.

Because aviation has been my life from early teen years until just recently, flying and airplanes will probably overwhelm the narrative. But I feel it might be worthwhile to pass on to future aviators or even some non-aviators my impressions as a pilot of the handling characteristics and idiosyncrasies of my generation's high-performance and a few low-performance aircraft. Hopefully, any reader who doesn't share my fascination, some would say obsession, with manned flight will bear with me and look for other tidbits of the past that hold some interest to the non-flyer. For starters, I've met a lot of interesting people in my flight through life. A few of them have heard my stories and said, "You should write a book". I'm sure they didn't mean it, but maybe this will serve as a warning to anyone tempted to use that phrase at cocktail parties. Somebody might actually do it!

I'll begin the tale with my immediate family to include a detailed introduction to my parents and siblings. They helped provide a framework for my own life and their influence will perhaps become obscured by events that were more central to my own path through life. I'll summarize immediate family ties at the outset and interject profiles of others as we go along.

So, autobiography, aviation adventure yarn, or both, off we go…..

The Family and Early Days

My family roots, while not completely atypical for the time, were a little different. My parents were born in France, later to become naturalized citizens through the familiar American process of enrollment by way of Ellis Island, New York. They were both born in the northern industrial town of Roubaix, France, were the same age, but did not know each other as children. They came to New York as children and learned to speak English with no trace of a French accent although they remained fluent in spoken French all their lives. They were typical hard-working people so common in those years among the immigrant population.

My mother was, as they say, a saint. My father was something else. More about that later. The kids were numerous. More about that later, too. On the subject of my mother, I find it difficult to be totally objective. She was one of the most courageous people I've ever known, having, to begin with, brought up five kids, single-handedly in the midst of the Great Depression. She was uneducated with some schooling in France, more in the U.S., but only at the grade school level and only long enough to be able to go to work in the textile mills and contribute to her family's income. Despite the lack of formal education she was smart, articulate and well-informed. In later years I would marvel at the skill with which she would compose a letter, knowing that spelling words in English required a mighty effort. And she was tough! I used to love to watch her bargain for the last penny's worth of vegetables from depression-weary grocery clerks. She never lost the battle. When I was ten or so I had a job delivering groceries from the corner delicatessen, but the job occupied my time only in the afternoon. To kill some time during the day I would often deliver Mom's lunch, with a cold or hot thermos, to the textile mill where she worked. I used to sit quietly while the half-dozen or so women ate lunch, told stories and discussed world affairs, no small thing since we were in the midst of World War II. Mom usually sat quietly, too until some outrageous statement was more than she could bear. She would then hold forth as long as needed but no farther. Conversation stopped and she had the group's undivided attention.

She was, in fact, the group's leader although she would laugh at being called "leader" of anything.

Nothing was easy in Mom's world. The calamity of World War II was actually a break from the multiple calamities that stretched from one end of her existence to the other because it meant full employment on the home front. She had many crosses to bear but the heaviest was life with an abusive, neglectful husband. Which brings me to a subject I would rather ignore but can not, in the interest of full disclosure, skip over. That subject is "The Old Man".

Even in my early octogenarian years I find it difficult not becoming furious at my father for his role in the loss of my childhood innocence. Seared into my memory is the image of my father, a six foot four brute of a man, beating my five foot two mother in full view of his terrified children. I must have been at most three or four years old, but the picture is still fresh. As an aside, it instilled in me a lifelong hatred of bullies of any ilk, whether of the abusive husband type, the schoolyard bully variety or the foreign dictator kind.

Physical violence was not the old man's only diabolical character trait. He thought nothing of abandoning his wife and five children at the height of the great depression with no financial support whatsoever. He would return home when it suited him, expecting to be welcomed like the prodigal son. We, his children, treated these homecomings with great trepidation, knowing full well that it was only a matter of time until his next eruption. He was a skilled craftsman and even constructed a fairly nice model railroad layout for my brother and me. But he did all of the work himself. We learned nothing. Later in life I built a model railroad layout for my kids, and I admit with some reluctance that my interest in the project was probably inspired by the old man's layout. The difference was that I encouraged the kids to work with me on the project. Even though it probably took twice as long that way, we had fun and the kids learned a few things about workmanship. As adults, they're all much better with their hands than I ever was, so maybe my training methodology did something for them if not for me.

I'll leave this subject, hopefully for the remainder of the narrative, because I find it highly distasteful, and besides, it could be the subject of another book about life with a borderline sociopath. However, I can't help but wonder what we five kids might have achieved if we had had a loving father teaching and supplying guidance. It will, probably, be impossible in later portions of the narrative to totally ignore the old man since his presence, or absence, had such a long-term effect on the central theme of family and on the individuals involved. I will make appropriate references as necessary, but reluctantly, and with luck he won't make another appearance at all.

I mentioned numerous kids earlier. Five is numerous when there's only one parent and only one income. The five DeGroote kids were all very different in looks, personality and passions. But there was always a common thread binding them together--the family, the thing that we all subliminally knew had to survive and be protected. In that regard, I think a thumbnail sketch of my siblings is very much in order.

First born was Irene, birth date 23 February, 1921. Irene, being 11 years older than I, was always an authority figure to me, more a second mother or live-in aunt than sister. Being the eldest, she caught the brunt of the old man's temper tantrums and deflected it from the other kids, especially me as the youngest. She bore the scars of that relationship throughout her life and played an unnatural role by trying to be tougher than he was. She maintained this façade, earning her the sobriquet from my brother, Bud, of "The Lion". She refused to attend the old man's funeral, but after his death she seemed to come to an agreement with life and reverted to the reserved, loving person that was the real Irene. She was married to Jack Gardiner, a small, quiet man who was the prototypical nice guy and one of the few people in the world who could have survived daily life with "The Lion". She had four wonderful children, Jackie, Mimi, Jimmie and Janice. As of this writing, Irene is the only DeGroote child to have passed on, and I think she died a happy woman, knowing that she was, next to Mom, the pillar of strength of the family, and knowing that she passed on to her own family the kind of love that had been denied to her by her father. "The Lion" was no more, replaced by a docile but contented kitten.

Doris was next. Born December 2, 1925, she was destined to become the "child-in-between". Whereas Irene was forced to grow up fast in order to help Mom survive the absence of a breadwinner father, Doris had to fight to be recognized as capable of helping. She was in a lonely position, with Irene the designated backup quarterback, and the three remaining kids, closer to each other in age, forming a sub-group that often left Doris isolated. Irene worked in close proximity to Mom, working, in fact, right next to her in a small "invisible mending" shop, a business Mom established to earn money to buy depression era food. "Invisible mending" is a lost art which was used to mend holes in the clothing of depression-era people who couldn't afford to replace the garment. The fabric was repaired, thread by thread in order to make the hole literally "invisible". Talk about labor-intensive work! In any case, Doris was excluded from learning that skill since there are only so many pants with holes in them in one neighborhood. Smart, ambitious, and determined to help the family survive, Doris quit school as soon as she was able and went to work as a cashier at the Baltimore Market, one of the new-fangled grocery outlets known as "supermarkets". In those days there were no optical readers of bar codes. New cashiers had to memorize the price of every item in the store! I used to sit on the bed with Doris and test her by picking random items for which she would have to recite the price to me immediately. I was amazed at the almost total absence of error and I wondered if I could do as well if I ever had to. Brother Bud and I worked briefly at the "Baltimore" delivering grocery orders to customers in our little red wagon. We were not employed by the store and worked for tips only, but it gave me an opportunity to watch my big sister, the fastest of the cashiers, as she typed memorized prices into the then modern cash register, never looking at the keys. Doris married Bob Nober a returning veteran from the war. Bob was another nice guy, a butcher by trade, who reminded me of the lead character in the movie "Marty". Ernest Borgnine played Marty, "a very good butcher". Unfortunately, Bob and Doris had vastly different ideas about lifestyles and the marriage failed after producing two children, Bob Jr. and Ronnie. Fate would later bring Bob Jr. and me together in, of all things, combat. More about that later. Doris later married Tony Daniele, a talented, romantic Italian and the love of her life.

Next was Dolores. Born August 2, 1928, Dolores was the golden girl. With beautiful blond hair and a peaches-and -cream complexion, Dolores was not just pretty, she was a knockout. During my teen years, working at the corner delicatessen I found myself constantly in demand by other teen-aged males who thought they could get an inside track on a date with Dolores by working through her little brother. None of their forlorn attempts ever worked out. Dolores was anything but the prototypical dumb blond. In fact, she was smart, very smart. The most coveted award out of the Edmunds Grammar School was the American Legion Award, given for academic excellence, leadership and other achievements. Dolores won the award hands down. Dolores became the first of the DeGroote kids to graduate from high school, but there was no money for college and girls in those days were expected to marry and produce kids, not go after degrees. Dolores worked for a Philadelphia business after high school, later married Tom Quinn, an ambitious, tough Irishman. She had four lovely children, Tommie, Ellen, Susan, and Jane, and has had a good life. But I can't help but wonder if her life would have been brighter with a college education financed by a doting father. Perhaps not-we'll never know. Tommie, her first born, incidentally, was seriously injured in a sledding accident and has had a difficult life, enduring one surgery after another. An amazing kid, Tommie has managed to keep his sense of humor despite the lousy hand life has dealt him. He's one of my private family heroes. Dolores, while seeming to enjoy projecting a tough-as-nails persona, is actually a pussy cat. When the old man was dying from lung cancer and found himself in desperate need of help, it was Dolores who stepped forward to look after him in his final days. She enlisted Doris in the project of compassion and they administered to his needs virtually around the clock until he died. I greatly admired the two of them, knowing full well that I was not a good enough human being to have done the same for a man who had spent his life spreading misery among those who should have been closest to him.

Last of my siblings is Gilbert Jr., "Bud" to all of us kids. Born on 3 September, 1929, Bud was the designated family rebel. Dolores and I were the family scholars, always striving for, and usually getting straight A's in school. Bud was anything but a scholar. He was somewhat contemptuous of my academic achievements, considering "book learning" pretty much a waste of time. He was interested mostly in being able to fix things and learning how to do things that would earn him money. Not that he had a love of money itself. Cash was only good for buying things, like clothes, to make him look good and to allow him to have fun. Always nattily dressed, he made me, with my usually very conservative garb, look like the poor country cousin. He was a fast learner, and I always secretly envied his ability to take something, like a car, apart and put it back together with no written guidance whatsoever. I was pretty good at making things, like model airplanes, as a kid, but Bud put me to shame when it came to useful pursuits like fixing the family Plymouth. He, of course, had to learn everything on his own since the old man was never around to mentor. Considering school a waste of time, Bud quit at age 16 and went to work, eventually landing a job with an electrical manufacturing and repair company which provided him with technical training and a good living.

A good living was badly needed since Bud continued in the rebel mode by marrying Katie, a very beautiful but very young neighborhood girl. They proceeded to produce eight(!) children, each of whom could pass as a movie star.

Although I was three years younger than Bud we tended to travel in the same circles and had the same friends. This continued through our pre-teen and teen years until Bud was eventually drafted into the Army.

Bud always impressed me when we were kids as having a much more cynical outlook on life than I. But one incident in our pre-teen period is, I think, a more accurate reflection of Bud's character than any of the many vignettes that I could recite. The incident stands as a monument to the stupidity of young boys who inevitably become bored with city life in the summertime. Our neighborhood group would frequently hang around the single track railroad that passed behind our house and past the Peter-Paul candy factory that dominated the neighborhood. We would call out to the candy factory workmen to toss us some raw caramel chunks in paper bags from the factory windows. They would often do so, interspersing the occasional bag full of water, for their own amusement. We didn't resent the occasional soaking since, after all, it was summertime and we all laughed as hard as the workmen at the poor boob who caught the bag and the soaking.

The Siblings & Spouses L-R: Irene, Author, Dolores, Doris, Jack, Bud, Tony, Kate, Tom

A far more hazardous activity that we engaged in to relieve our boredom involved the railroad, which spanned a deep chasm with a steel girder bridge mounted on massive stone pilings. We decided that to remain a member of our group each of us would have to prove his manhood by inching along the bottom flange of the steel girder from one stone piling to the next across the chasm. To assist in maintaining balance, the person crossing could grasp the vertical flanges, stretching from one to the other while shuffling along the bottom flange. A fall into the chasm would probably be fatal. Nonetheless, we all made the crossing. All, that is, except Bert. Bert was the awkward one of the group and the last to cross. Visibly frightened, Bert began his crossing and to our horror froze at the halfway point, screaming in panic. Those of us watching contemplated calling for help but didn't think it would arrive before Bert in his state of panic lost his balance and fell. Suddenly, Bud swore silently, stood up, and went back out onto the steel flange while ordering Bert to shut up and calm down. He reached out, taking Bert's hand in his and guiding him step-by-step back to safety. None of us said anything but there was no doubt that everyone admired Bud who risked being pulled off the girder by a panic-stricken kid into the chasm below. And there was no doubt that I, for the first time, felt very proud of my big brother.

-So much for some of the people and events that influenced my early life. A quick introduction to my family members is, I think, indispensable to the narrative since they all altered my life and development significantly. Now on to my recollections of how that life has played out until now.

The Airplane Obsession

When I was very young, say, five or six, I was already fascinated by the concept of flight. The idea that a man could step into a machine and fly through the air impressed my childhood mind as the most wondrous event possible. There was in the newspaper at the time a  comic strip, "Smilin' Jack", featuring an intrepid aviator named Jack, naturally, who went from adventure to adventure, always while flying some of the most modern aircraft of the day. I used to cut out the pictures of the airplanes, always being disappointed when the cut-outs didn't look like three dimensional reproductions of the aircraft shown in the comic strip. I began thinking of

Smilin' Jack, model airplanes. I also determined, without the
©Zack Mosley least shadow of a doubt, that I was going to be the incarnation of "Smilin' Jack". I was not only going to fly through the air, I was going to be the man in charge of the machine. I was going to be a pilot.

I began, however, to become adjusted to a simple fact of life. It was much easier to announce my intention to the world that I would be a pilot than it was to actually <u>become</u> a pilot. The first obstacle I encountered was a notable lack of enthusiasm on the part of my mother as to my choice of vocations. She was full of admiration for our family doctor, Joseph Toland-I think my middle name came from him-and Mom thought it would be much nicer if I became a doctor rather than a wild-eyed daredevil pilot. I also was earning points with my grade school teacher by writing articles for the school newspaper, "The Edmunds Bulletin", which my teacher happened to edit. Mom thought that if the medical profession was closed to me, being a newspaper writer might be a respectable profession for me to follow.

Then there was the money problem. I learned early on a fact about aviation life that would be with me all my life; that is, flying airplanes is expensive. I attacked this problem head on by going to work as a grocery clerk and delivery boy at Costello's corner grocery store.

This brings me to another person who had a great influence on my early years, Bill Costello. Bill was a young, ambitious business man whom I met when I was ten or so years old. He ran a grocery store, the kind that everyone patronized in the 40's before supermarkets became popular and eventually made the corner grocery store a thing of the past. Bill's store was a block from our house and I decided to show up, uninvited, with my little red wagon outside his store in hope that some housewife would ask me to deliver her groceries and reward me with a tip, usually a dime in those days.

With Bill Costello, 1953

Bill didn't really need or want me hanging around his neatly kept place of business, but he tolerated my presence and I eventually became part of the operation. It didn't occur to me at the time, but I think Bill had heard about the fatherless group of kids living in the neighborhood and felt sorry for me. I further ingratiated myself by helping to unload bulk groceries delivered from the warehouse and by doing small clean up jobs. Bill was a devout Catholic and had several teen-aged boys, all Catholic, on the payroll. But he eventually took a liking to this non-Catholic brash kid, and later put me on the payroll as a full-fledged grocery clerk (when I was old enough to be working legally).

Bill became my male role model. I found that he was scrupulously honest in all of his business dealings and refused to work with any supplier who didn't measure up to his standards of integrity. I was at a very impressionable stage of life and could easily have gone in the wrong direction had I not had Bill's example to follow. He was, in short, the closest thing I had to a father and I am forever indebted to him for his guidance. I think Bill knew that he played an important role in my life, and he would frequently invite me to dinner with his wife, Peg, and take me to a movie, always one with a moral message, afterward.

In any case, I worked at the grocery store, with only a few months' interruption, from my red wagon days until I entered the Air Force after two years of college. My primary motivation was to earn enough money to pay for flying lessons. While working part time during my high school years I earned the princely sum of ten dollars a week plus a few bucks in tips for the occasional delivery job (I had graduated by now into delivering groceries in Bill's beat-up Chevrolet rather than the red wagon). Flying lessons at the suburban airport cost ten dollars an hour, including instructor, or eight dollars an hour solo. In other words, virtually my entire week's salary went toward flying lessons. It never occurred to me that it should be any other way.

The War Years

World War II was another defining period in my young life. I came to understand its importance at a very early age. My earliest recollection was the fall of France. Since that happened in the summer of 1940, I would have been seven years old. We were living at the time on Lieper Street in northeast Philadelphia. My memory of our dwellings before that is weak. I vaguely recall that we lived in Yeadon also in Philadelphia. The old man was living at home during that time making a good living as an insurance agent and we lived in a fairly nice neighborhood. After that, he decided he hated the insurance business and pulled one of his disappearing acts. With no income, Mom was forced to move the family into an apartment over a barber shop on Unity Street. I remember that the hallways in the apartment were lit by gas jets! Our apartment could best be described as a tenement, but we didn't think it was all that bad. We eventually moved around the corner, however, to a rental house on Lieper Street. It was a significant improvement and actually had a back yard complete with a fruit-producing peach tree.

But back to Lieper Street and the war. I knew something important was going on because Mom was spending hours away from her hyper-busy existence in order to listen to the war news on our Atwater-Kent radio. By listening myself and by asking questions I learned that she was intensely worried about her family members in France, which was being overrun by the Nazis. She was especially concerned about her sister, my Aunt Germaine and Germaine's sons, Charlie and George, who were on duty with the French army.

On December 7th, 1941, I sensed that something serious was happening. I made my way to the Atwater-Kent and discovered that Mom was very upset because the Japanese had just bombed a place called Pearl Harbor. At age nine I was very happy to stay close to my mother while she speculated on the chances of "her kids" coming under attack. The United States were under attack but to Mom the most serious thing was that her kids might be in danger. I remember feeling a little worried, but I also remember feeling very angry and wishing that I were old enough to go after the bastards.

I followed the war news as if it were describing a sporting event and I couldn't wait for the "Evening Bulletin" to arrive with its daily updates. My interest in the war soon combined with my interest in airplanes, and the seed was planted that would eventually grow into my determination to become not just a pilot, but a fighter pilot. I discovered that this, too, was easier said than done.

I spent the war years pretty much like any other kid in a big city. I went to a series of big city schools including Marshall and Edmunds grammar schools, Harding Junior High and Frankford High School. I was good at schoolwork and pretty good at athletics even though I was slightly undersized. I enjoyed school for the most part, particularly Frankford High. I started slowly at Frankford until I realized that I had to study for the first time in my scholastic life. Once convinced of that, I ended up with straight A grades and was president of my senior class. The straight A grades were not the result of any particular brilliance, but more from a knack I had, which served me well throughout life--that is, being able to foresee which subjects would be covered in the exams, allowing me to better prepare for them.

I built model airplanes by the dozen, scraping together enough cash to buy a model plane engine which usually refused to start. The World War II years came to an abrupt end with the atomic bombing of Hiroshima but they had made a profound impression on my young mind. Without the war I would probably not have felt called to serve in the military and probably would not have pursued my strong desire to become a fighter pilot. As it was, the model plane habit, with my having built models of most of the WWII fighters, had one very positive outcome. It led to my first ride in a real airplane.

I was setting up to fly a control-line model airplane that somewhat resembled the P-51 Mustang, arguably the best fighter of World War II. As usual the engine was resisting my best efforts to get it to run. It was several months after the war ended and I was laboring over my recalcitrant engine at a local park, attracting several onlookers. One of the onlookers was a slender young man whom I guessed to be in his mid-twenties. He observed that the model looked like a P-51 and volunteered that he had just been released from the Army Air Force where he had been flying P-51s. That made him an instant hero in my book.

We struck up a conversation and he asked me if I had ever flown a real airplane. When I told him that, regretfully, I had not, he offered to take me for a ride. My model plane was thrown unceremoniously into the trunk of my car as I eagerly jumped at the chance to actually fly!

We drove to a nearby grass strip, Boulevard Airport, and my new friend rented a beautiful, red Taylorcraft. After all my subsequent years of flying, I still remember most vividly the excitement of that first takeoff. Expecting the feeling of high speed, I was struck by just the opposite. Everything seemed to slow down as we climbed out away from the airport. The local landscape reminded me ever so much of a model train layout. I was thrilled, and I was hooked! If there had been any doubt about my being a doctor, a newspaper writer, or a pilot, the issue was now settled.

Needless to say, Mom was less than thrilled about my taking off in an airplane with no effort to seek her permission and with a total stranger at that. But she began to slowly accept the inevitable, and I thus embarked on my next mission which was to get a student pilot's license. At age 15 I was old enough to take flying lessons, but not old enough to fly solo. Nevertheless, I began pressing Mom, whose permission was required, to visit her idol, Doctor Toland, in order to get the required medical clearance to fly. That medical clearance was, in effect, a student license as well as a medical certificate and as such vital to my plans. Hoping that the good doctor would provide some support and encouragement to Mom, I was badly disappointed. On examining the FAA paperwork, his first comment was, "you're gonna break your neck, kid!" This led Mom, who had to sign off on my application as a minor, to ask me, teary-eyed if she was signing my death warrant. Such was the public's perception of flight safety in the '40s. I began a slow campaign which took many years aimed at convincing Mom that flying was not daredeviltry. Many years into my professional flying career I flew Mom from Philadelphia to Long Island in a T-34, a tandem

Air Force trainer that had been declared surplus and acquired by the base flying club for which I was an instructor. Mom had to wear a headset and looked for all the world like an elderly Amelia Erhart. But she loved it, and I think I finally convinced her that she had made the right move in signing off on my student pilot's license all those years earlier.

Takeoff

My tattered first logbook shows entry number one on July 30th, 1949 in a Piper J-3 Cub, one hour of flight with an instructor named John Founds. I was sixteen and a senior in high school. I remember feeling that I had wasted too much time getting started on my aviation career because of limited funds. But, feeling slightly over the hill at my advanced age, I was determined to make the best of it.

Since I couldn't afford to fly more than once a week, John usually spent the first half of each lesson reviewing the previous week's work. Already exhibiting some of my later fighter pilot's cockiness, I felt that we were wasting time with review work since I had already gone over it a hundred times in my mind. In retrospect, I'm sure John was right. A week between flights is too long for a beginner and I clearly needed the work.

And my finances didn't afford me the choice of flying more frequently. To illustrate how tight my budget was, I'll review the ground transportation problem. Flushed with early post-war prosperity, Mom had bought a car. She couldn't drive, but she had two eager sons who could. So, Bud and I shared the 1938 Dodge which Mom acquired after taking our dubious advice at a used car dealership. Mom, of course, had priority if she needed to go somewhere. Bud had second priority since he had a job, thus cash to fill the gas tank. I, therefore, frequently found myself with an airplane to fly but no easy way to get to it. My alternative when I couldn't afford to gas up the Dodge was to walk several miles to the Route 66 street car, ride it to the end of the line and walk several more miles to the airport. This was a kid who wanted to fly!

John worked me hard. He was a shouter, a technique used by a lot of instructors, but one to which I never responded very well. In any case, after nine weeks, with a total of nine hours in my log book I found myself shooting landings with John shouting what I considered to be nit-picking corrections back to me. While I was taxiing back for another takeoff, John suddenly said, "drop me off here. Let's see you do it yourself". "Well, I'll be damned!", I thought, "I think he wants me to solo". John jumped out of the front seat and I was immediately surprised- pleasantly- that I could see much better over the nose. I stopped at the end of the grass strip and made an unnecessary additional check of the magnetos while gathering up my courage, smiled inwardly and pushed the throttle forward. The little Continental 65 horsepower engine seemed to instantly detect that a considerable portion of the payload, i.e., John, was no longer its responsibility and it made the J-3 fairly leap into the air. I was very busy tracking straight, making smooth turns at the right altitude, and was generally determined to put on a good show for John who I mistakenly assumed was worried sick. I did, however, allow myself to relax briefly on downwind leg while thinking to myself "Damn!-I'm flying this thing all by myself!" The self-congratulatory interlude lasted about 30 seconds and it was back to being a pilot-cut the power, establish glide, trim, turn base, then final-keep that nose down, slip off a little excess altitude, round out, hold it off, <u>touchdown</u>! So, on October 2, 1949 I became a pilot. Oh, I had a long way to go before the FAA recognized that I was really a private pilot and gave me a license, but in my mind I could now fly an airplane on my own, and my world had changed forever.

I was still a high school kid when I soloed, and I was enjoying life. I never had enough money to fly as much as I wanted to, even though I was now working 30 hours a week at Costello's-part time during the afternoon and evening, and on Saturdays- and earning the magnificent sum of $30 a week. I had a girl friend, a spectacular blond named Joan, and chasing her made a serious dent in my available flying dollars. I was elected senior class president for no particular reason except that I was a good student who got along pretty well with my classmates and teachers and stayed out of trouble most of the time. Anyway, it was a ceremonial job that involved making a few speeches but it didn't take much of my time.

During my senior year in Frankford High School I began to think seriously-as most kids do-about the future. There was no doubt that I would be terribly disappointed if I were unable to follow my dream of flying airplanes for a living. I graduated from high school in January of 1950, still pursuing the requirements for my private pilot's license. I read a recruiting advertisement in a magazine in the local barber shop while waiting my turn for a haircut. It talked about the Air Force's Aviation Cadet program. The ad immediately had my undivided attention! Here was a way to not only fly for a living but also to get training in the best, hottest aircraft in the world! But there were things to be done. After graduating from high school I had taken a job as a file clerk with Republic Steel Corporation, working at a sales office in downtown Philadelphia. The job was undemanding and rather boring, but it did supply me with needed cash to continue flying and, incidentally, save some money for possible higher education.

On the subject of higher education, there is a sidelight story to tell. I tell it reluctantly, but in the interest of full disclosure as they say. It can serve as the paradigm for the expression, "dumb kid". To begin with, I received a letter from the famed Philadelphia Science Museum, the Franklin Institute. It stated that after reviewing my high school transcript, they were offering me the opportunity to compete for a full scholarship in a science discipline. I was required to go to the Franklin Institute on a Saturday to be interviewed and to take a written exam. I did so although I resented having to miss a day's work at the grocery store and the day's pay that would cover my hour of flying time. A few weeks later I received another letter stating that I had done very well in the Physics competition and that I should go back downtown to the Franklin Institute for further evaluation in the scholarship process. This is where the "dumb kid" part comes in. I decided on my own--I had failed to keep Mom advised that any of this was going on--not to go. In my way of thinking, I had already missed one day of work and I wasn't about to miss another if these clowns couldn't make up their minds. Now, I would like to think at this late stage in life that I would have lost out in the competition and wouldn't have been awarded the scholarship anyway; but passing up the chance to compete for a free college education for a $30 paycheck certainly redefines the meaning of "dumb kid".

Looking back on the scholarship episode, it occurs to me that another factor was in play. The Air Force's Aviation Cadet program required only two years of college. The thought of accepting a four year commitment because of a scholarship did not appeal to me at all. I simply did not want to wait another two years to begin flying those beautiful airplanes. I had saved some money from my job at Republic Steel, and with Mom's encouragement and financial help I took steps to enroll in the cheapest local college I could find, Temple University in Philadelphia. I remember being appalled that the first semester was going to cost me $200 of my hard-earned cash!

While I had enjoyed my high school years, I can't say the same for my two years at Temple. I arranged my classes so as to be able to work at the grocery store--Bill had asked me to come back after my sojourn at Republic Steel--for 30 hours a week. So I was busy, but the hard work didn't bother me. The Korean War was going on and I had to subject myself to the indignity of applying for a 2-S deferment. The 2-S was, in my opinion, a slick way for kids who could afford to go to college to avoid going to war. But if I wanted to become an Aviation Cadet I had to finish the two years of college and the 2-S was my only way to avoid the draft while doing so. I knew I would end up in the military, but I still felt like a slacker, especially since Bud had been drafted and most of my friends had either been drafted or had enlisted in the Air Force.

So, I continued in the distasteful role of college student, flying whenever I could afford it, and working toward the goal of licensed private pilot. Finally, after filling all the required squares as ordained by the FAA, I scheduled myself for a check ride with an FAA Examiner. The flight was uneventful, and my log book bears the examiner's illegible signature attesting to the fact that on June 12th, 1951 I qualified to be a private pilot. I flew with my first passenger, Bert McGrath, a fellow grocery clerk at Costello's and a very trusting soul, the following week.

The months went by and sometime in the spring of 1952, armed with my transcript showing exactly 60 semester hours college credit and my private pilot's license I visited the local Air Force recruiting sergeant who was more than happy to tell me about the Aviation Cadet Program. He never had an easier selling job. He helped me get scheduled for several days of written exams, physical exams and various psycho-motor tests, as they were called, at Sampson Air Force Base in upstate New York. I sweated out the results for several weeks before an official-looking letter arrived from the Department of the Air Force. Opening it with great trepidation, I was ecstatic to discover that I had been accepted for a pilot training slot with class 53G! I was to make arrangements to be sworn in to the Air Force and report for pre-flight training at Lackland Air Force Base in San Antonio on October 30th, 1952. Life was good! There was only one complicating factor in that life. Her name was Marion.

Marion

Earlier, I mentioned my high school sweetheart, Joan. Sometime during my time at Temple, Joan and I came to the mutual conclusion that our romance was not really made in heaven and we decided to split. I then swore off girls forever. Forever lasted about a week.

Previously, I had introduced my best friend, Ted Hantwerker, to a high school acquaintance, Isabel Francis, also a friend of Joan's. Joan and I had frequently double-dated with Ted and Isabel. Upon discovering that Joan and I had called it quits, they decided to repay my earlier playing Cupid for them by arranging a blind date for me with one of their friends, Marion Cresson.

Young Love

It didn't occur to me at the time, but I probably could have selected a more romantic spot for a first date. As it was, I selected the midget auto races at Langhorne Speedway. Wearing my best striped purple T-shirt, I nervously arrived at Marion's house to begin our first date. A beautiful young thing came down the stairs, but, to my regret, introduced herself as Ruth Cresson. A second beautiful young thing then descended the stairs looking exactly like the first. I thus discovered that Marion had an identical twin sister. They obviously enjoyed being twins and I was soon to find out that they liked to have fun with their cloned identity. We went to the auto races with Ted and Isabel going along as chaperones. I found that I was very comfortable with this cute little girl who very quickly brought me out of my natural introversion and got me to talk a lot--something I rarely did. Before the night was over (my judgment on first date locales being further eroded by a tragic fatal accident on the track) we had agreed to another date. And so we were off!

We went to movies together, went dancing, something at which I was especially inept, and I even subjected her to the ultimate test of compatibility, a ride with me in the Piper Cub. We found that we liked being together, and soon I discovered that I didn't want to be away from this perky, little girl for any period of time. She introduced me to fun and games for twins on a couple of occasions. For example, she and Ruth set up one poor guy at a college dance. Ruth went with the guy, who was named Bill Wunder and knew nothing about a twin sister, to the dance where Ruth excused herself to go to the ladies room. Marion, dressed exactly like Ruth, then came dancing by in my arms, waving coyly at Bill as we passed by. All poor Bill knew was that his date had just taken up with some guy he had never seen before. I soon noted that Bill was talking to his friends and he looked angry. With that I called off the practical joke before it got ugly. Bill, seeing his date then emerge from the ladies room, looked open-mouthed, back and forth at his date and her double. Realizing he had been had he joined in the fun.

Marion seemed to enjoy being with me almost as much as I enjoyed being with her, and she made me happy by accepting my invitation to "go steady", the pre-engagement ritual of the period. The relationship would soon be put to the test since I was about to depart for 14 months of pilot training as an Aviation Cadet, a rank which carried with it a prohibition against marriage until training was complete.

There was no doubt in my mind that we would survive the separation. I was 20 years old and clearly in love with my Marion, but she understood that the relationship would involve a mistress named The United States Air Force. She accepted the relationship on those terms, and vowing to write every day, I climbed aboard a Lockheed Constellation airliner bound for San Antonio and pre-flight training in the Aviation Cadet Program.

Lackland

Certain parts of this narrative will prove to be better researched and documented than others. My three month stay at Lackland AFB as a pre-flight Aviation Cadet is one of those parts. The simple reason for the more detailed recitation is that Marion has, for over 50 years, preserved all of the letters I wrote to her. Since I wrote to her only when I was assigned to duty where she could not be with me, the stacks of letters are from Lackland AFB in San Antonio, Marianna Air Base in Florida, Foster AFB in Victoria, Texas, Williams AFB, Arizona, and Moody AFB, Georgia. All of these were pilot training bases. Later, I would be assigned to one-year so-called "remote" tours where dependents were not permitted. These tours included Thule Air Base, Greenland and Bien Hoa Air Base in South Vietnam. From each of these locations I endeavored to write to Marion every day and I very nearly achieved that goal. My letters are obviously a more accurate depiction of my life and times than the workings of my very old and very unreliable memory. All credit for that accuracy belongs to Marion who, despite my exhortations to "get rid of the junk", insisted always that we move her trunk full of letters to our next location.

Lackland was the start of almost two years of letter writing and painful separation from Marion. My letters were frequently lists of complaints because Lackland had much to complain about. We, as luck would have it, were the first Aviation Cadets in post war times to be based at Lackland. Previously, Cadets had done their pre-flight training at one of the many operational training bases which at the time were run by civilian contractors. For some reason the Air Force decided it would be better to consolidate all pre-flight training at one location. My class was re-designated from 53G to 54ABC. And the pre-flight training period was doubled to three months. This was demoralizing in itself, but more disappointing to me was the fact that there were no airplanes or even runways at Lackland. We cadets felt very much like run-of-the-mill grunts at basic training.

Since we were the first class to try the new system, we had no upper class. So, to keep this from detracting from our training in military discipline the Air Force sent in dozens and dozens of freshly-minted second lieutenants to be "Tactical Officers". The duty of a Tac Officer was to make life miserable for cadets. At this they succeeded admirably.

There is probably nothing in the world less capable of organizing something than a second lieutenant. The Air Force knows this and tries, therefore, to assign a good sergeant next to every second lieutenant to keep him out of trouble. This didn't happen with our class and organization suffered badly. I was, for example, not issued uniforms for about a week. Since all the civilian recruits were in the same boat we soon became a vile-smelling lot. Fortunately, our class was composed, probably by a 60:40 ratio, of former enlisted men to civilians like me. The enlisted men were tremendously helpful in teaching us displaced civilians the rudiments of military living--like how to make a GI bed, how to spit-shine shoes and the rest. I felt sorry for these guys as I watched them unsew the stripes, some as high as Tech or even Master Sergeant, that they had worked so hard for. They were willing to trade in their stripes for cadet epaulettes because they wanted to be pilots. Watching them sacrifice helped me to realize that I didn't have it so bad. I seldom complained--except to poor Marion.

In spite of the disappointments and disorganization, quite a few interesting things happened at Lackland, and after all these years I have come to realize that it was a good experience that helped me to mature. A pleasant surprise was the arrival, soon after our own arrival, of the NATO cadets.

The United States during this time had taken upon itself the task of training pilots from NATO countries. I don't know the politics involved, but the policy certainly presented an opportunity for young officers-in-training to make long standing friendships with their foreign ally counterparts. Our squadron had French, Italian, Danish, Dutch and Norwegian cadets. They ranged from very good to very bad, probably depending on the selection system of the various countries. The Scandinavian cadets were especially well qualified, and most of them spoke English better than the Americans. The Italians, on the other hand, had a very hard time.

There were about a dozen Italians who began the program and 14 months later, one graduated. I'm certain that they were simply not prepared for the rigors of a United States officer training program. I befriended an Italian living at the bunk next to mine, and with a mixture of my poor French (which he spoke haltingly) and his very poor English, he managed to tell me his story. He had been a partisan in daily combat during WWII, and was quite unimpressed by the childish discipline administered by the crew of second lieutenants we had over us. He also refused to do routine tasks like making his bed the G.I. way. He explained to me that as an officer candidate in Italy he had an enlisted aide to take care of such details. Within a few weeks he had contacted the Italian Ambassador and was gone.

With Pierre At Lackland

More successful was my friendship with a French cadet who lived near me in our open bay barracks. Pierre Fortin was not your typical French cadet. Generally speaking, the Frenchmen were a study in indiscipline and contrasts. When I first saw them they were marching in formation under the leadership of a French officer. I and my fellow American cadets were impressed! With their beautiful black uniforms and their cleated shoes they looked and sounded like a prize class from a military academy. But once they were integrated into our squadron under American officers, they began acting like the teen-agers that most of them were. Whereas we Americans had to be at least 20 years old, the French cadets could enter training at age 18. Anyone who's raised teenagers knows that those two years can be significant in terms of maturity.

But they were fun, and I soon took a liking to many of them. They gravitated naturally toward me because of my rudimentary proficiency with French. Pierre was a special case. For starters, he was 22 years old and had little time for the antics of his younger compatriots. His English, while far from perfect, was better than my French. In any case, having an interesting new friend ameliorated my disillusionment with pre-flight and my adjustment to this strange and unfriendly environment I had been thrust into.

Pre-flight training was tough on all cadets but tougher on those, like me, who entered training directly from civilian life. The curriculum was split about 50:50 into classroom work and drill, physical and military training. I had little trouble with the academic work although I found courses like "Air Force Administration" a crashing bore. The physical training was easy for me also and I especially enjoyed the intramural touch football games. Military training was not my strong suit and I accumulated a long list of demerits, barely escaping marching punishment tours on the parade ground on weekends. While I complained a lot in my letters home, I never had any intention of quitting. In fact, my greatest worry was an upcoming physical exam which I dreaded, fearing that some medical bureaucrat would find something that would disqualify me from the flight training I was so eagerly anticipating. In fact, when it came time for me to take the physical, I passed it easily. Two cadets in our barracks were not so lucky and were eliminated, leaving in silence, broken-hearted.

So, pre-flight training passed slowly and unpleasantly, but I was adjusting, and several occurrences popped up unexpectedly making it much more tolerable. The first was a decision, wholly unexpected, from our leaders to grant Christmas leave to all cadets. I didn't have enough money to buy an airline ticket back to Philadelphia, but simply being broke was not about to keep me from seeing my beloved Marion again. I was prepared to hitch-hike, but that became unnecessary when my friend in the bunk below mine, John Gantz, revealed that he had a car and, being from Pennsylvania, was looking for riders to share expenses. I not only took advantage of the opportunity, but also got to take my friend, Pierre along to share in an American Christmas. Although I had been in the Air

Force for only six weeks or so, no leave could have been better timed to salvage my sinking morale.

With six of us crammed into my friend's car, we drove straight through to Pennsylvania, stopping only for gas and an occasional pick-up hamburger. Marion and I made the most of our windfall vacation and Pierre was delighted at being able to communicate in fluent French with my mother.

Christmas leave passed all too quickly and we drove silently back to our lonely life at Lackland. In the barracks I showed Pierre some snapshots of home that he had not yet seen. After looking at the first few, he handed them back to me with tears in his eyes and said "I can not to look".

The second event that broke up the routine of Lackland was Dwight Eisenhower's first inauguration. West Point and Annapolis were to

Pierre With Twins, Xmas Leave, Marion On Right

have their usual large contingent of cadets and midshipmen in the inaugural parade, and since the Air Force Academy did not yet exist, the Air Force was to be unrepresented. Some one decided that this was unacceptable and some one else discovered that a huge group of blue-suiters sat in San Antonio without gainful employment. And, besides, they marched a lot.

Overnight we cadets went from being the lowest of the low to representing the entire U.S. Air Force before the President of the United States! We knew that we'd better do it well. For the next ten days we did nothing but march. Officers up to the rank of captain suddenly appeared from nowhere to bark commands and reprimand anyone who had the misfortune to swing his arm too far forward or too far behind. All of these officers were graduates of West Point or Annapolis. After ten days of this, believe me, we looked good!

Secure in the knowledge that we could march as well as anyone, we went by bus to Kelly AFB on the other side of town to be loaded into a half dozen or so C-124 Globemasters. The Globemaster was the Air Force's largest cargo/troop carrier aircraft at the time and was known, affectionately as "Old Shaky". The airplanes were in max load troop carrier configuration, meaning that there was a lower deck of wall-mounted canvas seats and an identical upper deck overhead. I was in a lower deck seat which turned out to be a less than desirable location. It's a long way from San Antonio to Washington, D.C. and Old Shaky made the trip at very slow speed and very low altitude. The cabin was hot, the air was turbulent, and the passengers very quickly went into air sickness mode. That's where my lower deck seat became a liability. Never susceptible to air sickness myself, I became very adept at dodging stray vomit from the upper deck. This was my first flight in an Air Force aircraft. It may have had something to do with my choice of fighters rather than transports later, but at the time I remember thinking that the Black Hole of Calcutta must have been something like this. We landed, mercifully, at Bolling AFB in Washington, a place that would become a part of my life much later.

We were quartered in the base gymnasium in triple decker bunks with rigid rules governing use of showers. The best part of the trip for me was that Marion was able to come down to Washington (with Mom playing chaperone) and spend the day with me after we marched. We were very pressed for time, of course, but we made the most of the few hours we had. As for the parade, the narrator observed when the Air Force group marched by that we "were the equal of the cadets and midshipmen." We weren't thrilled with that assessment since we thought we were better. I caught a glimpse of Ike on the reviewing stand as we did an "eyes right" while marching by.

The following morning we re-boarded our C-124s and made our way back to Lackland where we had some academic work to make up because of the time lost to the inaugural. We didn't mind-we were almost finished with pre-flight. A week or so later I had a scary incident that could have changed my life forever, but I got lucky.

I had a series of shots scheduled that morning and one of them or a combination of several caused me to pass out in the chow line. I woke up immediately with some of my buddies fanning me. Fortunately for me no one in authority witnessed my fall. I didn't know it at the time but losing consciousness is a sure way to get grounded until they find a cause--if they find a cause. As a lowly cadet, I'm sure I would have been washed out of the program. As it was, I, in my ignorance, simply went back to the barracks, cursing the fact that I had missed lunch, never knowing that I could have missed my Air Force career. I never discovered why I fainted and I have never in my life fainted again. Shortly afterward I got my new assignment--the 3300th Pilot Training Squadron at Marianna Air Base in the Florida Panhandle. The sound of "Pilot Training Squadron" was infinitely better than "pre-flight squadron" and I was excited about the future.

The Pennsylvanians in our group once again took advantage of John Gantz's Buick and headed eastward toward Florida. Unfortunately, my friend Pierre had been assigned to another training base in Malden, Missouri and we said goodbye, expressing the hope that we might get together again in basic training. That was not to be, and after exchanging a few letters, Pierre and I, both being extremely busy, lost track of each other. There was, however a sequel to the story which I'll go into later.

As luck would have it, we reached New Orleans while Mardi Gras was going on. John, at 27, was the old man of our group, but even he admitted never having seen a party quite like the one put on by "The Big Easy". We used up another day of our travel time to allow a better look.

We stopped for an early dinner, on the second day, at a place we thought to be a hamburger joint. The hamburger joint we chose turned out to be the world famous gourmet restaurant, Antoine's of New Orleans. A sympathetic waiter, recognizing us for the babes-in-the-woods we were, steered us toward the less expensive menu items, but we got an instant education in the marketing of haute cuisine when the check arrived. The next morning we left, poorer but wiser, for Marianna and flight training.

Marianna

We drove into Graham Air Base outside Marianna, Florida at 11AM, February 12, 1953 after spending the previous night in Panama City. We found ourselves once again in a ground-breaking situation. Marianna had been a WWII training base but had been closed since the end of the war. It was being re-opened for the Korean War buildup and we were, as at Lackland, the first class to arrive. New facilities were under construction, but in the interim we were quartered in a large WWII barracks building which had no amenities, like a heating system, for example. The dining hall was new and operated by a civilian contractor, but there was no BX, movie theater, or any other recreational facility. There was, however, one thing to warm my heart--a working flight line.

Another part of our ground-breaking status involved the airplanes. We found ourselves part of an Air Force experiment in beginning flight training. In recent years, the Air force had started fledgling pilots entering training in the North American T-6. The T-6 was a WWII trainer, but was previously designated the AT-6, The AT standing for "advanced trainer". Changing the aircraft from the machine which graduating pilots flew just before checking out in combat fighters, like the P-51, Mustang into a beginning trainer was a somewhat radical idea. But it seemed to be working well. However, in the "re-inventing- the-wheel" category of decision making from on high came the thought that if we start pilot trainees in a smaller airplane, we'll weed out the obvious ham-hands more quickly and at much less expense. Those of us arriving in class 54ABC were thus selected to perform this noble experiment. We found, therefore, standing neatly on the empty ramp 25 brand new Piper PA-18 Super Cubs.

This was a surprise to all of us and one about which I had mixed feelings. I had anticipated with great excitement flying the powerful T-6, and was disappointed that I would be delayed in doing so. But there was certainly an upside, too. I was, after all, a licensed private pilot, fully qualified to fly Piper Cubs. The Super Cub was just a very nice, more powerful version of the J-3 Cub that I flew as a civilian. I deduced, correctly, that this would give me a huge initial advantage over my classmates, most of whom had never flown an airplane of any kind.

There was also an advantage in being the first class at Marianna. While we had to suffer the lack of recreational facilities and absence of heat in the barracks, we didn't feel in the least deprived because our upper class was not in place. The plan had been to transfer the upper class from a base in North Carolina to Marianna before our class arrived. But since construction of new living quarters and other needed facilities was so far behind, it was decided to leave our upper class in North Carolina until facilities were completed. This left us without an upper class to harass us, much to our delight. There were the inevitable Tac Officers, but not nearly enough of them to really make our lives miserable.

February 16 was a landmark day for me. I flew my first flight at the controls of an Air Force airplane even though it was the familiar Piper Cub. I was actually thrilled to be flying anything, but the Super Cub was a Cadillac compared to the J-3s I had flown in civilian life. They had electric starters, better instrumentation and most of all a 115 horsepower Lycoming engine rather than the 65 hp Continental I was used to.

The instructors, incidentally, disliked the Cub intensely. Most of them were WWII veterans who had been flying the T-6 for many years and most had very little light plane time. I found myself on several occasions pointing out to my instructor where some gadget was in the cockpit, something I had to do with a certain amount of discretion and appropriate humility. But I enjoyed it!

There were only two cadets in our group with any appreciable flying experience--me and one other. Because of our previous time we were assigned to the "squadron commander" (so called despite being a civilian) as his students. This was because he was busy with administrative work and had little time to fly. The Air Force required 8 hours of dual time before solo, and my instructor happily vacated the back seat as soon as I accumulated my eight. My Air Force first solo on March 6th, 1953 consisted of making three takeoffs and landings under the watchful eyes of my instructor. The traffic patterns and landings were routine and my instructor seemed pleased with my work and relieved that he wouldn't have to fly in the Piper on every flight.

We had one bizarre occurrence during the Piper Cub phase, and it happened to one of our lower classmen, shortly after he and his classmates arrived at Marianna in mid-March. None of our lower classmen had accumulated the necessary hours to solo, and this particular young man had just a little over three.

It seems that his instructor was teaching him spins. Now, the PA-18 is a very stable airplane which has to be forced into a spin. It also tends to spin fairly nose high. This instructor who, like most, had little light plane time and was accustomed to the nose-low attitude of a spinning T-6, somehow decided that the aircraft was in an uncontrollable flat spin. He ordered the student to bail out and without waiting for the student to do so unceremoniously jumped out himself.

The student spent a short amount of time positioning himself and working up his courage to make his first parachute jump when he noted that the aircraft, its center of gravity having been changed by the instructor's vacating the rear seat, had recovered from the spin all by itself. He then wisely decided that there was no point in jumping out of a perfectly good airplane, especially since he could see the runways of Graham Air Base just a few miles away.

He throttled back, joined the traffic pattern and made a not-very-good landing, but one which left him and the Piper undamaged.

The student reluctantly made the obligatory first solo speech in the dining hall that night, and the hapless instructor was invited by Graham Air Service to seek employment in some other line of work.

Shortly after the arrival of the lower classmen, activity at Marianna picked up significantly. Our living standard made a giant leap forward when we moved into new barracks--brand new with heating and air conditioning, four men to a room. We had little time to enjoy our exalted status over the lower classmen since our upper class finally made its appearance a few days after the lower class' arrival.

The upper class' arrival was a bitter-sweet event. We knew that we'd be in for non-stop harassment, but then our tormentors arrived, noisily, in shiny yellow T-6g's. By the end of the day the Marianna ramp, previously desolate looking with our 25 little Piper Cubs, was

T-6G At Marianna, FL. That Big Radial Engine Was A Bit Intimidating To Piper Cub Pilots--But We Loved It!

suddenly transformed into a massive flying operation by the arrival of 96 T-6 Texans. The sound of the Texans' radial engines was like a symphony to me, and I decided instantly that no amount of badgering by upper classmen would keep me from enjoying my future life flying these beautiful machines.

The badgering began almost immediately, but I found that I had developed a very thick skin and was unruffled by the various insults and criticisms directed at me. I now found it humorous and my greatest problem was to keep from laughing at my tormentors, a sure way to gather demerits.

I found it even easier to ignore the annoyance of military discipline the week following our upper class' arrival because I finished the Piper Cub phase of training and began, with a new instructor, flying the T-6.

It's hard to imagine the effect on a twenty year old kid, who's already crazy about flying, of an airplane like the North American T-6 Texan. I was stepping out of the 115 horsepower Super Cub into a radial engined 600 horsepower machine only one step removed from the WWII fighters that I had dreamed about while growing up during the war. I literally felt like I had died and gone to heaven.

On March 30th I had my first flight in the T-6 with my new instructor, Cecil Johnson. Cecil (who we addressed as "sir") was a small, wirey guy who was a no-nonsense type, but not a shouter--in other words, the perfect mentor for me. I started the big Pratt and Whitney and was smiling from ear to ear as it exploded into life. The T-6 is a tail wheel airplane and taxiing it with the big engine blocking your forward view is something of a challenge. Cecil showed me how to "S" turn to enhance forward visibility. I made the takeoff with Cecil following lightly on the controls and was elated by the feeling of sheer power that went with the deafening roar of the Pratt and Whitney. We climbed out and Cecil demonstrated acrobatics, which I had never done, other than spins, to show me what the airplane could do. Some of my friends complained to me later that the acrobatics made them feel queasy but I had no such problem. I loved every minute of it. I made the landing with considerable help from Cecil and learned quickly that the T-6 had built-in directional control challenges and was not to be trifled with on landing roll. All in all, I knew I had a lot to learn but I also knew I would love the learning.

Under Cecil's watchful eye I began to get accustomed to the demands of a complex aircraft. I had never before flown an airplane with retractable landing gear, flaps, controllable pitch propellor and a full set of flight and engine instruments. The need to compensate for the greatly increased amount of engine torque on takeoff and the requirement to maintain directional control on landing added to my need to learn as much as I could from Cecil as fast as I could. I spent many hours sitting in the cockpit of a T-6 on the ramp simply finding switches and valves with my eyes closed.

After five or six hours in the airplane I began to feel comfortable in it and began to be convinced that I could do it alone. I was not kept waiting long before I had to prove that my optimism was well founded. The Air Force required a minimum of 10 hours instruction time before solo, and right at the 10 hour point Cecil had me taxi back to the ramp where he got out with his parachute, patted me on the shoulder and said quietly, as if it were all in a day's work, "give me three takeoffs and landings and I'll see you back in Operations".

I was to check out in many airplanes during my long career in aviation, but I never again felt quite the thrill or satisfaction of my first solo in the T-6. I had made the leap from Sunday pilot flying Piper Cubs to professional pilot operating a complex, modern machine. My three landings were good and Cecil, becoming as demonstrative as he ever became, said, "nice job", and went on to the next subject. Five of our class soloed that day, so I can't claim to be first in the class to solo the T-6, but I was certainly in the first group and that in itself was satisfying. Cecil's other two students were officers, so it gave me considerable satisfaction, as a lowly cadet to be the first at our table to solo the big bird. We were required to have three "supervised solos" meaning that the instructor flew with us for a short period during each of our next three flights to make certain there was no regression and then released us to fly on our own. Soon I was, indeed, on my own, practicing the maneuvers I thought I needed to work on and making my own decisions. Heady stuff for a 20 year old!

The days began to fly by since we were busy constantly with academics for half a day and, the part I loved, flying the other half. We alternated with the other squadron, flying mornings one week and afternoons the next. The classroom work was sometimes dull, but I knew it would all prove useful and I was motivated to work hard at it. The classes, with subjects like Navigation, Weather, and Instrument Flying, were head and shoulders above the yawners we had during Pre-Flight. My study habits paid off and I never had to worry about my academic grades.

I grew to love flying the T-6, especially acrobatics. I was to find later in my career that just about any airplane that I flew, because all were more modern than the T-6, would be much lighter on the controls; but there was a certain feeling of being part of the airframe when you had to muscle it through a slow roll using heavy aileron and rudder pressures. Instrument flying was different, and most of my friends complained bitterly of having to sit under the "bag" (an instrument training hood that covered the rear cockpit eliminating the outside view completely). But I liked any kind of flying and considered flying by instruments to be a challenge that for the most part I enjoyed. One exception was the "blue box", a WWII contraption that was supposed to serve as a flight simulator. It had little wings that were supposed to make you feel like you were in an airplane. They didn't, of course, but the rotational motion of the box was sufficient to bring on spatial disorientation which induced air sickness in more than one intrepid young aviator. It was very difficult to escape the opprobrium of having barfed in a machine that never left the ground. Happily, I wasn't susceptible to motion sickness and I successfully logged 20 hours or so in the blue box, more formally known as the "Link Trainer"

Toward the end of June we began night flying and I had the first high-adrenalin flight of my career. I will, by the way, spend considerable time in this narrative discussing the high-stress flights that I was involved in. This is obviously because such flights are more interesting and because there usually was an important learning component involved. It's important to point out that I firmly believe that air travel is by far the safest mode of transportation ever devised by man. Probably ninety-nine percent of my flights were routine, bordering on boring--especially in my later career as a corporate pilot. But I must admit that the fighter plane is a different breed of cat. It's not designed with safety as the prime consideration. It's designed to fight, and sometimes safety takes a back seat to mission accomplishment.

Having said all that, I'll return to my introduction to night flying at Marianna. To begin with, there was a certain amount of tension in the air among the flight trainees. A few weeks before our group began night flying one of our upper classmen was killed during his first night solo flight. He had just taken off when the airplane rolled hard and impacted the ground. Although we never saw the accident report it was generally believed that it was a case of "spatial disorientation" which simply means that the pilot, deprived of a visual horizon by weather or nighttime conditions, chooses to believe his senses instead of his instruments, a frequently fatal error among inexperienced pilots. I was particularly impacted by the accident since I knew the pilot well. He lived next door to my barracks room and was constantly harassing us, as an upper classman, with room inspections. He was a nuisance, but none of us wanted to see him die in order to get him out of our hair.

It appeared that night flying to Graham Air Service was an annoyance to be tolerated and dispensed with as soon as possible. The instructors had to work at night when they would rather have been home with their families, and Graham probably had to pay them overtime. So they and all the students were brought in at once and students were assigned to instructors helter-skelter with the objective seemingly to be to get the maximum number of students soloed out in the shortest time possible. To me, this meant that I would be flying with an instructor I had never met before. I spoke to one of his regular students, a Danish cadet, who said to me, "Don't worry, he'll clear you for solo" and with a chuckle, "even if you're not ready".

I introduced myself to the instructor who seemed very low key and friendly. He said that he would fly with me first, which pleased me since I was looking forward to flying at night. I had not, after all, ever flown at night, even as a passenger, except for my flight to San Antonio on my first full day in the Air Force.

It was a completely moonless night, and while I was too much of a rookie to realize it, flying in the darkness would be all that much more difficult without moonlight. Visual cues are available from reflected moonlight which enhance depth perception and simply make night flying easier. We were to do it without a moon and in an area of Florida where there were few lights on the ground to provide a defined horizon. When I took off into the inky blackness I instantly recalled the admonitions of my flight instructor and ground school instructors to trust the flight instruments, not your middle ear sensations. I made constant cross checks on my artificial horizon and had no difficulty in keeping the airplane right side up.

We were required to have a minimum of three night landings with an instructor, and on entering the traffic pattern I became aware of the fact that the T-6, so wonderful a trainer in daylight, left much to be desired as a night flyer. For starters, the aircraft weren't flown regularly at night and the lighting systems, which were not very well designed in the first place, were not maintained. They had burned out bulbs and had an appalling tendency to dim, almost to the point of being extinguished, when the power was retarded. The dials and needles had a fluorescent paint on them which was virtually invisible. It was very difficult to read critical instruments, like the airspeed indicator, on final approach. But I attributed it to my lack of experience and didn't complain to the instructor.

My first landing, although I found myself feeling for the runway because my depth perception was so poor compared to daytime, was not bad. My second was a disaster. I rounded out too high and tried to salvage a bad landing rather than execute a missed approach. The result was a poor touchdown with momentary loss of directional control to the point that my left wheel left the paved runway and rolled briefly on the grass before I regained control and took off again from the runway. The instructor's laconic voice over the intercom commented, "I believe we went off the runway a tad on that one didn't we?" "Yes, sir, I believe we did," I replied. I didn't think we did, I knew damned well we did.

My third landing was acceptable, but I thought it must have been a flunking ride because of my getting a wheel on the turf on my second attempt. I was sure my regular instructor would make me, at the very least, repeat the lesson. Instead, my fill-in instructor said, "drop me off at operations and go fly an hour in the practice area. We'll de-brief when you get back." I was dumfounded, but vastly relieved that I would not have to face Cecil's wrath at my inept performance.

I taxied out and took off into the blackness, remembering last week's fatality and paying close attention to the poorly lighted flight instruments. I began to feel better and actually found time to survey the beauty of night flight with winking stars above and points of light on the ground. I knew there would be dozens of other inexperienced pilots like me milling around the traffic pattern, getting in their hour of night time and landing as soon as possible afterward. I decided to reduce the risk of collision by wandering farther into the training area out of sight of the Marianna airport. I was still admiring the new sights and beauty of night flight when it occurred to me that the radio, which should have been full of chatter from all the aircraft airborne, was strangely silent. I decided to return to the airport.

As I came closer to Marianna flashes of lightning, which I had noticed in the distance earlier, seemed much closer to the airport. I then heard a weak radio transmission from the control tower, and I thought my call sign was part of the call. I pressed the mike button and said, "Graham Tower, this is Graham 32. Were you calling me?" The tower replied in an exasperated voice, "Graham 32, we've been calling you. Flying has been called off. There are thunderstorms approaching the field."

I suddenly realized why the radio seemed so quiet and peaceful while I was flying far out in the training area. I had a weak radio and had missed the weather recall. The real shocker came with the next transmission, this time from the mobile control unit which was always in place during student flying. Mobile was always manned by an instructor, but I recognized the voice of <u>my</u> instructor, Cecil, who was not supposed to be there. If they've put my instructor out there to talk me down, I must be in big trouble, I thought.

I was right. Cecil said, in a voice with practiced calm but with just a hint of desperation, "DeGroote, we've got a direct crosswind of 25 knots and it's gusting to 50. So keep that wing down and keep the nose straight down the runway." He must be kidding! Twenty-five knots is way beyond the crosswind limits of the airplane, and 50 is impossible! But I had no options other than to somehow get the airplane on the ground. Marianna had only one lighted runway, and trying to go to another airport was out of the question. I had no night navigation training and even if I could have found another airport, chances are that I'd get involved with one of the thunderstorms that were popping up in all quadrants.

I was in position for a straight-in approach so I ignored the now empty traffic pattern and reported on a two mile final. Cecil, who had taken over the air traffic control function quietly acknowledged. I was crabbing into the wind at a frightening angle and wondered if there would be any way that I could straighten the nose down the runway at touchdown. Strangely enough I didn't feel frightened. I was more worried about all the fuss I was causing by missing the tower's recall transmissions. But if I had had enough experience to know how serious my situation was, I surely would have been frightened. As I rounded out, Cecil admonished one last time to "keep that nose straight".

As I rounded out I dropped the left wing steeply into the crosswind and kicked almost full right rudder to align the nose down the runway. To my utter amazement the aircraft touched down lightly on the left main wheel and the tail wheel simultaneously. A perfect crosswind landing! But I had only seconds to enjoy my triumph because as soon as I lowered the right main wheel to the runway the savage crosswind raised my left wing high in the air. Full aileron had no effect in lowering the wing and the T-6 swerved right heading off the paved surface. Cecil's words of wisdom at many previous briefings came back to me. "If you can't get a wing down, let the airplane have its head even if you're going off the runway. Otherwise you might ground loop, dig in a wing tip and roll it up in a ball". My T-6 was indeed headed off the runway. I let it go and tapped right brake which immediately slammed the left wheel to the ground. My only problem now was that I was charging into the unlighted blackness on the grass and could only hope to get stopped before I encountered a pothole or a tree.

I braked hard and to my relief came to a complete stop. The radio became filled with chatter since nobody was sure where I was. With the power in idle, the navigation lights and landing lights dimmed along with the rest of the lights and the tower couldn't see me. Someone opined that I had gone off the runway but he wasn't sure where. I swung the airplane around to face the tower with my landing lights and asked for clearance to taxi back across the runway to the ramp. Relief in the voices on the radio was palpable since everyone now knew that the fire trucks standing by would not have to be employed. The tower even sent out a follow-me Jeep to lead me to the ramp.

I, however, far from feeling relief, was consumed with worry that I had really fouled up and was headed for disciplinary action of some sort. I shut down the T-6 and carried my parachute back into Operations expecting the worst. But I was pleasantly surprised when Cecil appeared with the faintest trace of a smile on his lips. He patted my shoulder and bestowed on me his highest compliment, "Good job".

I think Cecil was genuinely concerned for my safety, and the management of Graham Air Service was mightily relieved to not lose a second student to night flying in a month and, incidentally, happy to get their airplane back in one piece. I was something of a celebrity among the cadets since just about everyone got the word that "DeGroote is still airborne" and witnessed my exciting return to earth. But celebrity had a shelf life of about a week among cadets and my adventure was soon forgotten. My room mate, Randy Fisher, had the same sort of notoriety around the same time. While flying in the training area he had a problem with smoke in the cockpit. The smoke quickly blossomed into flame and Randy had a serious engine fire on his hands. He followed emergency procedures but the fire got worse. An instructor listening to the radio chatter suggested that Randy part company with his T-6 before it blew up. Randy thought that a wise bit of advice and bailed out, landing unhurt in the local lake, Blue Springs, where we cadets frequently went swimming on weekends. Randy's fame was similarly short lived and within weeks no one remembered who the cadet was who dumped a T-6 in the woods surrounding Blue Springs. Randy kept the rip cord from his chute as a souvenir.

While they didn't match the excitement of Randy's bail out or my night checkout, we still had some tension producers left at Marianna. We were all required to take check rides with Air Force check pilots who were specifically assigned to make certain that Graham Aviation was turning out the product that the Air Force had contracted for. There were five regular Air Force check pilots assigned to Marianna, and all had the reputation of being good guys who were demanding but reasonable. All, that is, except one. He was a jerk who had a reputation of trying to intimidate students to see if they would crack under pressure. Guess which of the five I drew for both my check rides?

While I was nervous at having drawn Captain Jerk for both check rides, it was the old adage of how your pending execution at dawn helps to focus the mind. I flew well on both rides and ignored his frequent sarcasm and his condescending manner because I knew he couldn't flunk me after I had performed well. After finishing my second check ride I felt an enormous wave of relief. I still had some navigation flights, a few instrument rides and some solo acrobatic work to finish, but that would be fun flying with no pressure. I was going to make it through primary training! I felt fortunate because the wash out machine was working overtime. One of my best friends, Al Binney had ground looped a T-6 recently, had trouble with night flying, and after a massive loss of confidence decided to resign. Another friend, Homer Haight, had recently been washed out because of "flying deficiencies". Homer was a fellow Philadelphian who raised his hand with me taking the oath of service back in October and driving with our group on Christmas leave and through New Orleans en route to Marianna. It was painful for me to see the disappointment in my friends' eyes but it redoubled my determination to get through the program or die trying.

That determination was put to an early test. I was in an ecstatic mood! I had nothing to do but fly some fun rides to finish basic training. And even better, Marion had arranged to fly to Marianna to visit me, twin sister Ruth acting as chaperone. They were to arrive on the daily Lockheed Lodestar flight from Jacksonville on a Saturday morning. It seemed too good to be true!

And it was. As luck would have it some one scheduled a parade on the Saturday of Marion's arrival. After the parade we were to have a standby inspection of our barracks. Okay, we were used to that sort of thing--no problem. Unfortunately, one of the four occupants of our four-man room had just washed out. A second was called home on emergency leave and the third was sick in the dispensary. That left me--with the clean up work usually done by four. I didn't make it. I had just finished cleaning the third man's part of the room when the inspecting Tac Officer walked in. He had no trouble finding a long list of things that were not in inspection order. To his question, "What's the meaning of this?" I gave the standard Aviation Cadet response, "No excuse, sir!" I actually had some damned good excuses but Cadet protocol did not allow for the use of logical argument. I was ready to accept a string of demerits and time marching on the tour path, but the lieutenant had his own ideas on how to instill discipline in this young miscreant. He bellowed, "You're restricted to base for the weekend. I'll be back to re-inspect Monday morning, and it had better be ready!"

Restricted to base with my Marion waiting for me in town? Like hell, my friend, I thought. But I shouted the obligatory "Yes, sir!" and stood at rigid attention as he left the room, satisfied that he had re-militarized another young rebel. I had already reasoned that the lieutenant was going to spend his Saturday playing golf, not looking for me on base. So I gave him five minutes while I changed into civilian clothes and followed him through the main gate to find my Marion.

Now, disobeying the direct order of a superior is a serious offense. Being absent without leave is even more serious. I weighed the seriousness of my planned rebellion against the disappointment of not seeing my Marion, and it was no contest. The power of logic is no match for the raging hormones of a 20 year old fighter pilot to be. Hell, rebelliousness is what makes a fighter pilot! Twenty minutes later I met Marion and Ruth at the Hotel Chipola in downtown Marianna. We had a great weekend and I slipped back on base unnoticed.

The Tac Officer who had been so difficult on Saturday never showed up for his promised re-inspection, for which I had prepared thoroughly. Nor did I receive any demerits or punishment tours. Since he seemed willing to forget the whole incident, I was more than willing to do likewise.

I was able to spend nearly every evening with Marion, since as upper classmen we were allowed off base whenever we were off duty. One scheduled night flight caused my only absence. Ruth was a pleasant and cooperative chaperone. I was, of course, deluged with requests from my fellow cadets to be introduced to Marion's beautiful twin sister, and my repeated explanations that she was spoken for by a friend back home fell on deaf ears.

Primary Training and Marianna came to an end in mid-July, 1953. Marion and Ruth, sadly, went home after a wonderful week and I reverted to my previous status of ordinary aviation cadet. Our class then had a graduation party at the newly completed cadet club. After the party five of us went out in search of a restaurant and further adventure. All-night restaurants were hard to find around Marianna so we stole a watermelon from a farmer's field and continued our search. I dozed off but fortunately I have always been a light sleeper. I was in the back seat of the car and awoke to the sound of a blaring truck horn. I instantly became aware that everyone in our car was asleep, including the driver! I pounded the driver awake and the truck driver whose lane we had been occupying went by, horn still blowing. The Air Force had come very close to losing five partially trained pilots in one stupid accident. Appropriately aware of our incredibly bad judgment, we drove back to the base to close out this phase of our lives. For me, it was assignment to Foster Air Force Base in Victoria, Texas for a course entitled Basic Single Engine Pilot Training.

Foster Air Force Base

Our group from Marianna was split up for Basic Training. The first split assigned trainees to either single or multi engine training bases. Since nearly everyone wanted single engine, i.e. fighters, the bottom of the class went to multi engine schools. I was happy to have made the cut for single engine training. Foster was one of several single engine training bases. We had ten days or so to make our way from Marianna to Foster and I once again got lucky with transportation, still having no car of my own. An acquaintance, Gene Kirby, lived in upstate New York and agreed to drop me off in Philadelphia and pick me up after a few days' leave time so we could proceed together to Foster.

I spent several wonderful days at home, most of them with Marion with whom I was beginning to mention the word "marriage" more and more frequently. The time went all too fast, and I was soon on my way to Texas.

I signed in at Foster on July 27th, 1953 for a program that was to include 55 hours in the propellor-driven T-28 and 80 hours in the jet-powered T-33. I was happy to see the flight line loaded with both models. There would be no waiting for aircraft to arrive this time. My morale was low after having to leave Marion so quickly, but it improved with my first flight in the T-28. The airplane was much more modern than the T-6 and was bigger and more powerful. Instead of the T-6's 600 horsepower Pratt & Whitney it had an 800 horsepower Wright-Cyclone. My first impression of the T-28 was that it was easier to fly than the T-6. I wondered why the Air Force would have a trainee go from harder to easier rather than the other way around. That question was never answered for me, but the reasoning probably was that the T-28, with its tricycle gear and rapid roll rate, would probably better prepare us for the jet aircraft we'd soon be flying.

On my first flight I did the usual tap dance on the rudder pedals during landing roll out that I had done in the T-6. My new instructor gently pointed out that it wasn't necessary to anticipate directional control problems with this airplane. "It's not a T-6", he said with a chuckle. I was especially impressed with the rapid roll rate of my new mount. A simple lateral flick of the stick and the airplane did a perfect roll, little or no rudder pressure required. While my first love was the T-6, the T-28 was a good candidate for alienating my affections.

T-28 At Victoria, TX. The T-28 Was Actually Easier To Fly Than The T-6.

My instructor was also a pleasant surprise. My experience with Air Force pilots had been gained from just a few rides with the check pilot, "Captain Jerk", at Marianna. Since all instruction henceforth would come from military pilots, I was expecting the worst. The surprise was that they all seemed reasonable and helpful. My instructor was a mature captain named Markle who I discovered had been an enlisted pilot in WWII, flew Spitfires, flew in the Berlin

Airlift and was hoping to retain his officer rank until retirement. I don't know how his career ended but it seemed inconceivable to me at the time that the Air Force wouldn't take care of a man with his service and experience. He was an excellent pilot who actually treated his students with respect. I had lots to learn and hoped that some of his experience would rub off on me. He seemed quite willing and able to accommodate me.

My stay at Foster was to be an abbreviated one but I didn't know that on arrival. I was cleared for solo in the T-28 after three transition flights with an instructor and settled into the Foster routine, enjoying the almost brand new T-28s. We did the usual things: instrument flying, navigation, night flying and pattern work. I greatly appreciated the excellent cockpit lighting system during night flying. That, along with the huge bubble canopy made night flying a real pleasure after the T-6 with its restricted tail wheel induced loss of forward visibility and its dim-out cockpit lighting.

There was a new wrinkle, however, in the T-28 training program. We were introduced to formation flying, and I loved it! To this day I consider the close up view of an airplane, with gear and flaps up, in flight to be one of the most beautiful sights in the world--a virtual work of art. Formation flying provides that view automatically. I learned the new skill quickly, felt confident at it and thought that I was pretty good at it. Many of my classmates felt very stressed when flying that close to another airplane, and some washed out because they couldn't get the hang of it.

Victoria, Texas was in the midst of a very bad weather year and it was to affect my future. In an effort to catch up on flight time the leaders at the base decided to send some students along with behind-the-line base pilots on cross country flights during weekends. I was chosen to be one of those students. I didn't mind flying on weekends, but flying straight and level for two thousand miles isn't very good training. The major I was flying with was a staff officer, not an instructor, and I was aware that his interest was in getting from point A to point B in the shortest time possible. Since I couldn't do anything about it, I decided to fly straight and level for once and enjoy the ride. But it turned out that I lost about

10 hours of valuable instrument training that I had to fit in on my own later.

The rain in Victoria continued for weeks on end. We did some flying in the weather but since students were not qualified to fly solo in instrument conditions an instructor had to be on board each airplane. We got farther and farther behind on solo time. This in turn delayed our transition to the T-33.

By mid-September a few members of our class completed the T-28 phase and began to fly the T-33. Included in this group was one of my two room mates, Bud Kavanaugh. My other room mate was Tony Hutters, a Danish cadet. They were both good guys and we got along well together, even chipping in 10 dollars each to buy a radio-phonograph so we could share music in the room. I was happy for Bud, though a little envious, that he was progressing and I was cooling my heels. My envy disappeared, however, when word got around a few days later that one of our T-33s had crashed. The crew turned out to be Bud and his instructor and both had perished. We used to joke with Bud about his instructor who looked like a movie star. His wife, who was a dazzling blond, used to pick him up in their new convertible--the car and his wife never failing to draw admiring glances from the cadet group. A feeling of deep gloom fell over the base. It didn't seem possible that two young men could die so quickly with their lives looking so promising. Tony and I were, of course, devastated. I wanted very much to talk to someone about it, but I elected not to tell Marion that I had lost my friend.

Life, of course, had to go on. The Korean War had just ended, but pilot training continued unabated since the cold war was far from over. We knew, however, that standards would be raised and that those coveted silver wings would be ever more difficult to obtain. At this point the weather broke for a few days and I was able to get in my final formation training flights to complete the T-28 phase.

We were issued the required helmets and oxygen masks so we could take training in the altitude chamber. We had two "flights" allowing us to learn about high altitude problems like hypoxia. It was fascinating and useful training. When it was over I had nothing else standing in the way of my checking out in one of those shiny, sleek T-33s that I had been admiring for months.

The T-33 was an easy airplane to love. It was a product of the Kelly Johnson famous "Skunk Works" at Lockheed Aircraft. It was actually a two-seat version of the P-80, the United States' first practical jet fighter. (The first U.S. operational jet fighter was the Bell P-59 Airacomet which was underpowered and slower than contemporary piston fighters--thus it never reached widespread operational usage). The T-33 was officially called the "Shooting Star", but was known to all pilots as the "T-Bird". For reasons that puzzled the designers, the T- Bird turned out to be slightly faster than the single seat P-80 (later redesignated F-80)

The T-Bird, if not quite at the leading edge of technology, was very close to it. Jet power was very new, the Germans having pioneered it with the Me-262 which revolutionized air warfare and forced the Allied Powers to vastly accelerate their development of jet engines. The T-bird's 4600 pound thrust J-33 engine was a copy of the RAF's first practical jet engine. It was simplicity itself with a simple centrifugal compressor being turned by a single turbine wheel powered by ejected gases provided by a series of burner cans which burned a fuel-air mixture. The simple but efficient jet engine when married to the excellent Lockheed airframe produced an airplane that was a joy to behold and to fly. It remained in service for decades despite being the first practical U.S. jet, produced in the heat of wartime by technicians under pressure to get something flying now. It's hard to overstate the feeling of pride and self-satisfaction in the heart of a 20 year-old who was about to get to fly this thing!

On the 26th of September, 1953, one day before my 21st birthday, I was scheduled for my first T-33 orientation ride, the so-called "dollar ride". It was called that because the student had little to do but get used to the sights and sounds of jet flying while the instructor did most of the flying. And was I impressed! The almost total absence of vibration was the first thing that got my attention. After that was the roll rate. The ailerons were hydraulically boosted, and the old-timers could usually recognize a new pilot by the way the wings rocked after takeoff.

I was looking forward to attacking the T-Bird course of study as vigorously as possible when the Air Force threw me another curve ball. The bad weather at Foster made it impossible for the instructor cadre to get enough flying hours in the time remaining.

The answer was to send part of our class to bases with better weather. I was one of the chosen and went hurriedly back to the barracks to pack my belongings for a flight the next morning to Williams Air Force Base in Chandler, Arizona. I had mixed feelings about the move. On the one hand I was glad that I would get to see the desert southwest, but I was apprehensive about learning a new area and new local procedures. In any case, the next morning found me boarding a B-25 (the model of bomber used by Jimmie Doolittle to bomb Tokyo) for a flight to Williams Air Force Base. The move had been so hastily ordered that I had to call Marion long distance on the phone, an expensive way to communicate in those days.

I spent my 21st birthday for the most part in the plexiglass nose of the B-25, which provided me with a remarkable view of the desert Southwest. I dozed off several times, awakening startled to find myself hanging in space in the glass nose. All in all, not an entertaining birthday but one I've always remembered. Several vibration filled hours later we landed at Williams Air Force Base, known as "The Fighter School"

Williams

I was afraid that our arrival at Williams would not fill the local instructors' hearts with joy. I was right. The locals saw us as a nuisance and an interruption to their well-planned curriculum. We arriving students found ourselves trying to learn new procedures that our classmates who had started at "Willie" were by now very familiar with. We ran into bad attitudes from almost everyone from the ground school instructors to supply people and, worst of all, from some of the flight instructors. This was patently unfair and we "new guys" became very resentful with justification. Our attitude manifested itself in criticism, probably unjust, of the local flying operation where every mistake we saw was magnified in our eyes. In a letter to Marion, I unloaded:

From what I've seen of the flying around here, I'd like nothing better than to get up in formation with them. I think I can fly the pants off any of these meatheads but they won't give me an airplane to prove it.

I chuckle today at being unable to detect the slightest hint of humility in the words of a young man who was, after all, still very much a novice pilot. But the Air Force's motto at fighter schools was, "Every man a tiger", and I guess by now some of that had rubbed off on me.

In any case, we began to be absorbed in the Williams way of training albeit slowly. We were required to show that we were caught up on all ground school requirements and all administrative work before flying. To make matters worse, I contracted a bad cold, probably from my instructor who was grounded from having one. It ended with my going from my first jet flight at Foster on September 26th until my first flight at Williams on October 19th. That's a long time between flights for a low-time pilot checking out in a jet for the first time.

My first few flights went well enough, but I learned at the outset that I had a problem with my instructor. We didn't like each other. For starters, all of the instructors, except mine, were Korean War veterans. Mine had done nothing but train students since he had been commissioned. I had been looking forward to learning something about combat flying from one of our squadron's veterans, and my disappointment may have been too obvious. In addition, my instructor, a freshly minted captain from Wisconsin, was a stickler for military discipline and protocol. I considered him to be a martinet. I was probably right. A few final irritants to me:

With My Trusty T-bird At Willie Field, Arizona. A Wonderful Airplane.

His personal call sign was "Shakey", not exactly the ringing battle cry of a fighter pilot attacking. The same was true of our flight call sign and I was forced to submit to the chuckles of my friends with call signs like, "Rocket" or," "Red eye", when they heard our flight call in as "Wimpy".

From his perspective, I probably appeared to him to be an East Coast smart alec kid who rebelled at regulations and badly needed a lesson in discipline. He, too, was probably right.

But the greatest problem we had in instructor-student relationships was that I was already a better pilot than he was, and I think he knew it. That was probably not his fault. He had been an instructor from the day he had finished pilot training, and instructors, while they flew lots of hours, seldom handled the controls. His lack of proficiency was most apparent in formation flying. As luck would have it, that was always my strong suit, the portion of training that gave me no trouble at all. I would giggle silently while he bounced around trying to demonstrate good position holding to me. I would then solicitously inquire, "Can I try it, sir?" Next, I would glue the T-Bird into position and quietly hum the melody of a recent movie, "Anything you can do, I can do better". Very bad judgment on my part, but I loved it. He would retaliate by making me do pushups on the ramp wearing my parachute if I failed to hold the nose wheel off after touchdown. I did lots of pushups but I also got to be pretty good at holding the T-Bird's nose wheel off during landing roll.

In any case, I liked Willie much better as I got more involved in flying. It was, without a doubt, better equipped than Foster. They had, for example, a "boom bucket". The boom bucket was more correctly called the ejection seat trainer. It was a set of vertical rails 100 feet or so high. At the bottom of the rails was a fully functioning ejection seat, which in those days, used a 20 millimeter cannon shell to provide motive power. We students all got to take a ride on this contraption which was actually good training and fun besides. When my turn came, the seat did not fire instantly when I pulled the trigger. I looked down to see what the problem was--a mistake because the seat then fired giving me a stiff neck for a month.

On the flight line, things were going well and I soloed out in the T-bird after four familiarization rides on October 27th. So, a year after leaving Philadelphia and a month past my 21st birthday I was a jet pilot and was feeling pretty pleased with myself. The T-Bird was a masterpiece, and I was ecstatic to be able to fly it.

My instructor, however, had not given up on re-making this young jerk over into his idea of a true Air Force officer. Matters came to a head one day in November when I was scheduled for two solo navigation flights on the same day. Maintenance had been slow in servicing my airplane, so I waited patiently on the ramp until it was ready. I then flew my carefully planned triangular navigation flight but because I got my airplane late I was also late for the normal landing period. Since I was scheduled in the same aircraft for my second flight, I was once again late for take off and, consequently late for landing. It all seemed to me to be no big deal.

French Cadet Friends Demonstrate Their Highly Disciplined Approach To Flight Training

My instructor, however, was livid. His students were not late for anything, period! When I asked him what exactly he would have done, he suggested that I could have cut the second leg of my flight short to make up time. This struck me as inordinately stupid and I couldn't conceal my contempt for the idea. I pointed out that a good navigator would never pull a heading out of his butt in hopes that it would be close enough to get him home. I suggested that flying over desert country without knowing exactly where you were was foolhardy. I was right--but cadets seldom won arguments with captains, right or wrong.

The following day I discovered just how badly I had lost the argument. And it brought me in close contact with a man who would influence my future significantly. Enter Major Virgil Turgeau, known to all as "Tobey".

Tobey was the commander of our flight, Rebel Flight. He was rarely seen in the day-to-day training operation, leaving that to his instructors--unless there was a problem. For example, he de-briefed the group one day after observing some sloppy pattern work. He called on one miscreant to explain why he had made a low final turn. The unfortunate cadet, who should have known better, responded while still seated in his chair. Tobey, who was normally soft spoken, erupted with, "STAND UP"! Fully two thirds of the flight, including me, jumped to rigid attention.

So there was a certain fear factor associated with Tobey's presence in the briefing room. If his name appeared on the schedule it was inevitably to fly with someone who was in trouble. Usually, it was the first step in a student's trip through the "washout machine". Students scheduled to fly with Tobey were often never seen again in the briefing room.

Given that background, it becomes easy to imagine my reaction to seeing my name on the scheduling board in an aircraft with Major Turgeau in the back seat. My first reaction was fear. My instructor was trying to get me washed out of the program at this late stage, after all my hard work! I saw him across the room wearing what appeared to be a look of triumph on his face. I did not acknowledge his presence, but my fear instantaneously changed to blind fury! "Alright, you s.o.b.", I thought, "let's see you wash me out"!

Amid words of encouragement from my friends, who couldn't understand what had happened since I appeared to be doing so well, I sought out Major Turgeau. He briefed that we would do some instrument work, unusual with me in the front seat, and then some airwork at one of the auxiliary fields. I had hoped that I could demonstrate my strong suit, formation, but it was not to be. I suspected that my instructor picked instruments because I was still behind as a result of the wasted time of my cross country flight with the major at Foster. But I thought that I could hold my own by now and felt fairly confident on instruments.

We did a radio range orientation and low approach, and I nailed it! My inner fury had raised my adrenalin level and I was concentrating on every detail. I was going to have a good day! After the instrument work, Tobey cut the power for a simulated flameout landing. The auxiliary field was in plain view and I set up in the high key position easily. My approach was perfect and Tobey let me take it down right to touchdown. I squeaked the T-Bird onto the runway and without waiting for instructions said "going around". I was on a roll and wanted to fly some more. Tobey got into the spirit and decided to give me the ultimate test, simulating engine failure just after takeoff, wherein the pilot has to make an instant decision to either eject or bend the airplane around in a maximum performance turn, landing in the direction opposite to take off. I instantly chose the latter, narrating that in an actual flameout I would jettison the tip tanks, but we could make it okay keeping them. I then pulled a maximum performance 90 degree turn, reversed into a 270 degree turn, lined up with the runway, lowered gear and flaps, and made a perfect downwind touchdown. At that point Tobey, who had done nothing that I considered to be unfair, said, "I've got it. Let's go home." The tension drained from my sweating body. I knew I had passed and that I wasn't going to wash out.

After the flight, I saw my instructor talking to Tobey, and I managed to get just close enough to eavesdrop while stowing my parachute. Tobey was saying, "He knows it was a good ride". That was all I needed to hear.

My instructor was gracious in defeat, telling me that he did, indeed, schedule me for a check ride to "get my attention", and congratulating me on doing well. I was not so gracious, grunting an unsmiling acknowledgement. A serendipitous outcome was that my ride counted as my transition check, leaving only my instrument check ride to go. The other plus was that I had established a rapport with Tobey that would blossom later in my career.

My instrument check passed uneventfully in early December and it looked like I was home free. I allowed myself the luxury of thinking about Christmas leave and seeing my Marion again.

Before Christmas leave time came the commissioning ceremony for members of Class 54ABC. The whole class was sworn in as 2nd lieutenants, but only "A" Class had finished flying and received their wings as well. All of us from Foster had to wait a month for our wings. But having passed all my check rides and cruising near the top of the class in academics, I was sitting pretty. I had only about four hours of routine solo time left to complete Air Force pilot training.

My transportation home for Christmas was difficult since the closest I could get to Philadelphia riding in a friend's car was Indianapolis. From there I took a bus the rest of the way.

Christmas was wonderful and I made the smartest decision of my life by formally asking Marion to marry me. I didn't exactly do that right either. Thinking that a wedding ring shouldn't be my only gift for her, I purchased a robe as well. Marion caught sight of the large box from me and assumed that she would be getting something large, not a ring. We went Christmas caroling with a group of friends and Marion spent the evening disappointed in me. After caroling, I finally brought out the ring and asked her to marry me. Despite the fact that I had ruined her Christmas Eve, she accepted and we agreed to marry as soon as I completed advanced training. While I didn't relate it to Marion, I wanted to wait until then because so many fatal accidents occurred in advanced training, and I didn't want Marion to be a 21 year old widow.

After the holidays I managed to get back to Williams only because Ruth worked for Pan Am and was able to get me one of the few remaining seats on an airliner. I, once again displaying youthful irresponsibility, had failed to make any arrangements to get back to base. But I did get back and began to make the adjustment to being an officer. I had moved into bachelor officers' quarters (BOQ) and found my way around the officers' club, but I still felt very much like an aviation cadet. However, there was no denying that the life of an officer was vastly superior to that of a cadet.

I hadn't flown for almost a month and I was eager to get back in the cockpit. I flew four more flights, and on January 9, 1954 my log book shows I practiced acrobatics and it contains the simple entry, "completed basic single engine training". After 14 long months my work was done--or perhaps just beginning.

With Brand-New Silver Wings and Gold Bars

On January 16th we were given our Air Force silver wings at a formal ceremony. Many of the students had a family member present to pin on the wings, but I wasn't so lucky. One of my friends and I settled for pinning each other's wings on. In any event, I've never been more proud, before or since, to receive any award.

My instructor invited his four students to dinner with his family--one child and a pregnant wife. They were very gracious, but he and I remained a bit cool toward each other. In retrospect, I should have been more mature and gone along with his General Patton complex rather than risk my entire aviation career over nothing. On the other hand, he was a captain and he too should have been mature--at least enough to handle a strong willed post-teenager. I never ran across him again--maybe a good thing, but my encounter with him probably helped me to grow up.

The last thing to be sweated out at Willie was our next assignment. I wanted multi-engine jets because I was sure that I would leave the

Air Force and fly for an airline. The only opportunity was an F-89 assignment, and I was high enough in class standing that I got it. I reasoned, correctly, that the airlines in a few years would be seeking out pilots with multi-jet time. Events were to make me follow a different path, but for now it was off to Moody Air Force Base for F-89 training!

Moody

I left Williams on January 25th, 1954 in a 1948 Ford convertible owned by Jack Cronin, a fellow student at Willie who had gone through the program as a student officer. After a short discussion of the subject, Jack readily admitted that he had had a much more pleasant experience going through pilot training as a student officer rather than as a cadet. And the pay was a lot better.

We crossed the southern United States at a leisurely pace spending most nights at Air Force bases, including Lackland. We arrived at Valdosta, GA on the 29th, a Friday, and did not need to report for duty until Monday. That gave Jack and me the opportunity to move into our quarters at our leisure, and we did so as room mates.

We discovered upon reporting in that we'd be taking the Air Force's all-weather training course before checking out in a fighter. That course consisted of several weeks of ground school followed by 25 hours of T-bird flying, almost all of it under the hood. It sounded like work, but I liked the idea of getting intensive training on instruments. We also found that there was good news and bad news about our follow-on training. The good news was that we had been slated for check out in the F-89 which Jack and I preferred over the single engine F-94. The bad news was that Moody was being forced to give up a number of F-89s to operational air defense squadrons. That would result in a shortage of aircraft which would delay our graduation, in my case from April to July. This upset me and my raging hormones no end. I was ready to take up life with Marion and three more months of bachelorhood did not fit my plans. Jack, who had planned to marry a Phoenix girl, Polly, took matters into his own hands and arranged for a wedding at the Moody base Chapel a few weeks hence. I still wanted to finish advanced training before marriage because of the risks involved, but, more practically because I couldn't yet afford it. So, I groused a lot and got a new room mate, Dick Miller a classmate from Williams. I went to Jack's wedding a few weeks later and pressed on.

The stretched out program caused me to not fly enough for my liking, but I thought the training was excellent. My instructor problems were over as I was the sole student of a 24 year old Korean War vet who had flown F-86s and F-84s in combat and was a West Point graduate to boot. He liked the way I flew, I liked the way he flew and I worked hard to learn from his combat experience.

As a sidelight to my recounting of the training experience, a bit of philosophy is in order because of an upcoming and unforeseen event that intruded on my routine. It seems that in the life of every fighter pilot there comes a seminal event which defines his future and determines in his mind whether or not he cares to proceed in his chosen profession or, as many do, escape to a less demanding role in aviation. This defining moment in my case came at an uncomfortably early point in my development.

We were allowed a few hours of solo contact time in order to maintain our proficiency with contact flying while we were otherwise flying exclusively under the hood. Some of those hours were scheduled at night so we could keep our hand in flying after dark. During one of these routine night proficiency flights I was to come of age, well before my time, as a professional fighter pilot. I was challenged with a serious emergency and my very survival hinged on whether or not I was up to the job of handling it.

The evening of March 5th was clear and beautifully calm and I was looking forward to flying in the excellent conditions. I had flown at night twice in the previous week, once with an instructor to regain my night currency and once solo. I was fully current on night landings and the flight should have been a piece of cake. Departure was normal and I planned to sightsee in the local area while burning off tip tank fuel so as to be light enough to practice night landings. But climbing through 15,000 feet the yellow engine overheat light illuminated. I reduced power to idle and assessed the situation. Tailpipe temperature read zero, an indication that the circuit had been burned out and that I had an engine fire behind me. My instructor at Williams had discussed engine fires with his students many times. He was convinced that jet engines would explode in an instant if there was a fire, and at the first indication of one that the throttle should be stop cocked. I reacted mechanically to my training by stop cocking the throttle and turning off the main fuel shutoff valve. That immediately changed my sleek jet airplane into a very heavy glider. I set up best gliding airspeed and called Moody Tower to declare an emergency. I advised tower that I had had an engine fire and that I was preparing to eject. I transmitted my position, banked steeply left and right to ascertain that there were no populated areas below me and jettisoned the tip tanks to improve my gliding range.

Telling myself to stay calm I thought again about ejecting. Moody's well lighted 8,000 foot runway was clearly in sight and I was sure I could glide far enough to set up a flameout pattern. I advised the tower that I would attempt a flameout landing and told them to keep all traffic clear. Another factor influencing my decision to not eject was the very large Okefenokee Swamp below me. The thought of sharing that piece of real estate with its natural reptilian population did not appeal to me. My announcement that I would attempt a "dead stick" landing brought the Supervisor of Flying, who was on duty in the tower onto the radio for the first time. While noncommittal, he seemed to be in favor of my attempt. I knew that all decisions would be mine, but it was nevertheless reassuring to have an experienced T-bird pilot to talk to.

I had made many simulated flameout landings in my T-bird training but even practicing them at night was considered too hazardous, so I had never attempted one in darkness. I made several turns to lose excess altitude so as to arrive at the "high key" point over the end of the runway at 5500 feet. The procedure then called for a descending 360 degree turn to place the aircraft on final approach at the proper altitude to land. Needless to say, there would be only one opportunity with margin for error at zero.

Just before I arrived at the "low key" position, 3500 feet opposite the touchdown point, my aileron control became extremely heavy. I had forgotten that with a wind milling engine hydraulic pressure, which supplied aileron boost, would be lost. At the higher airspeed I had held approaching the pattern the engine had been wind milling fast enough to provide pressure, but could not do so at lower airspeeds. The Supervisor of Flying suggested that I turn the boost off to keep it from cutting in and out. I did so and realized that I would be making my first ever unboosted landing in the T-bird. My beautifully flying jet was suddenly handling like a truck. I lowered the landing gear, using the battery powered emergency gear lowering hydraulic pump. I worried that the aircraft battery, which had been carrying the entire electrical load for some time now, might fail on final approach, leaving me in a dark airplane. Fortunately, the battery was equal to the task.

I glided through "base key", my last chance to adjust my altitude by turning, at 1500 feet. Rolling out on final approach, I realized that I was high. I lowered partial flaps, further draining the battery, then, seeing that I was still quite high, lowered full flaps. I dove toward the end of the runway picking up unwanted airspeed in the process. Still high, I reverted to an old Piper Cub technique, throwing the T-bird into a steep side slip. Now, I had been told that side slipping a T-bird would probably result in loss of control, but I figured that without tip tanks those rules didn't apply. Besides, I reasoned that my choices were to side slip or end up in a fireball off the far end of the runway. It worked! I was still too fast over the end of the runway, but I planted the airplane, narrowly avoiding a "porpoising" bounce and stood on the brakes. I had enough rolling energy left to turn the airplane off at the last taxiway, allowing the tower to keep the field open. I evacuated the cockpit, looking for signs of engine fire, but saw only some smoke from the abused wheel brakes.

As with my crosswind landing incident in the T-6 the previous year, I had brief celebrity status among the student population, and as with the T-6 incident my adventure was soon forgotten. It did, however, have a lasting effect on me personally. If nothing else, I had proven to myself that I would not panic in a life-threatening emergency. On the other hand, it had a negative effect in that I started to believe my own publicity. I tended to become dogmatic in discussions about flying, talking when, still as a novice pilot, I should have been listening. I had to scare myself a few times unnecessarily before I learned that there was still a lot that I didn't know.

In regard to my dead stick landing, I've thought many times how I would have handled the situation today, after so many years of experience and after so many mistakes. For starters, if it happened to me today I would never react immediately because of something I had been told by some one who had never done it. I had been brainwashed to believe that jet engines blew up at the first hint of a fire. That was nonsense. The J-33 engine was surely a primitive machine, the first of its kind, rather like a Model T in a world of Cadillacs. But it had the virtue of Model T simplicity--and it didn't blow up. Given the indications of fire in today's world I would pull the throttle to idle and make a flameout approach, but I would never stopcock the throttle. I never saw an incident report on my experience, but I doubt that I actually had a fire. I think that going by the book could have cost me my life, and I think it took many years of experience before I knew when to go by the book and when to wing it. Some further examples will doubtless make themselves known as my narrative progresses.

Life went on at Moody. My instructor was suitably impressed by my short lived notoriety, but after brief congratulations got back to making me a better combat pilot. Teaching instrument flying bored him to tears and we soon established a ritual wherein the last 10 minutes of our flight would be dedicated to his showing me how to fly as he did in Korea-- at extremely low altitude. He liked to fly over water, usually at a beach, but close to land and buildings. We would usually pass by beachfront properties below the 2nd floor level at 450 miles per hour or so. Since we flew very early in the morning, I'm sure the wake up call was appreciated by the sleeping vacationers.

While we had fun, my instructor and I worked hard on honing my skills as an instrument pilot. Not too many Air Force pilots had been through the All Weather School, and while I didn't appreciate it at the time, it was invaluable training that probably saved my life during the next few years while I was a novice pilot building up experience. By the time I had completed the course I was sick and tired of being under the hood, but I felt as much at home flying on instruments as I did flying contact. How useful that would prove to be in my next assignment!

I completed the instrument course without fanfare and was unhappy to be facing several months of boredom. Our class was officially washed back because there were simply not enough F-89s to fly in training. I began several months of "country club" existence during which I became very familiar with the Officers' Club swimming pool and tennis courts. We were scheduled to fly a T-bird twice a week, day or night and had an occasional make-work job to do, but mostly we were off. Being a hard charging youngster I could not accept this as a stroke of good fortune. It seemed like an impediment to my wish to get on with my career as a fighter pilot.

I spent much of my time reading the F-89 Flight Handbook and frequently went into a maintenance hangar to sit in the Scorpion's cockpit. Before I had my first simulator ride I was able to find any switch in the cockpit with my eyes closed.

In early May a group of radar observers, freshly out of navigation/radar observer school, arrived to be teamed up with our group of freshly trained instrument pilots. I teamed up with a muscular young man named Gene Polhemus from Plainfield, New Jersey. We hit it off well and began what was to be a lifelong friendship. With no F-89s to fly Gene was happy to go along in the back seat on my T-bird flights. He had never flown in any jet, let alone one with dual controls. Since he had dreams of going through pilot training eventually, he was delighted when I offered to give him some rudimentary flying lessons.

We continued our country club existence and Gene got me to relax a bit. We decided to try our hand at tennis since the courts were just adjacent to the pool. Since we were so obviously bad at the game we attracted some attention. One interested onlooker was an athletic looking young man who appeared to be about five to ten years older than Gene and me. He offered to show us some fundamentals of the game and we gladly accepted. Introductions were made and we discovered that our new friend was Captain Ted Harris who was waiting, like us, for available F-89s. But there the similarity ended. We noticed that Ted's arms were scarred, evidently from burns. Coaxing the story from him we found that he had been a B-29 pilot in Korea and was shot down by MIGs. He was burned because his tail gunner failed to respond to Harris' bailout order. Thinking that the gunner may have been incapacitated, Harris made

With Gene Polhemus - New F-89 Crew, Moody

his way through the burning B-29 only to find that the gunner had already bailed out without acknowledging the order. Harris then bailed out and was taken prisoner by the North Koreans. He told us that he resisted interrogation but that his crew cooperated with the North Koreans even volunteering that Ted was the Squadron Intelligence Officer. Ted told us that after his release he requested a fighter assignment because he didn't want to go into combat again with a large crew.

I was impressed with Ted's obvious heroism, but was impressed much more so a year or two later when I picked up a men's magazine with the cover story about the last man out of Panmunjom, the prisoner exchange point after the Korean War cease fire. It told the story of a POW who had refused to sign a germ warfare confession as a precondition to being released. He told his captors that if he couldn't go home with his honor, he wouldn't go home at all. The North Koreans, exasperated with a prisoner who gave them nothing but trouble, finally relented and released him. The POW in the story was none other than our tennis friend at Moody, Ted Harris who became the Air Force's poster boy for conduct under POW conditions. I met many impressive people in my Air Force career, some of them heroes, but none more impressive than Ted Harris.

While we F-89 trainees waited patiently to begin our course of instruction, our friends who had been given F-94 training progressed rapidly. The F-94C was a sleek single, engine, rocket firing interceptor that was closely related to the T-bird. It had a radar observer's station in the back seat instead of dual controls, a radome on the nose and an afterburner equipped engine. One F-94 people-related story is worth telling.

One of my good friends was a classmate from pilot training named Wilfred "Satch" Handel. Satch was in the F-94 program and was returning from a training mission one day with his R.O., Pete Peterson in the back. They flew a beautiful traffic pattern and made an exceptionally smooth landing. Everything went perfectly except for one detail. They had forgotten to lower the landing gear. The smooth touchdown was, unfortunately, on the extended speed brakes and the aft fuselage. Since the F-94 normally sat close to the ground neither Satch nor Pete realized that they had landed gear up. Satch, wondering why the airplane had stopped so short without braking, added power to taxi clear of the runway. When the F-94 refused to move, Satch made what is surely one of the most classic radio transmission in the annals of air traffic control history. He pressed the mike button and said, "Say tower, we must have blown a tire or something. This thing won't move. Could you send out a tug for us?" Moody Tower personnel, after recovering from disabling laughter, sent the required tug along with maintenance people and jacks to put the only slightly damaged F-94 back up on its three wheels, landing gear handle down. Satch would later check out in the F-89 and become a member of my squadron where he was an excellent and respected pilot. The sobriquet "Landing Gear" Handel lasted only a short time.

"Satch" Handel With F-89, Moody AFB

As April came to a close the F-89 situation improved and we finally started ground school and flight simulator work. The simulator was primitive by today's standards of full motion machines but for someone who had flown only WWII vintage Link trainers it was miraculous. It was, in fact, a very good procedures trainer although it really did not reproduce the "feel" of the aircraft. It did, however, afford Gene and me the opportunity to run radar intercepts, a real time saver.

Finally, on June 3rd I began my transition training into the F-89. The first flight was of little value since it put an instructor in the front seat with me in the back with nothing but a radar scope which I didn't know how to work. It got me accustomed to the noise the airplane made but otherwise was a waste of time. The following day I got my "real" checkout, and it was a thrill. The F-89 was a huge airplane for a fighter. It weighed 45,000 pounds, roughly two and one half times the T-bird's weight. It had two engines and afterburners. There was no trainer version so the first flight had to be right. For a 21 year old who had flown only relatively small single engine airplanes it presented quite a challenge. There wouldn't even be someone to read the checklist since the people who designed the checkout program insisted that no instructor or R.O. could fly on the first two missions. Gene, displaying great courage, volunteered to go with me but was not allowed. Obviously the leaders decided that there was no point in subjecting more than one person to the hazards of initial checkout of a neophyte pilot. In any case my first two flights were uneventful and I found that the big machine was quite docile once I got used to the very long takeoff roll.

Once started, Gene and I became very busy and our country club routine ended abruptly. We flew almost every day, often twice a day. This was great for me since I wanted to finish training as soon as possible so I could marry Marion and end my lonely bachelorhood. We were trying to make plans for a wedding, but the plans were complicated by the fact that twin sister Ruth was also getting married. The possibility of a double wedding was there, but planning even one wedding was difficult since I had no idea where I would be assigned. Finally just after the July 4th holiday Gene and I got orders as a crew to proceed to the 65th Fighter -Interceptor Squadron, Elmendorf AFB, Alaska. My reporting date made it important that Marion and I get married very soon, eliminating the chance of a double wedding since Ruth and Don were not ready to move so soon. The only other possibility was for me to go to Alaska alone and continue my bachelorhood for a while longer. This did not appeal to me at all and plans were soon made for a wedding on July 31st. I finished up my flying hours and returned to Philadelphia with Gene.

I discovered that most people in Marion's family didn't understand the military and couldn't believe that the United States Air Force could be so unreasonable as to interfere with a double wedding for "the twins". One distant relative made it clear that she also didn't understand military rank. Our wedding invitations were printed using the classic old-fashioned script. Along with the usual wedding invitation niceties it announced that the groom was "Lt Albert J. DeGroote". Now, the classic script "L" looks a lot like an "S", and Marion's relative, apparently never having seen the abbreviation for "lieutenant", responded by wishing good luck to "Marion and Saint Albert". I explained to Marion's mother that her relative's reading of the invitation was OK since all fighter pilots were saintly anyway.

Our wedding took place as planned, the most remarkable thing being the weather which was 99 degrees and the reception hall which was un-air conditioned. While everyone sweated profusely my Marion looked cool and beautiful all day long. After the reception we left for a honeymoon in New England. Even there, I couldn't shake the urge to fly and I took Marion on a flight over the New England countryside in a rented light plane. She was suitably cheerful about it but I sensed that she thought I should have different priorities on my honeymoon. After New England, we continued our honeymoon in Brant Beach on the Jersey shore, a place that had wonderful memories for us. Then it was time for Alaska planning.

Alaska was still a territory in 1954 and I had to leave Marion until I found a place to live. So, once again we were separated but I promised her that this separation would be a short one. It turned out to be about five weeks. Gene and I arranged to meet a friend, Bob Hemphill, in Denver. "Hemp" was a pilot classmate of mine who was at Moody with us and was going to the same Alaskan squadron as Gene and I. He had a Ford that he wanted to drive up the Alcan Highway and was happy to have Gene and I share expenses for the trip. So, on August 27th, still recovering from my honeymoon, I boarded an airliner, with Gene, for Denver. Hemp met us as planned and it was off to Alaska!

Alaska

Hemp's back seat in his four door Ford was quickly filled with our "stuff", and we had to sit, all three, in the front. That might not have been bad, but my two traveling companions had a liking for cigars, and as soon as they discovered that it annoyed me, they doubled up on their smoke production. I resolved not to complain, knowing that it would have only a counterproductive outcome. When I appeared to no longer be annoyed, the stogies were pretty much dispensed with. We spent one night at Yellowstone, made a few tourist visits, and pressed northward with stops at Shoshone, Wyoming and the Air Force Base at Great Falls, Montana.

We drove into Canada and found the roads to be much worse than anticipated, with some potholes 10 feet in diameter. We were required by the Canadian authorities to have two spare tires in the trunk, a requirement we felt was not necessary. But when we had to use both on the first day we decided that the Canadians knew what they were doing. The unpaved roads were graded constantly and small spiral shaped shavings from the grader blades screwed themselves into the tires, causing leaks. We lost time having tires repaired at each of the very few service stations along the route. We spent a night at Calgary and took in a Canadian football game between the Calgary Stampeders and the Winnipeg Blue Bombers. From there we went through White Horse and continued north toward Alaska. It was nearly impossible to exceed 35 miles per hour for fear of damaging a tire on the gravel. The scenery along the Alcan was spectacular when it could be seen--which was almost never. The road was carved out of deep forest and all we could see from the car was tall trees on either side. By the time we reached Anchorage on the 7th of September we had had quite enough of scenery, dust, tire changes and each other's company. I became busy very quickly moving into the BOQ, checking out equipment and especially getting the necessary orders and bureaucratic forms needed to move my new bride up to Alaska. I felt good about the squadron. People were helpful and most seemed genuinely interested in my problems with relocating my young wife and any problems I might have getting checked out in the local area and in 65th FIS aircraft.

The squadron, somewhat to my surprise, had older model F-89Cs, which were slightly different from the new F-89Ds that I flew at Moody. The primary difference was in the armament. Whereas the D model was armed with one hundred and four 2.75 inch folding fin aerial rockets, the C sported six 20 millimeter cannons. Because of the differences in weapons, the radar fire control system was also different. The F-89C radar computed a tail chase while the "D" computed a 90 degree collision course allowing for time of flight for the rockets--a so-called lead collision attack. I personally thought that the "C,s" 20 MM guns were the superior weapon. We were scheduled to get new 89Ds in a few months but I was eager to fly the "C" model and my new flight commander was eager to put me to work.

F-89 Over Alaska

My checkout was a little informal. My flight commander, knowing nothing about the "D" model assumed it was the same as the "C" He said, "Go take 755 up and look around the area." I had already had several T-bird rides and was fairly familiar with the area anyway, so I said, "Great". This was one of my early mistakes as a cocky young lieutenant. I got into the cockpit with ever trusting Gene in the back seat and managed to get the engines started. We taxied out and were cleared for takeoff, so I lined up and pushed the throttles to full power. I then tried to lift the finger lifts on the throttles which in the F-89D would ignite the afterburners. The finger lifts wouldn't budge. I later discovered that in the 89C they were used only to stopcock the engines. The tower was growing impatient with my delay since I was blocking the runway while I searched desperately for a way to light the burners. Finally I noticed two small toggle switches on the instrument panel which I knew were not in the 89D. Looking closely, I saw a faded placard that appeared to read "AB". Maybe that means "afterburner" I thought and decided to flip them up, hoping they wouldn't jettison the tip tanks. I got lucky. The burners lit nicely and I took off, acting like I knew what I was doing. I spent the rest of the flight looking around the cockpit identifying as many switches and levers as I could find that were different from those in my familiar 89D aircraft. After I landed I sat down with the flight handbook, something I should have been smart enough to do previously, and sat in a parked 89C getting familiar with most of the equipment. My flight commander assumed I had been fully trained at Moody and happily declared me combat ready so he could put me on alert that night. Gene and I set up for alert and I, somewhat sheepishly, asked my flight leader how to fire the guns since I was now defending Alaska without the slightest clue on how to fire the six 20 millimeter cannon.

While busy, we were far from overworked and I had plenty of free time to get ready for my young bride to arrive. I opened my first checking account and bought my first car, a 1950 Dodge coupe. Next I put a deposit down on a one bedroom apartment and set to work on the mountains of paperwork required to simply get my wife and a few belongings to Anchorage. Since Alaska was still a territory the military considered it an overseas assignment, and the old adage of "If the Air Force wanted you to have a wife, we'd have issued you one" seemed to apply. Finally, the paperwork was completed and Marion advised me that she would arrive on Saturday, October 2nd. I was scheduled for alert on that date, but my flight commander gave me the day off agreeing to pull alert for me if need be.

I dressed in my Sunday best and drove to Anchorage International Airport to meet Marion. Her flight arrived on time and I watched as the passengers de-planed. Soon there were no more passengers and the crew came down the stairs. I asked one of them if there were any passengers still on board and was advised there were none. Slightly panicked I went to the airline counter and reported my wife missing. An agent came close to losing his life with an attempt at humor saying, "Don't worry, we lose wives all the time." I replied, "Not my wife, you jerk!" and stormed out to check for news at the base. Sure enough, there was a telegram at the Orderly Room from Marion saying that she had missed her flight at JFK (then Idlewild) and would be a day late. She had sent a so-called full rate telegram so that it would be delivered to me, but since it was a weekend the Orderly Room was deserted except for one airman who had been stuck with charge of quarters duty. The young airman had no idea what to do with a telegram so he did nothing. I briefed him rather forcefully on the duties of a CQ but was relieved to know that my young bride was not lost somewhere in the air traffic system.

The following day I was off duty until evening alert and was able to meet Marion's flight. This time she was on board and my annoyance at her missing the previous day's flight melted away when I saw her step off the airliner. I drove her to our apartment which was a very Spartan affair but better than the Quonset hut she had been anticipating. When I reported for alert duty at the flight line my flight commander was not sympathetic at all about the missed flight and let me know that it was my problem and Marion would have to spend her first night in Anchorage alone. A few hours later he thought better of it and found a volunteer to fill in for me on alert. So I was able to go home to my bride, proving that romance is not dead among fighter pilots. Marion adjusted very quickly to her role of Air Force wife, made friends rapidly, and soon knew more about things like base housing than I did. Since she had a civil service job in the U.S. she had no difficulty getting a job on base. She signed on with the Office of Special Investigations (O.S.I.) and soon had a Top Secret security clearance, much to my chagrin, since I held only a Secret clearance.

Marion was introduced to the rigors of being an Air Force wife early. Tragedy was, very simply, a part of Air Force life in the early 50's. Jet engines were primitive, and the Allison J-35 which powered the F-89 was the first axial flow engine to go operational. It was copied from the engine that powered the German Me-262, the first operational jet fighter. The F-89, a 45,000 pound airplane, was grossly underpowered by the two afterburning J-35s producing a total of 15,200 pounds of thrust. The engine was known in the gallows humor of the Fighter Lounge bar as the "Allison Time Bomb". Single engine performance in the F-89 was very poor and the high accident rate at Elmendorf was partly due to that fact. The other major factor was the very low experience level of the pilots. Most of them, like me, were fresh out of pilot training, a by-product of the Korean War buildup. The 65th Squadron Commander proudly announced at a party that the average flying time of the squadron's pilots was now over 500 hours. Compared to squadrons I later flew with, this was a ridiculously low figure, the level in those later years always exceeding several thousand hours.

These factors inevitably led to accidents. There were three F-89 squadrons at Elmendorf, each having 25 F-89s and several T-birds. The squadrons were the 64th, 65th and 66th. Our squadron was lucky, in that most of the accidents happened to the 64th and 66th. But the sound of the fire station siren was always enough to send a wave of fear through the squadron wives.

The sting of tragedy hit home after Marion had been an Air Force wife for only a few months. I learned that Jack Cronin, my room mate at Moody, who had transported me in his Ford convertible from Williams to Moody and whose wedding I had attended, had recently been assigned to one of our sister squadrons. I mentioned it to Marion and we invited Jack and his wife, Polly, to dinner on the next Friday night. When that Friday came, I was at the flight line when the crash siren sounded. I was relieved to find that it was not one of our squadron's aircraft that had crashed but devastated to find shortly thereafter that Jack Cronin was the pilot of the accident aircraft and that he did not survive the crash. I was forced to inform my innocent young bride that her first dinner party would not take place because one of the guests had been killed. She was obviously shaken by the news, but otherwise took it stoically. I had chosen my Air Force wife well.

Flying in Alaska was fun, but challenging. The F-89, despite being underpowered, had many good features. It was an excellent instrument aircraft with a good cockpit layout that included a huge directional gyro that made one degree heading changes possible. Our only precision approach was ground controlled approach (GCA) in which a skilled radar operator directed the pilot with heading and glide slope information right to touchdown. This combination of good instrumentation and equally good GCA probably saved my life more than once. I'll describe one of those instances shortly. The F-89 was also well liked by the Ground Controlled Intercept (GCI) people because it carried lots of fuel and could be left on combat air patrol (CAP) for long periods of time. This allowed GCI controllers to "park" our fighters in position to ambush incoming bombers during exercises with Strategic Air Command (SAC). Fighter pilots hated it because it was boring but the battle planners loved it. Unfortunately, it was necessary for the GCI controllers to position our F-89s carefully because if we got far behind the modern SAC bombers, usually B-47s, we had trouble catching them. It meant using afterburner extensively which ran us low on fuel in short order. This was a serious deficiency in the F-89. Its low thrust engines and archaic aerodynamics left the airplane just too slow.

The navigational facilities in Alaska were also well behind the times. The Anchorage low frequency radio range was the primary navigational aid in the area. This was 1930's technology and, while satisfactory for slow flying piston engine aircraft, was totally inadequate for fast moving jets. The final approach required intercepting the range leg and flying it inbound. Overshooting the leg was a recipe for disaster since a small mountain, Mount Susitna, occupied the space on the other side of the range leg. Several charred gashes on the mountainside marked the spots where pilots in the past had made the fatal mistake of overshooting.

The more modern visual omni range was not scheduled for installation in Alaska for some time. The Air Force did install a

TACAN station on a test basis at Elmendorf, and although it was not cleared for use, we found it helpful.

Because the Air Force jets burned fuel at a prodigious rate, we normally used a GCI/GCA approach. This involved the long range ground control intercept controllers controlling our descent over water and handing us off to GCA for a precision approach to the runway. This normally worked very well, but there were exceptions, one of which I was a part of.

It happened shortly after I had been made a flight leader. My wingman, after a routine mission running practice firing passes with me, joined up for descent and landing. It was also before the test TACAN transmitter had been installed. Clouds were solid beneath us so there was no way of monitoring my position. We were, as was frequently the case, wholly dependent on our GCI controller. I began my descent with my wingman in tight formation and we soon entered the undercast. At lower altitude we broke out between cloud layers and I was shocked to see mountainous terrain at our altitude on both sides. I immediately called for afterburner to my wingman and we clawed for altitude. Breaking out on top I was shaken to realize that only by dumb luck had we let down into a valley instead of the peaks on either side of our flight path. Later conversation with the GCI controller revealed that he had evidently confused our flight with another being descended on a different frequency, although he never acknowledged his culpability. While GCI never again failed me, I had learned a lifelong lesson. Always cross check your position, if at all possible with some other resource. That resource in Alaska became available when the TACAN was installed, and I took full advantage of it.

My learning curve continued to rise as I became more acclimated to my position as a junior pilot in the squadron. I was 21 years old and could have passed for seventeen. In fact, a couple destined to become lifelong friends at our next base, Jake and Barb Jacobson, saw me in church one Sunday wearing my F-89 lapel pin. They were in a sister squadron and we did not know them at the time. They later revealed that upon seeing this youngster wearing an F-89 pin they decided that he must have borrowed it from his F-89 pilot father. More about this later. I was a bit sensitive about my appearance, especially when dealing with the senior NCOs assigned as crew chiefs. I noticed the snickers among them when they observed this juvenile lieutenant coming to fly their airplane. I probably compensated, foolishly, by sticking my neck out more than necessary to show the world that I was as good as the grizzled veterans.

One such incident involved an adventure I had towing targets. One of our best missions was rocket firing on the Alaskan gunnery range. This involved firing live rockets, with dummy warheads, at a towed banner target equipped with a radar reflector to simulate a bomber target. The targets were towed by four-engined B-50 bombers owned by SAC. The B-50s were a very low priority for SAC and our scheduled firing missions more often than not were aborted because the B-50 didn't make it to the range for one reason or another. To the fighter pilots running our squadron this was unacceptable. So someone sat down to figure out how we could do it ourselves with an F-89.

The ingenious solution was to take the drop tank off one wing and mount a hook on the now empty pylon. That hook would have to be held up until airborne so as not to drag on the ground during taxi and takeoff. It could then be lowered to snatch the target cable from the ground. Now, the F-89 used "decelerons" that is, split ailerons, for speed brakes, and they worked very well in that capacity. The solution for securing and lowering the hook was to tie a piece of nylon webbing to the hook and secure the other end by closing the decelerons on it. The pilot could then, very simply, open the decelerons once airborne releasing the end of the nylon webbing thus allowing the hook to drop into position for snatching the target.

The hard part involved snatching the target, and the Operations Officer asked for volunteers. It involved very low level flying which I enjoyed, it was something nobody had done before, and it sounded like great fun. Up went my hand! I did notice that the hands of all the older, more experienced pilots stayed in their pockets.

A few days later a set of "goal posts" was installed at a nearby dirt landing strip called Campbell's Field. A loop of nylon target tow cable was placed between the goal posts with the long tow cable and banner target laid out along the strip. My job would be to fly my F-89 so as to snare the loop with my hook and snatch the target off the ground. What could be simpler? One problem was that the target wasn't designed to operate at greater than 150 knots of airspeed. That is precariously slow for an asymmetrically configured F-89, but no problem for a 21 year old lieutenant. The sergeant whose airplane was chosen for this noble experiment looked especially delighted when he saw that the squadron teen-ager would be doing the flying.

Target Banner Pick-Up Hook. Designed By Rube Goldberg - But It Worked!

Nonetheless, I started engines on time and proceeded to Cambell's Field. En route, I opened the speed brakes and, as planned, the hook dropped into place for pickup. I used a combination of speed brakes and afterburner to keep the engine RPM high while still maintaining 150 knots or less. I hooked the cable loop on the first try, closed the speed brakes and pulled the nose up in a steep climb to maintain 150 knots. I was anticipating a sharp yaw when the target itself left the ground creating sudden high drag on the hook.

But I was not sufficiently prepared for the tug I got! The nose yawed violently to the left and I had to immediately apply almost full rudder to cancel out the yaw. My first reaction was that I wouldn't have enough rudder to overcome the yaw, but it turned out to be just enough. I trimmed out the yaw and climbed to normal towing altitude of 15,000 feet. Since this was a test run there were no aircraft scheduled to fire on the target so I informed the ground party at Campbell's that I was returning to drop the target. I jettisoned the hook over the strip and proceeded to land at Elmendorf. The test was a ringing success and I think I noticed a new found respect on the part of the crew chief sergeant.

My log book shows that I flew eight more target missions with F-89s clamoring to fire at my banner. The other squadrons followed our lead but, unfortunately, some problems arose which killed the project. I had trouble jettisoning the banner on one flight and ran low on fuel making multiple passes before it finally came off. The emergency drop procedure was to fly low over a forested area and drag the banner off. This happened to one of the other squadron's tow planes but he was unable to drag it off. Running out of fuel he had no choice but to return to Elmendorf towing the banner behind or eject. He chose the former. The banner eventually came off when he was on final approach and draped itself over a dwelling, bringing on an instant solar eclipse to the unhappy resident. The incident made the front page of the Anchorage paper, higher headquarters suddenly became interested, and our tow target adventure came to a halt. I thought this a pity, but I did learn from the project. The old military adage, "Never volunteer for anything" comes to mind.

I had a number of flight commanders during the Alaskan tour, some good, some not so good. One of the best was Ralph Giehl. Ralph was a P-38 pilot in WWII and his specialty was low level flying. Knowing that I shared his liking for skimming over the terrain at high speed, he usually made it a point at the end of a training mission to put me in trail and buzz the Alaskan wilderness. He included in his definition of wilderness the Alaska Railroad which ran north and south through the territory. On one occasion, I was hanging on to Ralph's tail just over the railroad tracks, in his jet wash, and looking up at the tops of the trees. Now, Alaska's trees are tall, but not that tall! As we cleared a gentle curve I saw just ahead one of those four man utility carts being propelled along the tracks by the four occupants. The two facing us obviously saw us coming and dove off the moving cart. I never saw how the remaining two reacted. After landing I parked my F-89 and Ralph climbed up the side to meet me. He pointed out an official-looking civilian down the ramp with an official-looking lieutenant colonel beside him evidently interviewing a just-returned aircrew. Ralph said, "I think that guy's from the Alaska Railroad. Go home and I'll see you tomorrow". We escaped and were never interviewed about low flying jets over the railroad tracks.

Ralph also introduced me to shallow angle dive bombing techniques that he used against the Japanese on Rabaul during the war. This time we were in a T-bird which we had borrowed from the 64th Squadron to use as a target for practice intercepts. After our target mission, always boring, we had plenty of fuel for Ralph's mentoring. I was in the back seat and on Ralph's first dive bomb run I heard a loud thump as we pulled out of our shallow dive. Ralph said quietly, "I believe we nicked a tree". "I believe you're right, Ralph," I replied, "Look at the left tip tank". The left tip tank, normally cylindrical, was quite flat on the bottom and stained with green. I suggested that, since the tank was obviously damaged beyond repair that we jettison it in the designated area. Since tip tanks that didn't feed were common the dropping of one would not be questioned. Ralph, however, for some reason decided that the tip tank could be salvaged. I was more concerned about salvaging our butts when the 64th squadron commander found out that we had hit a tree with one of his airplanes. In any case, Ralph landed and taxied back to the 64th parking area. The T-bird's crew chief guided us toward the parking space very professionally until he noticed the fractured left tip tank. I could read the epithet forming on his lips even from my cramped position in the rear seat. He climbed the ladder up to the cockpit and demanded, "What the **** happened to the tip tank?" Ralph responded with conviction that I greatly admired, "We hit a bird, Sarge, a big green bird". And we walked away with the sergeant scratching his head and contemplating whether or not there existed some strange species of green wild fowl in the Alaskan hinterlands that was a hazard to air navigation.

I was not at the controls when Ralph collided with the tree, and I have never been at the controls of an airplane that collided with anything. But I seem to have an affinity for just being around whenever somebody runs into something with an airplane. A second instance occurred while I was still in Alaska with the third and last coming during a later assignment which I'll get to later.

I was flying as number three on an early morning intercept mission led by one of the more senior line pilots. After completing our intercept mission we joined up with the leader in close formation, still my favorite kind of flying. Lead thought we looked so good in tight formation that somebody else deserved to see us. Now, a favorite, but frowned upon, pastime at Elmendorf was a so-called "bubble check". This involved buzzing the radome (bubble) of the GCI radar site on Fire Island located just offshore from Anchorage. We fighter pilots felt sorry for the controllers stuck on a lonely island in a boring job. We sometimes asked the controller working our flight if we were cleared for a bubble check. Our controller on this day was especially delighted to clear us since it was early morning and we would probably knock his sleeping buddies out of bed.

All went well until we went from smooth air over the water to very turbulent air over the bubble. I was flying right wing and anticipated the jolt but the left wingman evidently did not and inadvertently grazed lead's stabilizer with his enormous right rocket pod/tip tank. I did a damage check and found no apparent damage on the left wingman's airplane, but lead's stabilizer and elevator tip were bent up at nearly a 90 degree angle. Lead did a control check and fortunately still had good elevator control. Gene and I heaved a sigh of relief to see lead land safely ahead of us, but we wondered taxiing in how much trouble we were in. We didn't have long to wait since the next morning three pilots, three ROs and one GCI controller were standing in front of the squadron commander's desk. Colonel Heatly, the commander, was an old fighter pilot and his mild reprimand was a lot less than I expected. I suspect that he had made a few bubble checks himself. He held the ROs blameless, as he should have, and the wingmen and controller to a lesser degree, while the flight lead caught most of the abuse. I, personally, thought the left wingman got off too easily. If he had taken care of a wingman's first responsibility--don't run into your leader--none of it would have happened. I hadn't yet learned that the buck always stops with the leader.

I continued to have perhaps more than my share of interesting missions while flying in Alaska, but I must, once again, emphasize that the great preponderance of my flights were completely routine. One that was more than routine involved me flying a target mission in the T-33 for my friend, Jim Hoffman, playing the role of attacker in an F-89. I had planned to fly solo, but the Operations Officer asked me to take along a major from higher headquarters who had never flown in a jet and wanted to go along for the ride. I was happy to have the company and I spent considerable time briefing him on what to expect. I put special emphasis on ejection procedures since he was new to the aircraft and the T-bird's ejection system was a bit complex. I told him that I would call for him to remove and insert the seat's safety pins at the proper time.

The mission went routinely and my passenger enjoyed watching Jim simulating rocket attacks on us. I let him fly the airplane for most of the flight at altitude, but I took control for the descent and landing. We were on top of an overcast at 25,000 feet and the ceiling at Elmendorf was at about 5,000 feet. I retarded the throttle for descent and the engine immediately flamed out. For the second time in as many years I found myself in a T-bird glider. I called Jim who had started his descent ahead of me, told him I was flamed out and asked him to try to find me before I went into the undercast. Next I went through the air start procedure and was relieved to note the engine lighting off. My relief disappeared, however, when I advanced the throttle because the engine again flamed out! I told Jim and the GCI controller of my predicament and went back to work on an airstart telling everyone that I was heading for Anchorage International because it was closer than Elmendorf. My intention was to enter a flameout pattern somewhere below high key and once again make a dead stick landing. This was assuming that I could make it to Anchorage International. It was going to be close.

All of this time my passenger had been totally silent. But when the engine quit for the second time he piped up in an obviously strained voice that he had checked his seat pins out. I couldn't resist a chuckle while telling him to stay with me for a while because I hadn't given up on landing this thing yet. I went through the air start procedure again, this time using the fuel filter de-ice system in case we had an icing problem. Whether because of de-icing or the lower altitude, the engine this time continued to accelerate when I pushed the throttle forward. I changed course to Elmendorf, entered the flameout pattern at low key and landed without further excitement. I told my passenger to insure that his seat pins were inserted while I taxied in. He grunted his compliance, and while I tried to make light of the incident, he didn't seem to find it humorous. I invited him to come back and fly with us at a later date and I promised to do away with the excitement, but we never saw him again.

Steven

One of the most popular pastimes for young couples in Alaska was producing babies. Most of our friends either had a little one already or were in the midst of a pregnancy. Not to be outdone, Marion and I joined the club. The Army base, Fort Richardson, adjacent to Elmendorf had the only pre-natal facility in the area, so all the wives, including Marion, enrolled there. Calling the Army's facility primitive would be an understatement since it was located in a WWII wooden barracks building. But despite its outward appearance, the facility was home to people who were dedicated to caring for the young mothers and their babies. Marion still claims that her care at Fort Rich was superior to what she had, during her subsequent pregnancies, at the Air Force Academy hospital and the New York hospital where Jackie Kennedy was born.

So, on September 26th, 1955, Steven Albert DeGroote entered the world in the Territory of Alaska. Had he entered the world on Eastern Time he would have been born on my birthday, the 27th, but it was close enough. Steve had an Air Force childhood living in various parts of the world and having experiences different from the average kid's. He was an active kid and a challenge for a young couple barely into adulthood themselves. We made many mistakes learning to be parents but Steve overcame them to grow into a model son. Somehow while in high school in England Steve suddenly transformed from a hard-to-handle teenager into a solid citizen. We would like to take credit for the sudden change, but the truth is we did nothing different. He just suddenly grew up.

Steve is our only son to follow aviation as a career. He graduated from Embry-Riddle Aeronautical University, flight instructed for a while, worked for me in corporate aviation, moved to Ohio for another corporate job, and later went with American Airlines where he still works as a pilot.

I taught Steve to fly in Laos, of all places, and he had to break out of the pattern at Vientiane Airport to make way for a Russian airliner on his first solo flight. That should qualify for a memorable first solo! Steve was a natural, probably the best contact flying student I ever had. There were times when I had to induce control inputs to force him to recover from unusual attitudes that most students got themselves into by mistake. I had him make landing after landing hoping he would bounce so I could teach him recovery techniques. I finally became exasperated and jerked back on the yoke just before he was touching down. The airplane, of course, ballooned and Steve looked at me as if I had lost my mind, added a small amount of power nursing the Cessna back to a perfect touchdown. He had some problems with instrument flying at first, and rekindled my interest in flying while giving him some hood time in a Cherokee.

After Steve graduated from Embry-Riddle I had the pleasure of having him work for me in a small flight department that I ran after retirement from the Air Force. He had been making his living as a starving flight instructor when our flight department became busy enough that we needed another pilot. We were operating a Rockwell 690B turboprop which was a fairly sophisticated corporate aircraft for someone with Steve's experience to be flying. I resolved to bring him along slowly and carefully.

He adjusted quickly, confirming my belief that he was a "natural". On one flight with several of our top executives on board, Steve was flying from the left seat when we had an emergency. The nose gear came down on its own, signaling failure of the main hydraulic

Steve, Left With Ex-President And Mrs. Ford, 2ⁿᵈ Company Pilot. The Fords Were Frequent Passengers On The "Westwind" Corporate Jet Steve flew.

system. We went through the emergency checklist and I said, "I'll take it for landing". Steve looked at me with a pained expression that made it clear that he was insulted that I should think that he wasn't capable of handling a simple emergency. With an inward smile I said, "On second thought, you fly and I'll do the checklist".

Steve was not the least bit disturbed by the emergency and flew the approach like a pro. The emergency systems functioned normally and the landing was routine. Had the emergency systems not worked we could have been faced with a gear-up landing. Some months later, when Steve had been checked out as pilot-in-command, he faced a similar situation wherein the gear did not fully extend. Steve ended up taking control from a slightly panicked co-pilot and landed the aircraft safely with partially extended landing gear. He was obviously ready to be the man in charge in the cockpit.

The smartest move Steve has made in his life was to marry Caren, providing us with the daughter we never had--not just a daughter, but a wonderful daughter. They also have provided us with two wonderful grandchildren, Nicholas and Jennay who are the light of our lives.

But, back to 1955 and Air Force life in Alaska...

My education as a fighter pilot continued and Alaskan weather nudged that education along. Alaska was a beautiful place with many crystal clear days where you could see Mount McKinley from a hundred miles away. But it was the Arctic, and the weather and terrain had to be respected.

Early in my tour I was scrambled as Red 2 on an overcast night. I was being led by Lt. Ed Cullivan, a well respected squadron pilot who was nearing the end of his tour in Alaska. We followed radar vectors for some time until GCI gave it up as a false contact---not an unusual occurrence. We were flying F-89Cs and because fuel was getting low Ed elected to have me join up for the descent, saving time and fuel.

Always confident in my ability to fly good formation I quickly slipped into position. Ed began his descent and almost immediately we went into the clouds. I had flown lots of formation including night formation in clear weather and daytime formation in weather, but never night formation in weather. I was a little surprised at the sudden loss of visibility. I could hardly see Ed's aircraft except for the wing tip navigation light which was blinding me. Ed selected dim on his lighting which helped significantly, but I then encountered a new problem--the dreaded spatial disorientation. I had heard many pilots, especially new pilots, complain of spatial disorientation, commonly mis-labeled as "vertigo" but I had never had a serious encounter and began to think myself immune--until now. I became convinced that Ed was turning hard into me, but a stolen glance at my attitude indicator confirmed that we were in a wings level descent as we should have been. I tried shaking my head but that only made it worse. I was now convinced by my senses that we had rolled inverted. Determined not to panic, I simply said to myself, "Okay, if Ed wants to fly upside down, so be it--I'll just fly upside down on his wing!"

I continued in my inverted state until we broke out beneath the clouds causing my senses to immediately right themselves. I realized that I was sweating badly and had been working much too hard. But it was a good, humbling experience for a young pilot who had been getting too sure of himself. I had to fly night weather formation many times during the remainder of my Air Force career and I always followed the same rule--stay in position no matter what your senses are telling you and you'll eventually get oriented. As my experience increased my problem with spatial disorientation diminished until it was nothing more than an occasional minor annoyance. My learning process continued and it sometimes involved teaching.

Gene, my RO, had been busily pursuing the application process for pilot training. While I hated to lose him, I encouraged him to press on because I knew he would make a good pilot and would enjoy the Air Force much more from the front seat rather than the back. He went along with me in the back seat of the T-bird whenever possible and I gave him rudimentary flying lessons. I worked him up to making takeoffs which is a bit difficult from the back seat because there is very little forward visibility. I was just beginning to relax while he was taking off, convinced that he had the hang of it, when he hit a brake at 100 knots. The T-bird has no nose wheel steering, and steering with the brakes is normal at taxi speed. But at

100 knots it can easily blow a tire. I decided that Gene could wait until pilot training before practicing more takeoffs. Despite this minor setback, Gene got his pilot training slot, and after serving time as an Air Force pilot, he went on to become a Boeing 747 captain with United Airlines.

Another learning experience came to pass when Gene was not flying with me. We were deployed to King Salmon, Alaska, a God forsaken spot in southwestern Alaska. I was teamed up temporarily with Pete Peterson, who was normally Satch Handel's RO. Pete and I were on alert, minding our own business around midnight when our flight commander decided that we should fly a radar verification flight. I tried to talk him into waiting for daylight, but he was adamant. Standard procedure at King Salmon was to return the airplane to Elmendorf if the airborne radar failed. Pete decided just after takeoff that the radar had failed. I suspect that a desire to return to Elmendorf, away from an unreasonable flight commander may have had something to do with his analysis of the radar's performance. Anyway, we flew toward Elmendorf enjoying the night time view of the Aurora Borealis and the perfectly clear weather.

We started our descent and GCI read the destination weather to us, as usual. But the weather report was anything but usual. It read, "indefinite, zero ceiling, obscured, visibility zero, fog", the hated WOXOF readout. I told Pete that there was obviously a mistake because I could see the lighted runway from where we were, 50 miles out. I continued the descent and went to GCA just for the practice. I could still see the runway clearly until 300 feet whereupon it and everything else suddenly disappeared! I had paid little attention to reserve fuel since the weather had been clear. My quick mental calculation made it clear that we did not have sufficient fuel to go to any alternate except Anchorage International which was also socked in. I had, through complacency, run myself out of any option except a zero-zero landing. Cursing myself for my own stupidity, I settled down to make my first blind landing. I was grateful to be in the much-maligned F-89, a very stable instrument aircraft with its huge directional gyro. When I told GCA that I intended to land despite the weather, the controller's voice changed.

The NCO in charge had obviously taken over the scope from a trainee. Glad to have the first team talking me down I concentrated on the one degree heading changes he was giving me. Pete was completely silent. The few minutes it took for GCA to guide me to touchdown went well and my wheels touched down firmly at the same instant that I caught sight of runway lights out the left side of the canopy. I had some difficulty staying at a constant distance from the lights and braked hard to a stop. The tower sent out a "follow me" truck to lead me back to the 65ᵗʰ area.

I had just learned an almost very costly lesson about ice fog. When weather conditions are just right, ice fog can form in arctic areas. Ice fog hugs the ground and vertical visibility downward is as if it's not there. But horizontal visibility is zero as I discovered when I entered the fog layer at 300 feet above the ground.

Pete and I left for home and didn't mention our midnight return to anyone. I was a slightly older but much wiser young fighter pilot. Marion was glad to see me home early from King Salmon, and you can rest assured that I was glad to be there.

One more "Smilin' Jack" adventure took place before Gene left Alaska for pilot training. I was sitting 5-minute air defense alert, something that we took quite seriously in the 50s since any unknown target in those cold war days was assumed to be a possible hostile carrying nuclear weapons from the Soviet Union. I was the leader of the pair of alert birds, and my call sign was "Red One" the call sign that identified the 5 minute alert aircraft to the tower and other air traffic control agencies. It gave the 5-minute birds absolute priority for takeoff and departure.

Red flight was scrambled by GCI and Gene and I rushed to our aircraft in order to get airborne within the allotted five minutes. Alert aircraft were parked in alert hangars at the end of the east-west runway and a short taxiway led directly onto the runway, allowing scrambled aircraft to make running takeoffs.

After start I called for Red 2 to check in and after he did so, I called, "Elmendorf Tower, Red flight, scramble". The tower responded, "Red One, cleared for takeoff". I lit my afterburners and began takeoff on the runway, which was covered with hard packed snow, as was the case throughout winter in Alaska. Now, braking action on hard packed snow is not as good, naturally, as it is on dry concrete, but as long as the temperature stays down, it's not bad. It was momentarily going to become a critical factor!

Unknown to me, events were taking place at the far end of the runway that were leading toward disaster. The alert aircraft always took off to the west, unless the winds were very strong from the east. The winds on this day were not strong, so I was cleared to take off downwind. The active runway for normal traffic, however, was west to east. It happened that a fully loaded KC-97 tanker was on the taxiway at the west end awaiting takeoff clearance to the east. To complete the recipe for disaster, The KC-97 was on VHF radio while we were on UHF, meaning that we could not hear each other. The tower, however, transmitted simultaneously on both VHF and UHF. The KC-97s call sign was "Rover One". When the tower transmitted "Red One, cleared for takeoff" on both frequencies, the KC-97 pilot thought he heard, "Rover One, cleared for takeoff", so he lined up to begin his takeoff roll. Imagine his surprise when he looked up and saw an F-89, a very ugly airplane in the best of circumstances, coming right at him at full speed. Imagine my surprise (or horror) to see a KC-97, loaded with fuel suddenly appear in my windscreen at the most critical part of takeoff! My F-89 was at max gross weight with a full fuel load and 104 rockets in the pods. I momentarily considered aborting takeoff but instantly decided that the fully loaded fighter would never stop on the snow covered runway. The F-89 was known as an airplane that used every bit of available runway, but fortunately it was mid-winter and the cold temperatures improved takeoff performance somewhat. Saying "Oh, ****" to no one except poor Gene, I continued takeoff for what would be either a spectacular near-miss over the tanker or an explosion that would register on the Richter scale. Fortunately, it was the former. We went roaring over the KC-97 clearing it by a few feet. I exploded at the tower asking who the screwball was on my runway. The tower responded weakly that they were investigating.

After landing, Gene and I were instructed to go to operations immediately. I filled out an Operational Hazard Report (OHR) in which I could not resist a bit of sarcasm, recommending that SAC pilots be briefed on the importance of looking both ways before crossing streets. Within minutes the operations office was filled with various lieutenant colonels, full colonels and even a general. Air Traffic control and control tower supervisors were there, and SAC was represented by several colonels who objected vociferously to my comment about crossing streets. The discussion got more and more noisy and strayed farther and farther from the point, which was to make sure it didn't happen again.

While the argument was raging, I noticed one lonely looking captain standing in a corner, being ignored as were Gene and I. I said to Gene, "I'll bet that's the KC-97 pilot". I introduced myself and, sure enough, it was the SAC aircraft commander. We discussed what had happened and decided that it was a combination of factors including the VHF-UHF hazard and the tower's failure to take it into account by not giving the KC-97 positive instructions to hold short of the runway. The captain observed that if we thought we were scared, we should have been in his seat with an F-89 bearing down on him and nothing he could do about it except wait for the collision. We somehow relayed our feelings to the various arguing colonels and the two aircrews parted on friendly terms.

I did not plan to inform Marion of our close call, but Gene happened to cross paths with her and blurted out, "Well, your husband nearly bought the farm today". I made it a point to congratulate him on his tact and sensitivity.

Gene departed and I was assigned a new RO, Ben Diggs, who was also very good at his job. Our tour in Alaska was coming to a close, and I had learned much about being a fighter pilot, somewhat less about being a good husband and father, and had formed questions that needed to be answered about my future in the Air Force. In any case, after a very nice farewell party given to us by our Flight, we departed Alaska for some leave time in Philadelphia and a new challenge at Suffolk County Air Force Base at Westhampton Beach, Long Island, New York.

Suffolk County Air Force Base

We arrived at Westhampton Beach after a month's leave staying with Ruth and Don in their suburban home outside Philadelphia. Ruth was now married to Don Dickson and we had unfortunately missed the wedding since travel from Alaska was beyond my 2nd lieutenant's pay level. Don is a Korean War veteran and truly a solid citizen. A somewhat gruff manner covers up a generous and caring human being. He was always available to help Marion and our boys when I was away on remote tours, something I could never repay. He also agrees with me that we both really lucked out by marrying the Cresson twins.

Fourteen-year-Old Fighter Pilot Between Jake And Beautiful Barbie, Off-Duty At Our Cottage On Long Island.

I had been promoted to 1st lieutenant while in Alaska and the first thing we did on arriving home on leave was to go out and buy a brand new 1956 De Soto, white with blue trim and tailfins. That pretty much took care of my pay increase that went with the promotion. When we weren't showing off our new car and new son we were making plans and looking forward to living in Westhampton Beach. We left for our new base and began looking for a place to live, discovering quickly that a lieutenant's housing allowance didn't buy much in the New York "millionaire's playground". We eventually found a summer cottage on Peconic Bay that was quite adequate for us. Marion, as always, made friends quickly. One was Barbara Jacobson, mentioned earlier, who discovered that Marion had been in Alaska and had attended the same church as they. She invited us to dinner and Marion went to their house earlier while Jake and I were to come from work. Barb was in the process of telling Marion about the young kid they saw in church wearing an F-89 pin that must have been his father's when I made my appearance. Jumping way into the future, I'll quote from a note I composed to Jake on his 80th birthday, because it describes the Alaskan church encounter and pretty well sums up the feeling we have over the friendship that we had and still have with Barb and Jake. It also provides a hint of the flavor of life in a fighter squadron in the 1950s. Here's the letter:

April 22, 2011

I guess this falls into the category of unsolicited testimonial. Nobody asked me to write it and I'm stuck with the distinct possibility that nobody really gives a damn what I think about the subject. But, the subject is my friend Jake, and I'm just not going to let something as momentous as his 80th birthday go by without some comments.

Jake and I faced life looking through the same window, generally speaking. Lots of differences, mind you-He was a long lean Texan with a positive outlook that only Texans seem to have and I was a short, stocky Philadelphian with the kind of East Coast cynicism that gets Santa Claus booed off the field at football games in December. But as many differences as we had, there were also lots of similarities. And the Air Force, somehow, apparently, sensing this, stirred these two dissimilar eggs into an acceptable omelet.

Jake and I were junior officers together, i.e., we were together through the awkward teen-ager stage in an officer's career. As in the life of any teen-ager, there are things like young love, and there are also things like pimples. The young love part came from a natural affection we both had for flying fighter aircraft. The pimples came from a few senior officers in our lives, who shall be nameless, but who seemed intent on having us do things other than fly fighter aircraft.

We both began our operational careers in Anchorage Alaska where, strangely enough, we didn't know each other. We were in different squadrons and our paths never crossed. Well, that's not quite true. We both went to the same church off base, and Jake one Sunday noticed that the young man with the offering plate was wearing an F-89 lapel pin. Jake opined to Barb that since this kid couldn't be more than fourteen, he must have been wearing his father's lapel pin. It so happens that I was 21 at the time, looked--okay, fourteen--and was very sensitive about playing the child fighter pilot especially around sniggering senior sergeant crew chiefs. More about this later, but had we met on that day it may have been the premature end of a beautiful friendship.

Anyway, Jake left Alaska for pilot training while I completed my tour and we were both subsequently assigned to Suffolk County AFB on Long Island, New York. We were assigned to the same flight and discovered that we had things in common, like our Alaska tour. I was soon invited to bring my wife to dinner at the Jacobson abode. Upon arrival, Jake motioned for me to join him directly at the grill while Marion went inside to introduce herself to Barb. They quickly established the Alaska connection, the church connection and the peculiarity of the teen-ager wearing the F-89 lapel pin. At that point I walked in, beer in hand, and Barb, in utter amazement, shouted, "That's him! That's the kid." After establishing who "the kid" was I concealed my chagrin at once again wearing the child fighter pilot label, and, as I recall, asked Jake if he had a cigar so I could establish myself at least, as a _mature_ fourteen-year-old.

Jake and I, for better or worse, continued to agree on most things, and together with a ne'er-do-well named George Jatras, decided to leave our mark on the 2nd Fighter-Interceptor Squadron whether the squadron liked it or not. We agreed first that the squadron was being mismanaged, and like most junior officers, were convinced that we could manage it better ourselves. We were also convinced, correctly, that we had the best-looking wives in the squadron--but I digress.

The primary objective of our professional lives was to fly fighters as much as possible, and after a short period flying the F-86D we began transitioning into the magnificent F-102. The "Deuce" was a joy to fly, but sadly upper management on the base was unable to support it logistically and at the outset we found ourselves flying it very little. It was at this point that I began to realize that Jake was something special and that I could learn from this guy. While I drank coffee and bitched about upper echelon mismanagement, Jake quietly began doing something about it. I watched in amazement while he actually volunteered to straighten out the squadron's administrative mess. By now I had learned, by flying with him, that Jake was a top-notch pilot. I thought that I was pretty good too, but Jake knew instinctively, at that young stage in his career, that being a good pilot didn't necessarily make you a good officer. I think that I began at that moment, reluctantly to be sure, to learn about becoming an officer as well as a fighter jock. Much later in my career, having been over-promoted to positions of some responsibility, I still carried with me those early lessons in leadership given to me, subliminally perhaps, by young Captain Jacobson.

Meanwhile, as our flying hours and our morale rose proportionally, we were determined to keep off-hours boredom at bay. Jake and Barb were always leaders in the social life of our on-base existence and they frequently entertained with relaxing dinner parties. One memorable night Barb had invited Marion and me, together with the Jatras' to one such dinner. I arrived with Marion, having been off duty that day, to discover that Jake and George had not yet arrived. It occurred to Barb for some reason that having flown that day, they might possibly have stopped off at the club for some refreshments. Barb then decided that I should go to the club to seek them out. Now, this was exactly like sending Jack-the-Ripper to rescue a damsel in distress. However, I saw my duty and rose to the challenge. Some hours later, which seemed like mere minutes to the three of us, we went in George's car, which had somehow suffered some minor collateral damage in the parking lot, to the Jacobson's residence. Barb, having seen her carefully prepared dinner ruined by our unfortunate sojourn at the club, decided to exact her revenge by balancing a bucket of water over the door jamb. Yes, this was the same sweet Barbie, homemaker, mother of her children, later the distinguished Doctor Jacobson, lecturer, world traveler, planting a liquid I.E.D. to ambush three innocent, lovable fighter pilots who were only seeking a square meal. Well, as I recall, Jake entered first, suffering a near-miss from the I.E.D. which he didn't feel at all. But I also recall a massive headache the following day caused, I believe, by skipping dinner the previous evening.

We also kept our off-duty hours filled by occasional trips to the nearby Big Apple, New York City. On one such trip Jake decided to wear his very best Gene Autry Stetson. This struck me as a not very good idea, but I kept my silence. Later, while walking in the big town, we were forced to ask directions from a local shopkeeper. The shopkeeper began giving us directions, then paused, stared pensively at Jake's Stetson and said, "You didn't bring your horse, did you?". That shopkeeper probably never knew how close we came to reducing the population of the Big Apple by one person that day, but I managed to steer Jake outside explaining to him that we Easterners were sometimes overwhelmed by really cool Texas finery.

So, life went on and, while we didn't appreciate it at the time, we were privileged to live the exciting life of fighter squadron people, in the middle of perhaps the best years of their lives. It was during this period, however, that I made a major mistake with my life. I decided that for career progression purposes I should apply for the Air Force Institute of Technology's engineering degree program. As soon as I arrived at the school I realized that I had made a major blunder. I had left my dream job to be just one more pencil pusher. I tried to make the best of it, but although my grades put me at the top of my class I found myself with chronic insomnia, no appetite and various other maladies that eventually put me on sick call. Today I would probably be diagnosed with clinical depression, but whatever I had, the Air Force gave me the choice of joining a later class or returning to the cockpit as a behind-the-lines pilot. This is where Jake stepped in. Having got wind of my problems, Jake went out on a limb to get me back into the fighter squadron. This was no small feat since the Air Force had a temporary glut of interceptor pilots and was actually sending some to other career fields. Even though he was still a junior captain, Jake pushed the bureaucracy like a colonel and somehow got me back to my first love, flying fighters. My first flight back in my beloved "Deuce" was one of the happiest days of my life, and it was all due to the tireless efforts of young Captain Jacobson.

I tell this story because it's a typical illustration of what friendship means when Jake is involved. If you're Jake's friend, you're not just a friend when it's easy. If you're Jake's friend you're his friend when you're down and you're his friend when other people aren't standing in your corner. There are a thousand vignettes I could relate about our decades- long relationship with the Jacobson family, but I've rambled on long enough. Jake, George and I continued our careers along similar paths, all of us having combat tours in fighters, all having tours as Air Attaches at various trouble spots in the world. And through the years, although separated by miles, always staying in touch. And always knowing that if we ever needed a friend, my friend Jake would be there,

Happy birthday, Jake
Al and Marion

Continuing with sketches of people that we knew and built abiding friendships with, we come to George and Stella Jatras. There were also Syd and Gage Mersereau and others, but George and Stella were our next door neighbors and I have an aviation story involving George that I tell reluctantly, in the interest of full disclosure, because it contributed to my development as a fighter pilot.

We arrived at Suffolk at about the same time and at a rather awkward time. The squadron, the 2nd Fighter-Interceptor Squadron, was about to begin converting from the North American F-86D to the supersonic Convair F-102A. Most of the new pilots, including George, had come directly from advanced pilot training in the F-86D and had a few hours in the aircraft. In my case a decision had to be made as to whether or not to check me out in the '86D since the airplane would be leaving in a few months. The Operations Officer left the decision up to me, and I immediately opted to take the opportunity to fly another fighter. So, I studied the Flight Handbook, went to Stuart AFB in New York to fly the simulator and proceeded to fly the "Dog" for about 10 hours.

I enjoyed flying the '86 which was very light on the controls compared to the F-89, but the airplane had many shortcomings. It was the first jet aircraft with an electronic fuel control. This was ahead of its time, but, unfortunately, too far ahead. The system used vacuum tubes! The transistor was not yet in widespread use and the 86D's engine often had a mind of its own because of the unreliable fuel control. We used to listen to the frequent ejections of 86D pilots while we were at Moody. An 86D school was located near Tampa, and the phrase "One a day in Tampa Bay" came into common usage. The airplane was also very limited as an interceptor, having very short range and armament that consisted of a mere 24 rockets--compared to 104 carried by the F-89.

Marion, Left With George And Stella Jatras, 1967

In any case, I was glad to have the opportunity to fly the airplane. But the '86D soon left the scene and we were relegated to flying the squadron's three T-birds since the F-102s were not yet operational. It was here that I had a close encounter with George Jatras. It was a night training mission. I was in the front seat of one T-bird and George in the front seat of another. I had a "new guy", Thurston Hurt, in my back seat while George and his back seater were both right out of flying school. I, on the other hand, considered myself much more experienced after my two year operational tour in Alaska flying with many pilots who taught me much that they had learned flying combat in WWII. I had learned to hold my own with a few who had actually shot down enemy fighters in war II--so I was pretty cocky.

I happened to see George's T-bird flying along, straight and level several thousand feet below me. I decided to show this new guy that he could be jumped even at night if he let his guard down. I rolled in to make a high side pass on the unsuspecting T-bird. I was relaxed and completely confident. I had, after all, successfully tangled with pilots in Alaska who had shot down Messerschmitts or Zeros. This would be a piece of cake!

As I rolled in for the kill I was astounded to see the new guy suddenly break hard into me, get me into an unexpected rolling scissors and within seconds found myself the hunted instead of the hunter with a T-bird on my butt which I couldn't shake. Thurston, silent throughout, was obviously not impressed.

On the ground I could do nothing but sheepishly congratulate George on his alertness and proficiency. And I put several lessons into my pilot memory bank. First, don't ever relax if you're going to attack someone, second, be prepared for the unexpected, and finally don't ever _ever_ underestimate your opponent. I might add that if you're going to attack someone at night, turn your lights off--an obvious lesson that I applied many times while attacking ground targets in Vietnam.

I couldn't spend much time stroking my wounded ego because at long last our F-102s arrived and a serious spare parts situation resolved itself. We began to fly the airplane and we all fell in love with it. While I probably have a deeper affection for the F-100 because of its mission and because I flew it in combat, the F-102 remains my favorite mount as an airplane to fly for the sheer joy of flying. We began flying it in earnest in order to get the squadron certified as combat ready. One of our missions was to deploy for short periods to other bases to give their ground crews an opportunity to become familiar with the new bird and establish some proficiency in refueling and re-arming it.

We launched a flight of three on just such a mission on a beautiful day for flying without a cloud in sight. We were led by Gage Mersereau who, after a few practice attack runs, signaled join-up for our flight and subsequently put us in trail formation. I was number three and noticed that Gage was working us closer to our intended landing spot for ground crew training, Otis Air Force Base on Cape Cod. Gage rolled our formation into a steep dive, and I noticed with some trepidation that we were pointed directly at the center of the Otis complex and picking up speed rapidly. Sure enough, the formation of "Deuces" slipped easily into supersonic flight. Gage uttered a quiet "Uh-Oh" over the radio and signaled the flight back into normal formation for landing.

When we parked there was much excitement among the ground crewmen. There was also the airdrome officer who immediately asked us if we had gone supersonic over the airport. Feigning shock that we might have been suspected of beating up their airport, we quickly diverted attention to our shiny, new F-102s and turned them over to the maintenance trainees. The airdrome officer seemed content, stating, "I didn't think it was a sonic boom; it was too loud for that." We didn't mention to him that three successive sonic booms from three deuces in trail would probably make one helluva noise! These were the days when supersonic flight was in its infancy, and there were few rules.

On the subject of loud, explosive sounds, we had an absolute classic example at the Suffolk County alert hangars. We were gathered as a squadron in the briefing room going over the schedule for the day when a tremendous explosion stopped all conversation. I immediately said, "That was a rocket going off!" I was sure of myself because I had heard that sound twice before, both times in Alaska. The first time was an accidental firing of a live rocket inside the combination hangar/operations building that housed the 65th Squadron on Elmendorf. In that instance, an armament technician had failed to clear all 104 firing tubes of a hangared F-89 before closing the firing circuit during maintenance. Fortunately, the rocket traveled only a very short distance before impacting a concrete wall. I had been sitting in Operations and I can say, unequivocally, that a 2.75 inch rocket going off indoors will get everyone's attention.

The second event took place as I was walking from my just parked aircraft toward Operations. Without warning, the entire right hand rocket pod of an F-89 parked a few spaces down the ramp fired across the north-south runway. A ground crewman had inserted the grounding plug into the rocket pod, as he should have, but when he switched on electrical power all 52 rockets fired. Now, we had always been told that rockets have no recoil. Maybe not--but I can attest to the fact that the right side of a 45,000 pound F-89 was propelled backward by something that left the aircraft situated at a 45 degree angle from its previous orientation. Most of the 52 rockets ended up on the Army base, Fort Richardson, which was on the other side of our north-south runway. Fortunately again, no one was hurt, but the Army was not pleased. We were told that a short circuit in the grounding plug caused the mishap.

Returning to my story of Suffolk County's accident, we pilots rushed outside to witness a raging fire at one of the alert hangars with the fire fighters and EOD people already engaged in containing the inferno. My initial analysis was slightly off since it turned out to be a missile rather than a rocket that I heard igniting. The fire ended up melting down one of the four hangars including the F-102 that was parked inside.

Investigation showed that the disaster sequence began when a pilot was setting up the cockpit, as was done routinely, for five minute alert. He was checking his fuel boost pumps, and just as he turned one of the four pumps off, the armament bay doors opened, a missile launcher extended, and a missile fired into the partially open hangar door. Now, according to the experts, none of this could have happened. The safety devices and procedures were double and triple redundant.

It was supposedly impossible to fire any armament with the fire control radar off. It was off. It was impossible to fire armament with the landing gear down. It was, obviously, down. It was impossible to fire armament without the joystick trigger being pulled. It was not pulled and the trigger safety pins were never removed. And on and on. The F-102 carried six Falcon missiles and twelve 2.75 inch rockets. All of them eventually cooked off during the fire. Some ended up in the nearby town. Miraculously, no one was injured. Needless to say, very detailed studies were launched to solve the mystery of the stray voltage that somehow overrode all of the safety devices and allowed the airplane to launch weapons on its own. For me, it was an education in the basic elements of missile and explosive safety in which I would later become involved. The moral of the story is that loaded warplanes can be very dangerous commodities.

In late 1958, as described in my letter on Jake's 80th birthday, I made the biggest mistake of my life by leaving my happy life as a fighter pilot to become an engineering student. We moved briefly to Dayton, Ohio where I enrolled in the Air Force Institute of Technology. My schoolboy genes were still OK and my grades were very good. But that was the only thing that was good. I was depressed so much by my bad decision that it affected my health. I was medically grounded for the first and only time in my life and was effectively rescued and returned to the squadron by the superhuman efforts of Jake. The only positive thing that came out of my stay at Wright-Patterson was a brief checkout in the classic twin Beech, known in the Air Force as the C-45--a fun airplane, a little like a twin engine T-6.

When I returned to Suffolk County I made an amazing discovery. The ops building was abuzz with talk of the new operations officer, already given the nickname "Nails" as in "tough as". It hadn't yet been decided whether he was tough but fair or just tough. When I learned his name I put everyone's mind at ease. Tobey Turgeau, my old iron-tailed check pilot, nemesis of the cadet corps, was the new ops officer. He remembered me from Williams AFB days and evidently went to bat for me while my return to the squadron was being negotiated. I assured everyone that Tobey would be meticulously fair, but if you screwed up you'd better own up to it and expect to hear some pointed words on the subject. Tobey put me on his wing for a couple of flights and decided, I think, that he had made the right decision on me back at Williams. I quickly was reinstated into my instructor pilot status in the Deuce and the T-bird.

It was nice to have the prestige of being an I.P., but it involved some sticky jobs. In those late 50's days the Air Force had quite a few pilots who were not jet qualified and the Air Force didn't like that state of affairs. So, to solve the problem they initiated project "Blue Flame" to get everyone who wore wings jet qualified. Some of the training was done at formal schools while some of it was done locally. I became involved in the latter. I discovered that quite a few rated pilots were not all that interested in becoming jet qualified--something that I found astounding. A few gave up their wings rather than fly these new-fangled blow torches.

My first encounter with a jet "student" involved me with a Wing Headquarters lieutenant colonel. I quickly learned that he had been perfectly happy flying the base C-47 support aircraft and was being dragged kicking and screaming into the T-33. I gave him ground school and quizzed him on systems and procedures. After a week of instruction his knowledge level was zero. I finally decided that if I could get him to learn the T-bird emergency procedures I'd consider it a minor victory. No such luck! He couldn't remember the simplest of procedures. Flying with him in the T-bird was equally adventuresome. I finished the airwork part of the curriculum, involving simple stalls and a few basic acrobatics, and thought I was making some progress--although I felt he was deathly afraid of the airplane.

I then decided to give some touch and go landings a try. Our normal 9,000 foot runway was closed for repairs, but the crosswind runway was available. It was 5200 feet long--a little tight but perfectly adequate for a T-33 flown properly. On his first landing he touched down hard and a little long but good enough for a beginner. Unfortunately, when he pushed the power up to full throttle, he decided on his own that the engine wasn't accelerating properly. Instead of asking me, he stop cocked the throttle! Even though my hand was firmly on the rear seat throttle, he almost broke my thumb snatching the lever to off which killed the engine. We had about half the runway remaining. I shouted, "I've got it!" Almost simultaneously, I shouted, "Get off the damn brakes". Too late--his lead foot blew the right tire. I finally won the struggle for control of the airplane and we stopped, with at least 1,000 feet of runway remaining, and with no further damage to the airplane. I was livid! The runway was closed while maintenance sent out a tug to tow us away. The base commander, Colonel Hook, showed up wanting to know why we closed down his only runway. I muttered something about "an incompetent S.O.B. on the controls" not specifying whether I meant me or the lieutenant colonel. But I think Colonel Hook got my meaning from my tight jaws. There was, of course, nothing wrong with the engine. My "student" had evidently never looked at the tachometer before and therefore never noticed the lag between throttle position and RPM--although I had pointed out to him earlier that this was a defining difference between jet and piston power.

I related my sad story to Tobey Turgeau and told him that in my opinion this guy should never fly a jet and should face a Flying Evaluation Board (FEB) to determine whether he should ever fly anything again. He was sloppy, lazy, prone to panic and totally undisciplined. Tobey agreed and I never saw the lieutenant colonel again near the flight line.

Shortly thereafter I was informed that I would be instructing another lieutenant colonel in the art of flying jets. This time it was Colonel McCoy, commander of the Bomarc missile site that was adjacent to our base complex. Needless to say, I was none too pleased with the prospect of a repeat of my last instruction job.

I introduced myself to the colonel and began going over the T-33 flight manual with him. I was surprised and delighted to discover that he had already read the manual from cover to cover and knew the normal and emergency procedures very well.

Things were looking good for me to start with his flight instruction, but events took a bizarre turn before we could begin.

Marion called and informed me that we had had a slight mishap involving our son Steven and automobiles. I went home to our base quarters and listened to the sad story. My Desoto was a very nice car but it had a design deficiency. It had, instead of the usual gear shift lever, a small box with push buttons. There was a button for Drive, Low, Neutral and Reverse. Notice that a button for Park is not included in the list. Yes, the designers at Chrysler had decided that a parking gear was not necessary and would break up the artistic symmetry of their push button box. The only thing that held the car in place on a hill was the parking brake.

Now, Steven was about five years old at the time and he and some of his friends decided to amuse themselves by getting into the Desoto to go on a make-believe trip. Steve noticed a shiny, silver lever, the parking brake, and managed to release it. The car was in our car port which was on a slight incline and it proceeded to roll backwards down the driveway, across the street and into a brand new Ford Thunderbird belonging to--you guessed it--Lieutenant Colonel McCoy. The Thunderbird was Colonel McCoy's pride and joy, and despite my profuse apologies he was obviously unhappy with his introduction to the DeGroote family.

But, life goes on, and the next day I met with Colonel McCoy ready to make amends by teaching him to operate another machine named, ironically, T-bird, just like his dented car. We took off and began airwork. I demonstrated stall series, some basic acrobatics, and a few emergency procedures. He learned quickly and I was very happy to discover that this guy was a good, professional pilot who simply needed to be checked out in a new kind of aircraft.

But once again fate stepped in to ruin my well planned course of instruction. We were operating about 50 miles out over the Atlantic in our usual training area south of the airlines' overseas routes. It was a good place to train, but a bad place to lose an engine in a single engine airplane. While Colonel McCoy was practicing maneuvers--and doing very well--I thought I noticed a very high pitched vibration. I asked the colonel if he could feel anything unusual, like a vibration. He, of course, was used to piston engine aircraft and could only marvel about how these jet airplanes didn't seem to vibrate at all. I said, "I've got it" and proceeded to head for dry land. Colonel McCoy was obviously displeased with my decision. He was having a good time flying this aerial hot-rod, his time was limited, and he didn't like my taking control.

I pushed the throttle to full forward which should have produced 100% RPM. The tachometer stopped at 96%! Something was definitely wrong. I climbed to get as much gliding distance toward land as I could. While I was in the climb, the yellow engine overheat light came on. I called Suffolk Tower, declared an emergency and told them that I would be entering high key for a simulated flame out pattern. The pattern was normal and I landed the airplane from the back seat, and taxied back to parking. Colonel McCoy was still grousing about losing his training time and it was clear to me that his take on the situation was that a young instructor was being overly cautious about an imaginary engine problem. I had lots of T-bird time and had never encountered the kind of vibration we had just experienced, so I was sure I had made the right decision. After we de-planed I looked up the tailpipe and was instantly vindicated. The single turbine wheel of the J-33 engine was almost completely destroyed! There was not a single intact turbine blade on the entire wheel! Some were completely missing, some were broken with half or less of the blade remaining and some had only a corner gone. But not one was completely intact. The amazing thing was that the engine continued to run and produce some power with the turbine wheel so out of balance.

Colonel McCoy was busy collecting his parachute, ready to leave what he still thought was a flyable airplane when I said, " C'mere a second, Colonel--I want to show you something." I gave him my flashlight and heard his words echo from the tailpipe, "holy ****!"

After withdrawing his head from the tailpipe, he looked me right in the eyes and said with conviction, "DeGroote, why don't you just stay away from me for a while?"

I was happy to do so, and I completely understood his reluctance to be in the same room with me, let alone the same airplane. As I recall, he completed his jet checkout without further problem, but with a different instructor. So ended my contribution to the Air Force's project Blue Flame.

Other significant events occurred at Suffolk County. I was promoted to captain along with Jake, George, and other contemporaries. I no longer looked like a teenager, although I was still "carded" on occasion by a suspicious bar tender. One of the most important events was my decision to change my career path in aviation completely. My plan had always been to put in my required mandatory commitment time as an Air Force pilot and take advantage of my jet experience to get a job as an airline pilot. The airlines were indeed hiring pilots with jet time to ease their transition into the sleek, new jet airliners. And the airlines had a problem similar to the Air Force's "Blue Flame" imbroglio. Many of their most experienced pilots were reluctant to get involved with this radical new form of propulsion. Despite the golden opportunity presented by these circumstances, I was hesitant to make the move. The primary reason was my love affair with the F-102. I looked at that delta-winged beauty and compared it with the sleek but massive airliners coming out and the airliners came in a distant second. There was also the matter of security. I now had a wife and child for whom I was required to put food on the table, and the possibility of failure in an airline career--although I was still cocky enough to think that was a very remote possibility--still had to influence my decision. I had won a regular commission in Alaska, making a military career quite secure. I had gone to Squadron Officers School (SOS) and emerged as a distinguished graduate, which in my mind cancelled out my failure at Wright-Patterson the previous year. All in all, the smart thing for me to do appeared to be to follow an Air Force career. As long as I was flying fighters I don't think there was any possibility of my making any other decision. Marion was delighted. I think she thought I looked too young to be an airline pilot anyway.

On January 18th, 1958 another reason for me to insure that my career and income were secure became evident. David Glenn DeGroote came into the world at the same hospital in the Hamptons where Jackie Kennedy was born.

David

While David's arrival into our lives was not a surprise, his disposition was. Steve was the only baby we really knew and David was as different from Steve as night is from day. To begin with, David didn't physically resemble Steve as a baby at all--not all that unusual for brothers, but it didn't stop there. Whereas Steve was moving at a hundred miles an hour even before he could walk, Dave seemed content to sit and observe life going on around him. He would often sit in his chair for hours, without demanding attention, happily amused by something as mundane as a clothes pin. David was so laid back, in fact, we were a little concerned that he might have a learning disability. We were quickly disabused of that notion when we went to his first parent-teacher meeting and were advised by a beaming teacher that, "David is a sponge when it comes to learning". It seems that we were harboring a quiet intellectual.

A few years later I bought David a toy plastic "computer" that actually did basic computations through a series of sliding, manually placed flat plates. We assembled the gadget and David was fascinated by it. We read the operating manual together and I discovered that it was actually a fairly sophisticated and ingenious toy. Its computations were predicated on the arithmetic base 2 rather than the conventional base 10. Since I had never worked extensively with the base 2, David and I were starting from almost the same point in reading and understanding the operating manual. I would have to read and re-read the same page, while Dave, who was about seven at the time, was impatiently trying to get me to turn to the next page. It was quite obvious to me that when starting a mathematical problem or function from the same point, David's comprehension was leaving me in the dust. I tried, unsuccessfully to get him interested in something else.

Dave was, and still is, a voracious reader. We tried with only limited success to teach him to discipline himself so that he wouldn't become absorbed in a book to the point that he lost the world around him. He was known to keep reading right through his stop on the school bus route and had to be told by the bus driver that the bus was at the end of the line and he'd have to call his parents to pick him up. We once "lost" him on a base in Thailand when he became engrossed in a book in the library's research room. When he failed to show up for dinner we searched the base for hours until we finally discovered the research room and David who had no idea that he was late for anything. He still occasionally gets involved in a new book and stays up reading it until the rising sun reminds him that he should be in bed.

But these are problems that most parents would like to have. We never had to fight things like drugs with any of our boys. In Dave's case, his daily regimen puts me to shame. Dave has a vision problem which we tried to get corrected surgically when he was very young with only limited success. His eyes operate independently making any sport or activity requiring good depth perception very difficult for him. Thus it was natural for him to gravitate toward activities like running. He runs competitively and has run in many marathons including the Boston Marathon. One day he announced casually that he was going on a 50 mile run, and he proceeded to do just that. As one who has to work up his adrenalin to drive 50 miles, I found this to be pretty impressive.

Dave elected to use his talent for mathematics by becoming an electrical engineer, getting his degree from Penn State. He made me very proud, especially after the way I had botched my attempt to become an engineer with the Air Force's program. Dave is different in that he's the only male in our immediate family who has no interest whatsoever in flying airplanes--meaning perhaps that he's the only one with good sense. For a while I could talk about "My son, the rocket scientist" since Dave actually worked for a company that launched satellites. He designed some of the software for the units that went into orbit. But he eventually became bored with working for a big company, returned to the Penn State area to live and designs software on his own. This always seemed to me, with my cautious, Depression era outlook, to be risky, but Dave, more than anyone else in the family, marches to his own drummer.

There is one thing further that I have to say about my second son. Dave is a wonderful human being. He's middle-aged now and has, it seems to me, spent most of his life doing things for others. If someone, even someone he hardly knows, has a problem with his computer, Dave is always there to fix the problem. When someone is sick or needs help moving something Dave is always ready to volunteer. His politics drive me crazy, but it's easy to overlook that shortcoming when he has so much else going for him.

--but with a few more adventures to relate about Suffolk County life, I'll return to the late 1950s and early '60s.

In late 1959 the squadron began transition into the F-101B, another of the so-called "Century Series" fighters that were re-equipping the Air Force's aircraft inventory. The "Voodoo" was, like the F-89, a twin jet, 45,000 pound, two place interceptor.

F-101B "Voodoo"

But the resemblance ended there! The Voodoo, with two afterburning J-57 engines, had more than double the thrust of the F-89. We were accustomed to phenomenal rates of climb in the Deuce, but the Voodoo left it in the dust, climbing to 40,000 feet in under three minutes! It was also faster than the Deuce, able to reach its red line supersonic speed of 1.73 mach compared to the Deuce's 1.25 mach.

There were, however, some drawbacks. For starters, no fighter pilot wants to admit that he needs help operating his aircraft and weapons system. We had been operating the F-102's attack radar and missile systems quite well for several years while flying the airplane. The thought of turning over a key part of the weapons system to somebody riding in the back was anathema to most pilots in the squadron, and arriving R.O.s were not warmly welcomed. I had a couple of years working with R.O.s and I knew that a good two man crew was far superior to a good one man crew. I talked this up at every opportunity with only limited success. Most of our pilots had to learn the lesson on their own. Fortunately it was eventually learned and pilots found themselves competing for the good R.O.s.

There was one other fundamental problem with the Voodoo. It was a handful to fly! After years of flying the F-102 with its docile response to all manner of pilot abuse, we found ourselves flying a marginally stable airplane that could reach out and kill you if you weren't careful.

By this time I was a fairly senior captain, respected, I think, by my peers and the command structure of the squadron, which included Tobey Turgeau. I was selected to be one of the first pilots to check out in the Voodoo and to become an instructor pilot charged with checking out other pilots. Jake and I were assigned to temporary duty with the Voodoo squadron at Dover AFB, Delaware and proceeded to get qualified in the aircraft. My first impression was not good. The airplane's wing loading was so high that the whole aircraft shook whenever 30 degrees of bank were exceeded. Whereas the Deuce seemed to want to fly, this machine had to be dragged kicking and screaming through its flight envelope. Once supersonic, however, the airplane was in its realm and was a pleasure to fly.

One of the jobs that fell to those of us who were newly checked out was to go to the McDonnell factory in Saint Louis to pick up new airplanes for our Squadron. On one such trip I picked up a brand new airplane and flew it back, uneventfully to Suffolk County. The usual procedure was to hand carry all of the aircraft's records with you and upon arrival at home base turn the records over to Maintenance, thereby "selling" the airplane to them. When we landed, however, my R.O. and I were hungry so we decided to have lunch at the Officers' Club before selling the aircraft to Maintenance. While we were at lunch, Maintenance needed a spare and discovered my airplane, in commission, on the ramp. Since the Form 781, the prime document for the airplane, was in the cockpit, there was no reason they could not assign it to fly. This they did, assigning it to Captain Don Willsie to fly on one of his first transition missions. Unfortunately, during the mission Don was forced to eject from the aircraft which then crashed and sank to the bottom of Long Island Sound. When I discovered what had happened, I went sheepishly to Maintenance with a stack of documents, attempting to establish their ownership of the aircraft. Needless to say, I had a snowball's chance in Hell of getting anyone to sign for an airplane that was currently residing in the depths of Long Island Sound. Although I was able to drop the records off as part of the accident board's paper trail, no one signed for them, and to the best of my knowledge, ownership of that aircraft is still officially mine.

Aside from the peculiarities of ownership, Don Willsie's accident raised some official eyebrows in the Air Force's F-101 community. Don was an experienced and well respected fighter pilot, and his accident could not be easily explained. He was doing some simple familiarization maneuvers, being chased by Bob Hafner, another well respected I.P. While in a tight turn he apparently exceeded the angle of attack limits and the airplane "pitched up". This was an aerodynamic peculiarity of the '101 caused by the wing tip vortices impinging on the stabilator during high angle of attack flight. This causes the nose to rise precipitously and, once started, upward rotation is aggravated by slipstream hitting the long nose section forward of the center of gravity. The Flight Handbook recovery procedure was to hold the stick full forward, deploy the drag chute, and wait for the airplane to start flying again, usually indicated by a violent roll which showed that one wing had started flying again. Don swore that he had followed the procedure but saw no sign of recovery. Bob Hafner warned him not to stay with it too long, and at 10,000 feet Don ordered his R.O., Dale Williams, to eject. Dale did so and Don followed shortly. They were rescued by a boat captain who had witnessed the event. They were unhurt except that the rapid pressure changes adversely affected Don's sinuses to the point that it ended his flying career.

When we advised McDonnell of the accident they were skeptical that Don had followed the correct recovery procedure. We found, however, almost incidentally, that pitch up flight testing had been done on an "A" model Voodoo, not an F-101B. The "B" was a significantly different aircraft, having two seats instead of one, different model engines and a fire control radar system mounted in the nose. McDonnell insisted it made no difference, but to mollify our many doubting pilots, agreed to have their chief test pilot, Don Stuck, repeat the pitch up testing sequence. He did so, taking the added precaution of using a large spin chute rather than the standard F-101 drag chute. Despite that precaution, Mr. Stuck found himself floating down in his personal parachute after the "B" model he was testing failed to recover from his induced pitch up.

The only solution to the problem was: don't pitch up, but if you do, make certain to eject by 10,000 feet. We squadron pilots soon adjusted to the Voodoo's idiosyncrasies and enjoyed its great performance as an interceptor while always treating it with the respect it demanded.

In my spare time I became interested in a much more stable airplane, the Beech T-34. The base had a flying club and a pair of surplus T-34s which the Air Force had used as a primary trainer for a number of years. It was a spin off of the famous Beech Bonanza but had just two seats in tandem, a conventional tail, and was, much to my delight, fully acrobatic. I decided to help the club by getting my FAA flight instructor's rating. I quickly became the club's most popular instructor when word got around that I didn't charge a fee for instructing. I also taught ground school for the members. Most of my students were squadron R.O.s, some of whom were hoping to go to Air Force pilot training. It was a satisfying pastime, and I loved doing acrobatics in the sweet handling T-34, but I soon discovered that I was getting bored teaching the same things over and over and that I simply didn't have the patience to be a good teacher.

I soon found that my time for instructing would be very limited because my Commander, Lieutenant Colonel Mike Culwell, asked me if I would mind filling in as the Group Flight Safety Officer, since the incumbent was transferring out and no replacement was due in for some time. Since it sounded interesting and the boss needed help, I agreed to take the job temporarily. It turned out to be another classic example of a case wherein I should have followed my old adage of, "Never volunteer for anything".

Dad, Befuddled By Tinkertoys, Base Housing, Long Island, With Steve And Dave Observing.

Without my knowledge, the Personnel troglodytes, seeing a new guy at the Safety desk, placed the entry level Flight Safety Air Force Specialty Code (AFSC) into my records. It seems that, by coincidence, the fighter wing at Thule, Greenland needed a flight safety officer and I was available. To make a long story short, my vehement protests went unheeded by higher headquarters, and I found myself announcing to Marion that I was going to spend a year away from her and the boys in the world's worst place doing what I now considered to be the Air Force's worst job. So, after spending several weeks at Westover AFB in Massachusetts getting re-current in the F-102, I said farewell to my friends at Suffolk County, moved Marion and the boys into an apartment in Warminster Pennsylvania and booked passage on a C-135 to Thule.

Thule

The worst part of a military career is the family separations. They usually come at the worst possible time, normally when the kids really need a father and when the wife really needs help raising those kids. There are a few to whom it doesn't matter all that much, and even a very few for whom it presents an opportunity to get away from an unloved spouse or unhappy family situation. My family situation was the absolute antithesis of that sort of situation. I found myself, from the minute I left Marion to board the C-135 bound for Thule falling into a state of depression that I would have to fight for the entire year on the Greenland ice cap. Thule was, in fact, a dreadful place. It was cold, desolate and boring. And I was in a job which I didn't like and for which I was unprepared, having not been to the Flight Safety Officers' course at USC and having had no time apprenticed with an experienced safety officer anywhere. But, prepared or not, I was now the Chief of Safety at Thule Air Base, Greenland.

The flight to Thule was uneventful and uncomfortable. The C-135 was a cargo aircraft with no windows, so it was like being transported in a time capsule. I entered the time capsule at McGuire in the sweltering heat of the last day of August, 1962. A few hours later the door of the time capsule was opened from outside by a sergeant wearing a parka!

I was met at the airplane by a captain, who turned out to be the temporary base Chief of Safety, and who couldn't wait for me to arrive so he could go back to his F-102 pilot job. He was accompanied by the safety technician, a grizzled master sergeant who had just a month left on his tour. The sergeant kept making remarks about how beautiful the Arctic landscape was. I decided that he had been there too long. All I could see was ice and rocks, a totally black and white scene, and I thought it was, hands down, the ugliest place I had ever seen!

But ugly or not, I was to become part of that landscape. I moved in with the fighter squadron people since I would be flying with them. The BOQ was an Arctic building standing on stilts which had been sunken into the permafrost by some sort of machine that used superheated steam to melt a hole in the permanently frozen earth. Virtually all of the buildings on Thule were of this basic design. They were made of metal and were, of course, heavily insulated in walls and ceiling. They were designed to withstand the Arctic hurricanes which blew snow from the ice cap with winds that could exceed 100 miles per hour. Someone had named these "Phase Winds" for no good reason in my estimation. I was wrong. The Phase I, II, or III designation proved useful in labeling the severity of the many storms I experienced.

After settling in, I met my new boss, a full colonel named David Tudor, the Wing Commander, who seemed a competent, nice sort of guy. I moved into my new office, determined to learn as much as I could about my new job and make the best of a bad situation. I had an administrative NCO who had been on base for several months and a ground safety technician who had arrived the day after I had. My administrative sergeant knew his way around and proved very good at keeping the new captain from getting into too much trouble before he got his feet on the ground. The ground safety guy, previously a teetotaler, could never adjust to the surroundings and ended up a hopeless alcoholic. He left Thule, having failed in his job, and after causing more problems than he ever solved, for a new assignment. I hoped he would recover from his addiction and I felt that I had somehow failed him although I have no idea what I could have done differently.

I checked in at the flight line as soon as possible and got checked out on the local procedures so I could start flying. One of the local peculiarities was that there were no alternates within the Deuce's range. You either landed at Thule or you crash landed on the ice cap. There was even a procedure for doing just that. If you were unable to land at Thule, you were to fly straight and level until the ice cap, which rose very gradually, came up to meet you. I quickly decided that I'd take my chances with a zero-zero GCA before I'd try the ice cap bit.

Soon after I completed my orientation flights with the squadron the Cuban missile crisis occurred. Although, as Safety Officer, I was not a line pilot, I was combat ready, and all combat ready pilots were on full time alert. Most of us were on 15 minute alert which meant that we were set up in an airplane and wore flight suits everywhere on base. All Americans who lived through the October crisis remember the tension that pervaded the country until the Soviets backed down. But I think it was more tense among those of us in the military since we were kept advised of classified intelligence that made us aware of just how serious the situation was and how close we came to an actual nuclear war. And while we at Thule were the tip of the spear, being closest to the Soviet Union, our worries were almost exclusively for our families back home for whom we could provide no assistance. Fortunately for civilization, a political solution was reached and we went back to our normal dull existence in the Arctic.

Three and a half months went by with me fighting a losing battle with boredom, when BLACK FRIDAY occurred. On Friday, December 14, 1962, Major Robert Daum, Operations Officer of the 332nd Fighter Squadron, a friend of mine, took off on a routine post-maintenance test hop and disappeared forever.

Normally, test hops of any kind are performed in daylight hours, but since there is no daylight in Thule during the winter months, Bob had departed in darkness. He made the routine radio check-in call with the GCI site located on "P" Mountain adjacent to the base. The GCI controller was Dick Brown, also a friend, who had been coerced into his present job after many years as a fighter pilot. Dick stated during the investigation that he had observed Bob's blip on one sweep of the antenna and turned his attention to a recovering flight during the next sweep. On the subsequent sweep, he looked back to where Bob's F-102 should have been and saw nothing. The F-102 had to have been within about 30 miles of Thule but had vanished! It has not been found to this day.

Shortly after the F-102 had been reported missing, the base's rescue helicopter was dispatched to search for the missing aircraft. When the 'copter pilot encountered some unexpected weather over the ice cap he elected to land to wait out the weather. Unfortunately, the ice cap was too steeply inclined and the helicopter rolled on its side causing major damage. Luckily, in this instance no one was seriously injured. But the 'copter was a complete write-off.

As bad as things were at this point, they were about to get much worse. The base C-47 support aircraft crew, upon hearing that an F-102 was missing, launched on a search mission. With the pilot flying from the left seat, the copilot was looking out the right side window for any sign of wreckage. Suddenly he felt that the aircraft was in an unusual attitude. He checked his instruments and confirmed that the aircraft was in a 90 degree bank. He seized the controls from the pilot who was apparently suffering from spatial disorientation over the pure white ice cap and tried to roll wings level. It was too late. The C-47 impacted the ice cap, skidding to a stop from cruise speed. The propellors disintegrated, throwing shrapnel through the fuselage and, tragically, killing the pilot and radio operator.

In the space of a few hours we had lost three good men, including one of my friends. I also found myself, with no prior experience, directing the investigations and proceedings of three major accident boards simultaneously. We were told, somewhat ominously, that the Air Force Chief of Staff, General LeMay, was personally interested in the investigative proceedings.

To round out the example of a perfect black Friday, I found myself at the center of a leadership crisis. As luck would have it, the Wing Commander, Colonel Tudor, had just gone on leave and was somewhere in the USA. His second in command, another full colonel, was an incompetent boob and a hopeless alcoholic to boot. I had prepared the vital first notification messages to higher headquarters, including the Pentagon, and found the man in charge too inebriated to comprehend the text. I decided to employ the old military adage, "Lead, follow, or get the hell out of the way", signed the messages myself, and sent them off. I then went to base operations, supposedly to assist the Director of Operations with the search and rescue operation. Upon arrival I found the D.O., a senior lieutenant colonel, literally in tears over the out-of -control situation and the fatalities. I suggested he go home and get some rest and that I would fill in for him. He gladly took me up on the offer, and the Base Operations NCOs seemed happy that this young captain, whoever he was, was willing to take charge.

Since our only support aircraft had already crashed, the decision to call off the search and ask for help from higher headquarters was an easy one. Support was quick to arrive and within a few days six RB-66s were on station photographing the area, while an exotic infrared detection aircraft was also pressed into service. Unfortunately, the Herculean efforts produced no results and Bob Daum and his aircraft were never found.

As technical advisor to three investigative boards, I was kept very busy. My administrator, Sergeant Burt, reminded me that I hadn't been to bed for three days so he intercepted calls allowing me to get a few hours of sleep. I spent Christmas day along with Sergeant Burt composing the final cover letters for the accident reports. The Wing Commander had by now returned early from his leave and things were back under control. He seemed unaware of the Safety shop's efforts during his absence on Black Friday. That was alright with me. I saw nothing to be gained by insisting on exposure of the shortcomings of his Operations and Command personnel operating under pressure. In retrospect, that was probably an error in judgment on my part.

Black Friday was a depressing and tragic affair, but in reviewing the disaster, it taught me a lot about accident investigation, something that I would find useful in the future, and about how people react under stress. I was no longer the boy fighter pilot, whether I liked it or not. I didn't look like a teenager any more and I was slowly but inexorably coming to the realization that I was an Air Force officer and that I would, sometimes on very short notice, be required to pick up the proverbial ball and run with it. Such were the lessons of Black Friday at Thule Air Base. While I didn't exactly come of age, I at least stepped out of my adolescence.

I had completed one third of my tour at Thule and I was still marveling at the strangeness of my surroundings. Loneliness was still my greatest enemy, and it was compounded by living in the unnatural setting some 1000 miles above the Arctic Circle. By

December we had gone well into the dark season, aptly named because the base was in total darkness 24 hours a day. Even climbing to 40,000 feet in an F-102 at noon did not uncover the slightest glimpse of sunshine. This continued until late February when hints of twilight began to appear on the southern horizon. It then began to rush toward the daylight season, and by May it was as bright and sunny at midnight as it was at noon. This too was disconcerting, but not nearly as much so as the dark season, which was very depressing.

Those of us who flew were given a two day indoctrination into survival on the ice pack. After a day of classroom work we were driven out onto the ice pack so that we could learn to build an ice shelter. The shelter was made from ice blocks that we sawed from the surface with the small ice saw that we carried in the survival pack we sat on in the Deuce. The shelter was roughly the size of a grave, and the ice blocks we sawed out were propped up to make a roof. Cracks were sealed with snow or chips of ice. Constructing the shelter was hard work and I found myself stripping to my winter underwear to keep from perspiring, since getting wet was the worst thing you could do. The temperature was well below zero, but I was quite comfortable working in my underwear. Once my shelter was completed I quickly dressed in my Arctic clothing, crawled into my double sleeping bag and managed to get a few hours of sleep. While I certainly didn't enjoy my Arctic adventure, it was probably a worthwhile exercise, and the kids enjoyed hearing about Dad's experiences in a letter I wrote to them.

The "Phase" winds, mentioned earlier became a problem on base. We were told that the weather station recorded more Phase conditions in January than the base normally experienced in an entire winter. Phase conditions were declared as Phase I, II or III, Phase III being the most severe. During Phase III conditions everybody was supposed to stay where they were, protected by the Arctic buildings' rugged construction. I once opened the heavy door of our barracks and took one step outside to see for myself the fury of the storm. I literally could not see my hand in front of my face. I quickly stepped back inside and closed the door securely.

The Phase winds came precariously close to claiming a victim on one midwinter day. A clerk working alone in an Arctic building decided to walk to another building a few feet away in order to use its latrine. He did so even though there was a Phase III storm condition in effect which emphatically mandated that you stay in the building where you were. He had made the short trip to the other building many times in good weather and was certain that he would have no problem navigating the few feet involved. He was wrong. He missed the building and was soon wandering aimlessly about in the zero visibility conditions, rapidly losing body heat. He then got very lucky, bumping into a dumpster. He, at that point, made the smartest decision of his day by crawling inside the dumpster and staying there until the storm subsided. He was later rescued, cold but unhurt, by the base rescue squad.

While we were all very conscious of the weather, we were probably even more conscious of the passage of time. This was far and away the slowest year of my life, and I complained about it constantly to my long-suffering Marion who had her own problems running a household with an absentee husband. All of the fighter pilots were bored and soon began searching for ways to beat the system and the boredom.

Someone soon discovered a requirement in the combat readiness training manual for flight simulator training every few months. Thule had no simulator, but Goose Bay, Canada did. And once at Goose there was no way to get back to Thule on a regularly scheduled flight except by way of McGuire AFB, New Jersey. That allowed at least a day or so back in the civilized world. For me it was a great morale booster since Marion had settled in an apartment in Warminster PA, less than an hour's drive from McGuire. I was able to take advantage of the training requirement twice during my year on "the rock", and developed a new affection for the simulator.

Another somewhat shady method of breaking out of our frozen jailhouse was the requirement that all F-102 pilots be fitted with pressure suits. These were to be worn any time flight was expected to exceed 50,000 feet. This required a flight down to McGuire with a follow on trip to Perrin AFB in Texas where the pressure suit would be fitted and test flown in Perrin's altitude chamber. This all took about a week and required Marion to buy an airline ticket so she could accompany me on the flight to Perrin. We had a great time and I actually enjoyed the claustrophobic experience of "flying" in the suit to 80,000 feet in the altitude chamber. The chamber's technicians put a jar of water in the chamber's anteroom, where I sat, to demonstrate what would happen to your blood at extreme altitude without the suit's protection. The water boiled instantly when the anteroom was explosively decompressed to 80,000 feet. The thought occurred to me as I was sitting alone in the chamber, watching the altimeter wind up toward extreme altitude, that I had just bet my life on the little valve assembly on the front of the suit that controlled its functioning. I immediately dismissed that negative notion from my mind. The valve worked beautifully and I went back to enjoying my impromptu vacation with Marion.

Back at Thule I was required to fly with the suit in an F-102 in order to become accustomed to the restricted movement that a pilot has when wearing the suit. My first flight didn't work out too well.

It was a simple training flight with a climb to high altitude under GCI control with some maneuvering to get the feel of the pressure suit. The weather was clear and cold with bright sunshine. The crew chief helped me strap in with a little extra effort required because of the suit. Taxi and takeoff were normal until I was airborne. I was then acutely aware of a rush of hot air filling the cockpit. The cockpit temperature controls on the Deuce are on a small central pedestal between your feet. I reached down to turn the temperature rheostat to full cold but was dismayed to discover that, because of the pressure suit I couldn't reach either the rheostat or the cockpit pressure dump switch. It was obvious that the cockpit temperature control had stuck in the full hot position. It was also obvious that I couldn't move far enough forward to do anything about it. I pulled up sharply onto a downwind leg, simultaneously declaring an emergency. I could feel perspiration running down my face from the extreme temperature. I reached for the canopy jettison knob, but by now I was turning a tight base leg and decided that I could make it back on the ground without dropping pieces of the airplane onto the base. I landed, deployed the drag chute and opened the canopy. The blast of Arctic air solved my heating problem and I never thought the air of Greenland could feel so refreshing. Taxiing in, I noticed that perspiration from my head had filled the bottom of my helmet up to my lower lip, and I had to release the face plate of the pressure suit to drain it. Needless to say, I sat down with the personal equipment technicians in order to make drastic adjustments to the suit's laces to allow me to reach all of the cockpit controls. My story made the rounds and everyone made similar checks, some finding that they had the same adjustment problem. That, I suppose, made my training flight a success. But I couldn't help but feel put upon by a cockpit temperature control failing for the one and only time in all of my Deuce flights on the one and only pressure suit flight I had ever made.

Time continued to move on, albeit at a snail's pace. I became sufficiently bored that I checked out as a missile loading technician with the armament shop which had received a poor report card on an inspection. Since I was also the base missile safety officer, I thought I should try to help. I decided that the best way to help was to find out what the missile loaders did and the best way to do that was to become one of them. The armament officer was glad to have my input, once he discovered that I was on his side and not another problem for him. And the loading crew chief was delighted to be able to order a captain fighter pilot around. I got to be pretty good at it and made a number of suggestions to improve safety procedures, some of which were actually adopted.

During the last few months of my tour I ran into one more unexpected problem. I took my annual physical exam given to me by Dr. Bob Hendee a good friend. The three staff physicians were very close to the fighter pilots and we socialized at the bar most days. During my physical Bob announced that I had a hernia. He was a neurosurgeon by training, so I demanded that a "real doctor" examine me. He brought in Dr. Charlie Graff, the Army surgeon on post, and later, Dr. Bob Goldberger, the other Air Force surgeon. They examined me independently and all agreed that I did indeed have a hernia. They gave me the choice of having the operation done in Thule or waiting until I rotated. I could then have it done at a normal medical facility, but I would be grounded until after the surgery. I accused them of plotting the whole thing for their own proficiency training, but agreed to let them operate. I didn't want anything to slow down my resuming combat readiness as soon as I arrived at my next assignment.

There began a steady back and forth among the doctors, nurses and fighter pilots. My hernia operation became the social event of July in Thule. Since my physical also revealed that I needed glasses, the pilots branded me a "blind old man with a hernia". I pointed out that I had recently pummeled several of them on the squash court and asked them how it felt to be beaten by a blind old man with a hernia. The nurse-anesthetist described her function and claimed I would have no secrets from her. I told her to simply feed me intravenously with Beefeaters Gin, and she promised to do so. In any event the big day arrived and, partially sedated, I asked a gowned and masked Bob Goldberger whether he had brought his rusty razor blade along. He acknowledged that he had indeed and that was all I remembered. The nurse-anesthetist claimed that the IV solution bottle was indeed wearing a Beefeaters label, but I was too far under to remember. In any case, the operation was a success and it provided a great topic for bar conversation for at least a week. One final vignette concerning the medical staff involved Doctors Goldberger and Graff who, just after my surgery, were making their rounds at the small Army base up the mountain adjacent to the air base. They were driving down the mountain in a jeep with Charlie Graff at the wheel. Now Charlie was a good doctor but he was from New York and had traveled everywhere on the subway. He learned to drive at Thule! The result was predictable. Rounding a curve, Charlie proceeded to roll the jeep one and a half times. The two doctors suffered only a few cuts and bruises, but the responding ambulance crew was mystified as to how the doctors had beaten them to the scene of the accident!

After a week in hospital I went back to my routine at the office and at various trouble spots on base like the armament squadron.

My new found knowledge of missile safety, it turns out, would prove useful in my next assignment. That assignment came from my long standing relationship with Tobey Turgeau, now a lieutenant colonel and a team chief on Air Defense Command's Operational Readiness Inspection (ORI) Team. Tobey knew I was on a one year tour in Thule and decided that he wanted me working for him again. He called me fairly early in my tour to invite me to join the ORI Team. Although I was reluctant to take a job that I knew would involve much travel and short time separations from my family, the idea of working for Tobey again and being home based in Colorado Springs was too appealing to turn down. I instantly accepted Tobey's invitation. I thought I had to sell Marion on the idea of taking a traveling job, but she was all in favor of it. She liked the idea of moving to Colorado Springs, and she was glad to see me go to a job that I wanted, working for a man she knew I greatly respected. Besides, the trips were short, usually a week to ten days. When the team wasn't traveling we had a very loose schedule with plenty of time to spend with the family.

So, at the end of August, 1963, the tour I thought would never end was finally over. Boarding the C-135 for McGuire was one of the happiest moments of my life. I'm reluctant to find anything good to say about an assignment that I so thoroughly detested, but in later years I had to admit that it had broadened me professionally.

Since I had had time on my hands I had at last re-started my college education and this time I stuck with it for the many years it took to earn my bachelor's degree and later my graduate degree.

Colorado Springs

Putting Thule behind me proved to be no problem once I found myself home with Marion and the boys. We were too busy to be bothered with the past. We had to get organized to move across the country, a project made more difficult by the fact that we were under pressure to get the boys enrolled in school as soon as possible. I briefly stopped to bid farewell to family and friends in the Philadelphia area, and the four of us piled into our aging Desoto and set out for the promised land of Colorado Springs.

We drove long hours thinking we'd see lots of interesting things on the way. What we saw mostly was the Great Plains with all of their flat, boring scenery. We were happy to be a family again, however, and we enjoyed the trip. But we were eager to make it to Colorado.

Social Life Resumes After Thule Exile

We finally saw the end of the Great Plains with the Rocky Mountains in the distance and Pike's Peak at the center. I was impressed by the massive mountain range, but I sensed disappointment from Marion. The mountains were snow free and somewhat ugly this time of year, and Marion had been expecting the snow capped majesty of the tourist photos she had seen. For my part it looked a whole lot more attractive than Mount Dundas in Thule. In a few months Marion had her daily view of the Pike's Peak snow covered beauty. We quickly found a house to buy, perhaps too quickly, but it fit our family well and we were happy. I insisted on a house with a nice lawn and flowers, something that would never have occurred to me before Thule, but was now very important to me. It was also important to me to spend time with the boys and we spent many hours working with model planes and trains, hobbies that they continued to follow in later years. Steven and David were enrolled in a nice school and we began to make friends and to get settled in. Gage and Syd Mersereau, old friends from Suffolk County, were our sponsors and were very helpful in getting us acclimated. It was time to go to work.

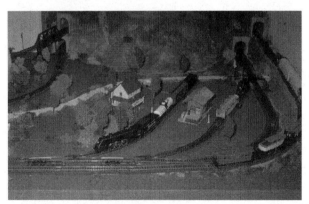

Model Planes And Trains Projects

Tobey Turgeau briefed me on the job and seemed distraught about my aircraft assignment. He told me apologetically that I would not be flying the F-101 and F-102, but the F-101 and the F-89! He explained that the Air National Guard had nine squadrons of F-89s and that he noted from my records that I had flown the '89 for several years. The team needed F-89 inspectors so it only made sense to make use of my background. He need not have been concerned. Gage, who had never flown the F-89 before, had already been checked out and had warned me to expect to fly the '89 rather than the Deuce. I put Tobey at ease, telling him that I had expected it when I discovered that the Guard was still flying the '89. Inwardly, while I was disappointed to not be flying my favorite mount, I was overjoyed to be getting current in three different airplanes-including the T-bird- at one time.

Tobey told me to take my time getting the family settled in, but I knew that the team was short of pilots, so I hurried along, making arrangements to get recurrent in the F-101 with the squadron at Kingsley Field, Oregon. Remembering that the Voodoo climbed like a rocket, I asked my instructor if he would mind my making an afterburner climb. He was more than willing, and I could feel myself grinning behind the oxygen mask as the Voodoo broke through 40,000 feet in under four minutes. I enjoyed my re-introduction to the '101, but as soon as I made my first 30 degree bank turn the airplane shuddered in its characteristic pre-stall burble. The airplane actually turned better while in a burble, and you got used to it after a while. But I remembered that this was not an airplane to be trifled with.

Next came recurrency in the F-89, an aircraft that would never be labeled as climbing like a rocket. After some time at home I went to Des Moines Iowa where the Air National Guard had a squadron of F-89s and a good reputation with the ORI Team. Flying the F-89 after seven years was like shaking hands with an old friend, but I had forgotten how grossly underpowered the airplane was. At roughly the same gross weight as the F-89, the '101 had more than double the thrust. To maintain proficiency in both aircraft at the same time I would sometimes arrange to visit a city that had an F-101 squadron based with an ANG F-89 squadron nearby so I could fly both aircraft on the same trip. This was very efficient, but flying the Voodoo in the morning with an afternoon F-89 flight was a real study in the extremes of jet engine thrust. While the Voodoo shot down the runway on takeoff like a leaping gazelle, the F-89 lurched forward like a wounded aardvark.

The ORI Team assignment was a three year affair. After that period of time the personnel people reasoned, correctly I think, that you would tend to become too dogmatic as a professional inspector. A large portion of our inspection activity consisted of simply flying chase on one of the local pilots and observing how well he adhered to Air Defense Command's published attack procedures. We all had our own pet theories on how these procedures should be implemented, so there was a good exchange of ideas during our inspections. My personal crusade was to improve formation flying during departure and recovery. The GCI controllers workload was automatically cut in half if aircraft departed and recovered as a flight of two rather than individually. So, my usual routine was to find the newest, green lieutenant, fresh out of flying school to lead me on a formation takeoff, after which I would drop back to chase him through the intercepts and attacks. When it was time for recovery I would rejoin in close formation and have him lead me through a formation landing. I would then have the squadron training officer assign a "ringer", their best pilot to do the same thing. That way I got to look at how their training was at both extremes of proficiency. I was always surprised at how often the "ringer" turned out to be the guy who needed the extra work rather than the new guy. In one instance I was making a night wing landing being led by a Navy exchange pilot. As we came over the approach lights he called for me to cut power, "now". Cutting power suddenly in an F-101 is like cutting the wings off. The airplane drops like a stone. I watched him sink below me and bounce halfway back into position. All this time I nursed back my throttles for a normal landing, touching down slightly ahead of him but keeping him in sight. At debriefing I questioned the wisdom of his power control and he confessed that he had never led a night formation landing in his life. I should have been more vigilant upon seeing that he was a Naval Aviator since controlled crashes are what they do for landings on ships. On the other hand, it would have done wonders for inter service amicability if he had told me before takeoff that he had never before led a night formation landing.

Speaking of formation flying, I promised earlier that I would mention one further incident wherein I was involved, though once again not directly, in a mid-air collision. One of our inspection requirements was to assure that the Command's aircraft that were on alert were in top notch condition manned by crews that were fully ready to fly. That would appear to be self-evident, but people tend to get careless about aircraft that have very little chance of flying. In any case, we devised a system that put a six man inspection team into the alert hangars, unannounced to verify the alert force. We did this by flying three T-birds on a flight plan to an airport near the Air Force Base we had singled out and changing destination at the last minute. We would then taxi into the alert area, have the live munitions taken off the alert aircraft and have them flown by the alert crews. Usually, we found the aircraft and flight crews fully combat ready, but every so often we found someone trying to beat the system. When we found someone like that it usually meant that heads would roll somewhere in the command structure. We had zero tolerance for corner cutting with the alert force, and the word got around quickly.

Anyway, we had just completed a successful Alert Force Capability Test (AFCT) and were headed home with our flight of three T-33s. We had to stop for fuel and did so in Kansas as I recall. Our leader, a full colonel, decided that we would make a 3-ship formation takeoff to avoid the need for an in-flight join up. This was fine with me, although I noticed that the runway width was 25 feet short of the width required in Air Defense Command (ADC) regulations. There was plenty of room to make a safe 3-ship takeoff. I didn't consider it important enough to point it out to the colonel, a serious mistake on my part, although I think he would have pressed on anyway.

We proceeded to line up for departure, the leader nodded his head forward, signaling brake release, and we were off. At around 100 knots of airspeed I saw a sudden stream of fuel from the other side of the formation. I said to my back seater, Tom George, an old Suffolk County buddy, "Uh-oh, I think two just ran into lead."

My worry was confirmed when number two spread out after takeoff and we could observe a rip in his left tip tank from end to end. We went to a discrete radio frequency to discuss our options.

We decided that if we returned and reported a mid air collision, it would generate an investigation, voluminous reports and much embarrassment. Option two was to return to Colorado Springs and dump the damaged tank in an area designated for getting rid of tip tanks that didn't feed, since the T-bird could not be landed with one full and one empty tip tank. Everyone would assume that it was just another case of a tip tank not feeding, and we saw no need to further enlighten them. The vote for option two was unanimous. Had there been any dissent, I was prepared to unleash my bombshell--the fact that we had taken off from a runway that did not meet minimum width standards--but it was not necessary. We worried that number two might not have enough fuel to make it to Colorado Springs, but, amazingly, the damaged tip tank fed out most of its fuel despite being ruptured He made a routine jettison in the tip tank drop area. We inspected lead's tip tank and found no damage except a scratch on the stabilizing fin. The fin had sliced two's tank with virtually no damage to itself. Thus ended our formation incident, having lost only a simple tip tank, and with me having survived my third and last involvement with airborne collisions, thank goodness.

A much more serious loss to the Air Force occurred some months later. I was flying on an administrative trip with the boss, Tobey Turgeau, in a T-bird. Tobey was in the front seat and I could see he was fidgeting trying to get comfortable. I asked him if he was OK and he replied that his back was giving him fits and that he was going to see the Doc when we got home. He did check in with the flight surgeon who scheduled him for further tests. The news we got from those tests was bad. Tobey had a tumor the size of a grapefruit pressing on his back. Small wonder it was giving him fits in the cockpit. Tobey was sent to the Brooks Medical center in Texas for treatment. Gage Mersereau and I visited him a few months later and found him his usual upbeat self but clearly unhappy with the hand fate had dealt to him. The Air Force was processing him for medical discharge, he had already been permanently grounded, and life as he knew it was over. We wished him well, but Gage and I had a somber flight back to Colorado Springs.

Some months later, Gage, Tom George and I were promoted to major and we immediately thought that there had to be a way to get Tobey back for our promotion party. He had, after all, brought all three of us Suffolk County warriors to the ORI team and probably helped to get us promoted. As luck would have it, another Suffolk County alumnus, Dick Gillette, ran the support flight at Peterson Field for ADC and Gage, Tom and I prevailed upon him to set up an administrative flight to Louisiana, where Tobey lived, to pick him up. He was transported, in style, in a T-39 executive jet. I'm sure this was all of marginal legality, but Dick was never one to quibble about rules. At the party, Tobey congratulated the three of us, and wished us well, while still implying that if we didn't make "his" Air Force a better organization, he'd come back and kick our butts.

We lost contact with Tobey for many years, while most of us were involved in Vietnam, and when the subject came up we worried that he might have lost his battle with cancer. But twenty years later we had a Suffolk County reunion, and who should come bouncing into the room, looking better than any of us, but Tobey Turgeau! He was too tough for even the big "C".

The real tragedy was the loss of a man like Tobey to the Air Force and the United States. Whereas most of us learned about leadership over the course of our careers, he was the prototypical natural leader. Tobey could walk into a room full of people and everyone would instantly know who was in charge. In my case, I had him as a mentor from my Aviation Cadet days until I was a field grade officer. No military academy could have provided a better curriculum. Tobey would have made an outstanding general officer, and it's too bad that it was not to be.

On the subject of top notch officers, one other of my contemporaries comes to mind. He was the only member of the so-called two man shop (i.e., two-place interceptors, the F-89 and F-

101) not to have been under Tobey at Suffolk County AFB. And it was probably appropriate that he, Chuck Aly, stood apart because Chuck was in every way his own man. He was, literally, larger than life. Most fighter pilots range, in physical size, from medium to downright diminutive. There's a good reason for this in that fighter cockpits are created by designers who are obsessed with saving weight and are thus inclined to include a cockpit as a necessary evil. The Air Force has maximum "sitting height" criteria which effectively eliminate large people from fighter cockpits. But Chuck Aly was a fighter pilot and sitting height be damned, he somehow made the cut. While I could easily fit my small frame into any fighter cockpit I used to marvel at the way Chuck could shoehorn his body, gargantuan by fighter squadron norms, into the claustrophobic confines of the T-33 cockpit.

We soon became accustomed to Chuck's physical size while we learned, more slowly, to adjust to the depth of his intellect. As I became better acquainted with Chuck I gradually came to realize that he fell into my very small group of "unforgettable characters" that were part of my education. Chuck, I discovered, came from highly educated and academically accomplished parents. The importance of education to his success in life was stressed over and over in his early years. So, Chuck in typical fighter pilot fashion, rebelled and joined the Air Force with only a high school education. Determined to prove that education has little to do with intelligence or competence, he qualified for the Aviation Cadet program and began a supercharged career as an officer. He was truly a self-educated man and I used to delight in watching him inject quotations from Shakespeare into fighter squadron banter that he had become bored with. Chuck was one of the most intelligent people I have ever dealt with and was living proof that formal education never overrides determination and natural ability. He was a superb pilot and a gifted staff officer. After a combat tour flying F-4s in Southeast Asia he continued his below-the-zone promotions, reaching full colonel whereupon, with typical Aly unpredictability, retired to devote more of his time to his family. As with Tobey Turgeau, the Air Force, in my opinion, lost a good general officer. Chuck was a good guy, hardworking, dedicated and in possession of a sense of humor that usually made the job at hand a pleasure. I consider it a privilege to have worked with him and to be his friend today.

The three year tour on the ORI Team was a fun job and time passed quickly. While not on the road we all had some spare time at home and I decided to make good use of mine by enrolling in a conversational French course. It was the same course as was taught at the Air Force Academy and the instructors were all native French speakers. I ended up taking the Air Force's language proficiency exam and was graded, inaccurately, I thought, as "fluent". This was to have some later significant effect on my career.

Naturally, we spent most of our time on ORI's, some more memorable than others. One that I've never forgotten happened at my old unit at Suffolk County Air Force Base. Since we seldom got back to Suffolk the base alumni, Gage, Tom and I were looking forward to visiting our old haunts. It turned out that we were too busy to do much sightseeing, but we enjoyed the trip anyway.

The Suffolk County Fighter Wing was under the command of Colonel Francis S. Gabreski, one of the most famous fighter pilots in the world. Colonel Gabreski had shot down 26 German aircraft in World War II and downed another 6.5 MIGs in Korea. With thirty-four and a half kills he was the Air Force's top ace who was still alive and, in fact, still on active duty.

On our arrival, the Colonel graciously invited the fighter crews on the ORI Team to dinner at his quarters. He served steak tartare as an hors d'oeuvre, presumably because he thought fighter pilots should eat raw meat!

The next day we launched our simulated war with dozens of targets assigned to "bomb" New York City while we evaluated how well Suffolk County and other bases prevented them from doing so. We took this mission very seriously, incidentally, since our tactics manuals even included techniques for ramming nuclear armed bombers if we were out of ammunition. The Cold War was serious business, especially after the Cuban Missile Crisis.

One of my jobs, after flying an early chase mission in the F-101 was to assess NADAR. NADAR was a recording tape contained in a can that was installed in the nose of the aircraft. Its only function was to record the display that the pilot flew during his attack. It was very simple. The pilot steered the aircraft, after the R.O. locked on to the target, so as to center a dot in a steering circle. The missile would fire automatically at which time a large "X" would appear. If the NADAR showed the dot centered when the firing "X" appeared, it was a "kill". If the dot was not in the center, it was a miss. Most of ADC's pilots were very good and misses were rare.

While I was assessing attack after attack, mostly hits, in walked Colonel Gabreski, NADAR can in hand, large cigar in his jaw. He had recorded two attacks. "Well, this should be easy", I thought. "Here's the Air Force's greatest living ace with a couple of simulated kills to add to the total." I suspect my jaw visibly dropped when the firing "X" appeared with the steering dot not centered. I had only one thing to say. "That's a miss, colonel". In reply, Gabreski grunted. The second attack came up on the screen and I could scarcely believe my eyes when once again the dot was not centered at firing signal. "That's a miss, too, sir", I said as quietly as possible. Gabreski grunted again and left the room. I suspected that the politics of a smart--ass young captain inflicting the humiliation of two missed attacks on the Air Force's greatest living ace might cause me some problems, but there were no repercussions. I think everyone realized that Gabreski was still number one. He was now dealing in a new skill set. He became famous in the "bank and yank" era of WWII and Korea when the outcome of an air battle depended on who could coax the last ounce of performance from a fighter before it met with structural failure. This was a different world, a world wherein precision instrument flying determined whether or not a nuclear armed bomber hit its target. I'm sure I could fly an attack in an F-101 better than Gabreski. But I'm also sure that if we squared off against each other in F-86s or better still in P-51s he would clean my clock. In any case, he never invited me back for steak tartare.

It was easy, as an ORI Team inspector, to become a little cynical and to start believing your own publicity. I mentioned this earlier in view of the personnel policy which forbade inspectors from staying on the job for more than three years. For those of us in Operations, witnessing the same mistakes from different squadrons drew us into the trap of anticipating the mistakes before we even observed them. That made us begin to believe that we would never have fallen into such a trap. In fact, some became, after a few years, insufferably arrogant. I was fortunate enough to have been beaten down early in my job by friends in the Des Moines National Guard.

I had become a well known part of the landscape at the Des Moines Guard, having become recurrent with them in the F-89. They were also close to Colorado Springs and I frequently went there to fly because it was convenient. On one such flight proficiency trip I was accompanied by Major Bill Truitt, one of our ORI exercise planners and a highly experienced Radar Observer/Navigator. Bill and I arrived in Des Moines looking forward to a pleasant couple of days flying with a good, professional outfit without the tension of an ORI in progress.

We briefed to fly as number three in a three-ship attack flight going after a high altitude target. The weather was perfect and we soon lined up in trail for a "snap-up" attack on the high altitude target. The snap up maneuver in the F-89 consisted of getting the old machine going as fast as it would go at intermediate altitude, centering the steering dot laterally but not vertically. The idea was to make a steep pull up at the last moments before missile firing so as to add as much of the airplane's velocity as possible to that of the missile thus allowing a hit on higher flying targets. After the fire control system performed its simulated weapon launch, the pilot would roll off in a wing over maneuver keeping the aircraft belly toward the blast. It was as close to an acrobatic maneuver as we ever came with the old F-89 and was great fun.

Bill expertly locked on to the target as I accelerated in afterburner and we completed an excellent snap-up attack for a simulated kill. I did the standard wing over and picked up a heading for Des Moines. At least I thought I picked up a heading for Des Moines.

There were two contrails ahead of me which I thought belonged to the other two aircraft in our flight. Bill and I sat back to enjoy the scenery and beautiful weather on a leisurely trip home. We were, in fact, totally under the influence of the aviator's worst enemy, complacency.

What was actually happening, while I enjoyed the scenery, was an insidious equipment failure. During my semi-acrobatic wing over after the attack, my directional gyro had tumbled. It was not supposed to do that, and if somehow it did, then a warning flag should have been shown on the gyro face. There was no warning flag and the heading I picked up for Des Moines was, in fact, 135 degrees off in the wrong direction! If I had simply checked the standby magnetic compass the failure would have been immediately apparent. But the reassuring two contrails were there and everything seemed right with the world. The contrails were probably from a pair of stray airliners that just happened to be going my way.

After twenty minutes or so I began to get uneasy since I thought we should be nearing Des Moines. GCI's radio transmissions were getting weak and my DME mileage suddenly started cycling. I finally checked my magnetic compass and realized that our directional gyro had failed. I called GCI, but the controller (the only guy who might have been even more complacent than I) couldn't identify us and his radio transmissions soon faded out. I announced to my master navigator in the back seat that we were hopelessly lost and that we had better find ourselves while we still had some fuel. While charts were flying frantically in the back seat, I saw a runway a few miles away. I then did the only smart thing I had done all day and headed straight for it. I told Bill that the runway looked plenty long enough for me to get the airplane stopped and we were going to land there, wherever it was! It turned out to be Rockford, Illinois, which is a long way from Des Moines, Iowa. After landing we found a frequency to communicate with the tower, and I apologized for barging into their pattern. They were friendly Midwesterners and welcomed us to Rockford, observing that they didn't get many airplanes as big and as ugly as ours into their little airport. We called the Des Moines Guard and they were greatly relieved that they would not have to explain how they lost one of their F-89s along with two ORI inspectors. A C-47 soon arrived to return us to Des Moines while dropping off a maintenance crew to repair the gyro.

We had a debriefing session for lessons learned. The GCI controller had assumed that I had joined up for recovery with one of the other aircraft. He, of course, should never have made such an assumption. But I took full responsibility for a fiasco nurtured by pure complacency. The Des Moines Guard, while sympathetic, did not dispute my finding and for the rest of my tour, whenever I flew with them they had the weather man brief the weather conditions at Rockford. It's hard to not have some humility as an ORI inspector under that kind of scrutiny.

Late in my tour at Colorado Springs I began working quite a bit with Major Sam (Ken) Shealy. Sam was a laconic Midwesterner who often threatened to "go home and bore sight the old mule". With my big city boy upbringing it was perhaps inevitable that the theory of opposites attracting would lead Sam and I to become close friends. Sam, as a ranking major, was chosen to be "Team Chief" a very responsible job on an ORI Team. Each ORI had its various teams assigned to inspect individual bases, squadrons, GCI Sites, etc. And each Team had its very powerful Team Chief. We were often reminded that senior officers' careers were made or broken on the basis of the inspection's outcome. Most outfits passed their ORI and people were all smiles. The team members were fair, objective, brilliant, and handsome. But to the unit that failed, the team members were stupid, unfeeling louts who knew nothing and should all be cashiered from the Air Force. As a new "Chief", Sam was given two units to inspect that on paper should have presented no problems. They were both Air Guard squadrons that had not had problems in the past.

Sam knew that one of my extra duties on ORIs was to edit the reports we wrote for content, accuracy, and everything else down to simple spelling and grammar. He decided with solid, Midwestern logic that if I went with him I could both write and edit the report thus saving one major step. I was, therefore, intimately involved in Sam's first two ORIs, within weeks of each other, both of which were supposed to be easy "passes", and both of which--you guessed it--turned out to be "flunks". Now, I have great respect for the Air National Guard, but State politics are very much a part of the Guard's military units. And when a military unit fails, finger pointing begins in earnest. Our big boss, the Air Defense Command Inspector General himself, Michael Ingelido, showed up at the exit briefings as did the States' highest ranking general.

To make two sad and long stories short, Sam handled the politics well and with his direct no B.S. approach convinced the Guard hierarchy in each case that they had problems that had to be solved. He was never arrogant, but he never bent an inch on our findings either. I was proud to be on his team. Sam and I were both at the end of our tours, but we would continue to have business with each other in the very near future.

There was one other major event that took place in Colorado Springs that made all the others pale in comparison. That was the arrival of Douglas John DeGroote!

Douglas

It happens that while we were stationed in Colorado Springs, Marion's twin sister, Ruth, and her husband, Don, were trying desperately to have a second child. It was a frequent topic of conversation between Marion and me, so one evening while we were driving to dinner at a local restaurant, Marion's question seemed to merit a simple, straightforward answer. She asked, "Guess who's pregnant?" I, of course, immediately replied, "Ruth!" Marion smiled and responded quietly, "No, me". Thus, I was apprised of my impending third try at fatherhood.

Douglas was born on November 19th, 1965 at the Air Force Academy Hospital in Colorado Springs. He was the light of our lives. It takes nothing away from the love we had for Steven and David to say that we were more delighted to have a new baby in the house than ever before, simply because we were older and could better appreciate what a joy a new child could be.

Doug was introduced to the itinerant lifestyle of the military family early in life. Well before his first birthday he was already traveling in the back seat of a Volkswagen from Colorado to Luke Air Force Base in Arizona. His first birthday was in Arizona, but he was soon in an airplane headed for Pennsylvania, having kissed his Vietnam-bound daddy goodbye for a year. While I was in Vietnam Marion moved to Huntingdon Valley, Pennsylvania for another year without a husband. Determined that Douglas would not forget his daddy, she taught him to respond to her question, "Where's Daddy?" with a response that had him toddle across the room to point to a framed picture of me. But when I returned his first response to the "where's Daddy" question was to point, as usual, to the picture. I remember that, while everyone laughed, as would seem appropriate, I felt a tightness in my throat realizing that I had missed one of the best years of my life and a year with my kids that could never be duplicated. When people talk about sacrifices made for the country by military people, something that military people themselves seldom do, that is exactly what they mean.

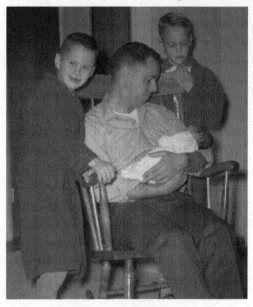

New Guy In Town

Doug and I got reacquainted while en route to our next assignment in London. We had a leisurely trip across the Atlantic on board the SS United States, since travel by ship was still authorized in those days. Doug was the unplanned star of the ship's show, sitting on the edge of the stage and waving his hands to keep time with the music. His proud father drank in the comments from the audience about the cute little kid on stage.

Our tour in London turned Doug onto a lifelong Anglophile, and as an adult he went to work in London and even acquired dual citizenship. But as a little boy he faced some practical problems. His little English friends had trouble understanding his American speech, so he learned to speak with an English accent. This was made easier since he started school in the local British system, learning to read with a perfect British accent. When he was at home, of course, he reverted to American so his brothers could understand him. One of our prized possessions is an audio tape of Douglas reading his English reader with an impeccable Bloke accent. He was, in effect, bilingual.

We took a family vacation to Germany and decided that Douglas was too young and would be bored staying in a nursery. We elected to leave him with his favorite English baby sitter while we went on a ski trip. Doug has never quite forgiven us for this slight, determined that we had deprived him of an irretrievable family vacation. To compensate he has become a world traveler, visiting not only all of the famous attractions of Europe, but also the less-traveled spots like Australia and New Zealand.

I can't escape the subject of aviation in any recitation of Doug's life, even though he opted to make his living away from the flying business. Doug was, like most kids, unsure of what he wanted to do with his life. He had a brief encounter with ROTC in college and decided, wisely I think, that the military life was not for him. I had been teaching him to fly because he was interested, but I did nothing to encourage his pursuing of an aviation career. It was very difficult to get started in commercial flying, and I no longer liked what I saw of the airline business. It was highly unionized and seemed to be going in the wrong direction. I remembered flying commercially in the 50s when all the male passengers wore coats and ties. Now you're lucky if the guy next to you is wearing shoes.

Dave and Doug were very close despite the eight year difference in their ages, and Doug was influenced by Dave's choice of engineering as a profession. That seemed like a sensible choice to me, so I let nature take its course and did nothing. As far as aviation aptitude was concerned, I never doubted Doug's qualifications.

During contact flying in the Cessna Doug didn't have Steve's "natural" touch, but not many did. On the other hand, while Steve had problems learning instrument flying, Doug amazed me by flying as though the instruments were stuck--his altimeter never seemed to budge!

Doug asked to join me at the recurrent training facility where I was scheduled to fly the Hawker 700 simulator. He had never seen a full-motion simulator and was curious. I finished my training session a little early and decided to give Doug, who was a private pilot, but had never flown anything bigger than the Cessna 150, a shot at flying the machine. I had the instructor set up an ILS approach, which Doug had never flown, and turned him loose. I played copilot, reading off power settings and making configuration changes as required. Doug intercepted the localizer smoothly, and while I was marveling at his beginners luck, he intercepted the glide slope and kept both needles pegged right down to landing. Whether it was his experience with video games or a natural flair for instrument flying, I don't know but I was impressed! So was the instructor who suggested only half jokingly that since somebody named DeGroote had to take an instrument check tomorrow that maybe I should let Doug do the next day's work.

Doug sometimes expresses remorse about not following an aviation career rather than his engineering vocation which he says is "boring". I sometimes feel that I made a mistake by not nudging him in that direction, but every time I travel in an airliner I decide that he and I did the right thing.

In any case, life was going on in Colorado Springs, my ORI assignment was coming to an end, and I had a major decision to make concerning a place called Vietnam.

Vietnam

I was on one of my last ORIs giving an instrument check to a young lieutenant in the T-33. He was doing fine and I told him so. I took over control and told him to relax while I flew us home and I struck up a conversation with him on the way. He told me that he was going to forward air controller school and was on his way to Vietnam after his training. From that moment on I began an internal struggle with my conscience, my sense of loyalty to my family, my sense of responsibility to the Air Force and my country, and finally my obsessive sense of simple fairness. This young man in the T-bird had half my experience, but he was going into combat, probably not as well equipped to do so as was I. The Korean War had ended while I was in pilot training. I had missed that war, and now this kid was taking my place in another war. It was probably not that simple, but in my mind it was black and white. When I returned to Colorado Springs I immediately went to see a friend in Personnel and told him to keep an eye out for a fighter assignment for me in Vietnam.

Marion, of course, was not exactly thrilled with my decision, but she once again played the perfect Air Force wife and stood by her man. I have a running record of my tour in Vietnam thanks once again to Marion who saved every one of my almost daily letters. One of those letters, written shortly after I arrived in country, accurately reflects my internal struggle at the time:

> ... *It's a terrible thing to feel completely alone. I could sense your loneliness in your letters, and I felt sorry for you but relieved to know that you needed me as much as I need you. I think the impact of how very long a year can be is hitting us both again. It's not a new feeling. We both went through it before when I was in Thule and to a lesser extent when I was in pilot training. I knew all this when I volunteered for this tour and I think you know the agony I went through trying to make up my mind. It was something I had to do, honey, like going to the doctor for surgery...Hearing you tell me about Douglas makes me realize just how much the decision to come here has cost me. I can only hope that I've done the right thing. Knowing that I've done this to us of my own free will can be very hard to live with...*

So, as much as I detested leaving my family again, after only three short years, I never thought I had a choice. Some tried to talk me out of it. My sister, Doris, lectured me about having responsibilities to my wife and kids. I said, "Doris, I'm a professional soldier. If someone's robbing a bank, you expect the police to do something about it." Doris was just being my big sister and to her it was more like Duty, Honor, Family than Duty, Honor, Country. A few of my friends resigned their commissions and went to work for the airlines. I simply could not do that. My decision was made and my friend in Personnel soon called to inform me that several requisitions had come through for F-100 pilots, ultimate assignment Vietnam. I told him to sign me up.

Now, it would seem that volunteering to fly fighters in combat should be, for a trained fighter pilot, a simple thing. Not so--first you must attend the Air Force's world wide survival school in the state of Washington. There are few things that I, the inveterate city boy, despised as much as survival schools. But it seemed that the Air Force had a clerk somewhere whose sole duty was to make certain that I attended every last one of them, whether on the Greenland ice cap or in the jungle. As for the school in Washington State, I survived but I was definitely not an honor student. I learned one thing--that I would make a lousy prisoner of war, and I resolved never to get captured.

Next came checkout in the F-100, a short course that included much needed training in air-to-ground gunnery. In my case, having spent most of my time flying interceptors, the work on the gunnery range was a new and exciting world. It was scheduled to take place at Luke Air Force Base in Arizona.

On my return from survival school we sold our house, feeling fortunate to do so without losing any money, and set off in a two car caravan for Arizona. My pilot training days at Williams had been in the September-January time frame and my memory of Arizona was full of scenes of pleasant weather. This time we arrived in July and the daytime temperature was 113 degrees. I had gone out to Luke previously in a T-bird and placed a deposit on a pleasant apartment with a palm tree surrounded swimming pool. Marion and the kids were pleased with my choice and the pool got lots of use. Had it not been for my imminent scheduled departure for the war, it would have been a very pleasant four month interlude. It happened that my ORI Team traveling buddy, Sam Shealy, volunteered for the same job as I and was to move into the apartment complex with us in a few weeks. We were delighted to welcome Sam, Marge and their girls to our new, if temporary, life. Sam added some excitement to our lives by becoming a patient in the hospital. He had complained to Marge about some abdominal pain, but Marge observed that men in general didn't know what pain was all about since they never had to bear children. Sam, being the prototypical Stoic decided to grin and bear it. Unfortunately it soon became unbearable and Marge, remembering that Sam didn't complain much called me to ask if I could take Sam to the hospital. This I did, and the verdict was ruptured appendix. This upset Sam a bit, but mostly because it pushed him back into a later class.

As much as I hated the thought of leaving the family, I had to admit that I was eager to get on with the job that I had been training for all these years. I had my first flight in the two-seat F-100F in mid July and I immediately liked the airplane. It performed very much like the F-102, although it was not nearly so forgiving. It was a rudder airplane and once you accepted that idiosyncrasy the airplane was fun to fly. Having cut my teeth on the T-6, I found the need to use lots of rudder not the least bit daunting.

With thousands of hours of jet fighter time in my log book, transitioning into the "Hun" was fairly easy for me. In-flight refueling was a new experience for me, but if you can fly good formation, then refueling is just an adjunctive skill to be learned. I learned it quite rapidly and enjoyed the competition of seeing who could get hooked up and refueled the fastest.

Unfortunately, I learned to my considerable chagrin, that air-to-ground gunnery, unlike the other new skills I was learning, did not come easily to me. Part of my problem stemmed from a bit of natural over-aggressiveness. The gunnery range was carefully controlled in order to keep accidents to a minimum. The range safety officers were very strict in enforcing the rules, and each student was allowed a maximum of three "fouls" while delivering practice ordnance. The first week I was awarded two fouls on the skip bomb (napalm simulation) target which involved high "G" maneuvering at 50 feet. Faced with elimination if I used up my last remaining foul, I became Mr. Conservative himself. I went through the rest of the program with no fouls, but I was slow to qualify and in general very dissatisfied with my performance on the gunnery range. Later, in Vietnam, there were no range safety officers and my skill level advanced rapidly. I always thought that the excellent safety record that the gunnery program at Luke enjoyed was to some extent achieved at the expense of the combat units in Vietnam where it was frequently necessary to "press" delivery parameters to insure a hit. You're supposed to train the way you fight, and I thought Luke's insistence on conservatism on the range led to later accidents on combat missions. Then again, maybe I was just a slow learner. In any case, I completed the course and just after Thanksgiving, 1966 I began the long flight to Southeast Asia.

The flight went from Phoenix to Los Angeles to San Francisco to Anchorage to Tokyo to Manila. At Manila I was intercepted by a sergeant who read my name tag and handed me a set of orders enrolling me in the next jungle survival school. My survival school clerk had caught up with me again!

I can't say that I enjoyed Jungle Survival School. But I grudgingly admit that I learned quite a lot about the jungle--a few things that might have saved my life had a bail-out been in the cards. The really fascinating part was the last night in the jungle when we were released individually to evade capture. The role of pursuer was played admirably by little guys (about 4 feet tall) who were indigenous to the Philippines. They were called "Negritos" and were skilled trackers. They made their living by tracking down pilots like me who were required to give them a chit good for one bag of rice if they succeeded in making a capture--which they always did!

I was released into the jungle at twilight and, crawling on my stomach, I spotted a loincloth-wearing Negrito across a ravine. Feeling superior, I continued to crawl away, sure that I had shaken my pursuer. About two minutes later I felt a tap on my shoulder.

Vietnam 151

There stood my tracker, palm extended for a rice chit. I figured it had taken him all of three minutes to effect my capture.

After accepting my rice chit, the Negrito waited, eyeing my flashlight. When I shook my head "no", he motioned for me to follow him. It was dark now and I thought, "Why not?" He led me about a hundred yards farther into the jungle, showing me to a small clearing with a brush-vegetation bed and a corrugated plastic roof! I had stumbled upon a Negrito-entrepreneur running the only hotel in town. He then made helicopter noises while whirling his arm to simulate rotor blades. His pointing to a clearing atop the next hill made it obvious that the rescue chopper would land there in the morning.

I settled down to get some sleep protected from the rain in my "hotel". Sleep was fitful at best. We had been warned about rats the size of small dogs and I was aroused by some type of critter, which I assumed was one of the rats, sniffing at my ear. I chased him away, knowing he would return. When he did, I was ready and struck at him as hard as I could with my hunting knife. I missed, burying my blade to the hilt, but he never came back, so I assume he went off to find somebody in a better mood.

At daybreak my new Negrito friend appeared holding--believe it or not--a plastic cup filled with coffee. I tasted the liquid gingerly, and as if on cue, the rescue helicopter arrived. I gave my friend all of my remaining rice chits plus my flashlight, knife and last chocolate bar. He had earned them and he smiled slightly as I left for the chopper. Another satisfied customer.

Upon my return from the jungle I found a message from the big boss from my ORI Team days, General Ingelido, who had been the Inspector General at ADC. He was now stationed at Clark as Deputy Commander of 13th Air Force. The general invited me and another ORI alumnus, Marv Miller, to dinner, and I looked forward to a feast after my days in the jungle. The boss did not disappoint and we had great stories along with pre-dinner martinis, various wines during a sumptuous dinner, and fine Cognac after dinner. Since my C-130 was taking off for Bien Hoa in Vietnam at 0330 in the morning, I decided to not allow the Cognac to make me sleep through my alarm clock and possibly miss my plane to Bien Hoa. Instead, I went to the terminal, checked in my bags, and settled in a seat to await my flight. In what seemed like a few minutes, I was awakened by a sunbeam shining in my eyes. In a flash of insight I recognized that sunbeams shouldn't be around at 3:30 in the morning, and I had missed my flight. My first day in the combat zone and I was late!

I walked sheepishly up to the boarding clerk to explain my problem and was given all the sympathy I deserved. "Major DeGroote", he intoned, "We paged you for a full half hour before we had to give up." I explained that I was a very sound sleeper--not mentioning the Cognac--and managed to talk my way onto a C-118 that was going to Tan Son Nhut, close enough to Bien Hoa that I could bum a ride to the squadron. At Tan Son Nhut I called an old buddy from Colorado Springs, Fred Roll, who led me to the right bus to Bien Hoa. I noticed that the window glass in the bus had been replaced by heavy metal grill work, presumably to keep grenades from being thrown in. Welcome to the war!

I got off the bus at the Wing Command Post to sign in and hopefully catch a ride to the 90th. I was shown around by a helpful young captain who was busy working a rescue operation. The captain explained to me that they had lost four aircraft that day, including an Army chopper and a Vietnamese Air Force A-1. I did some quick mental arithmetic, knowing there were three squadrons of F-100s with 25 airplanes each plus about the same number of A-1s and choppers. Let's see--125 total aircraft, 4 lost today--sounds like I'll be shot down within a month. I dismissed this negative thought immediately and, in fact, the 3rd Tac Fighter Wing never had another day of losses even approaching those suffered on the day of my arrival. The 90th Squadron sent someone to pick me up and show me around. They were very glad to get another pilot and everyone was quite helpful. The factor of my late arrival never came up and I certainly had no intention of broaching the subject.

I spent several days doing typical "new guy" tasks, such as reading "Rules of Engagement", Lyndon Johnson's methodology for fighting an air war while insuring that only Americans can get hurt. I checked out flight gear, helmet, parachute, emergency radios, etc. and was eager to get involved. I didn't have too long to wait as I flew my first combat sortie on December 11th, 1966, just four days after my arrival in country. It was a fairly routine mission to the IV Corps area, in the southern part of Vietnam. I was number four in a flight of four, and I was most impressed with the firepower that four F-100s could bring to a fight. In our case each aircraft carried four 750 pound bombs along with fuel drop tanks and four 20 MM cannons. Somehow flying close formation with fully loaded airplanes had a different feel than flying with wingmen carrying practice bombs to be dropped on a gunnery range. We found our Forward Air Controller (FAC) and dropped our bombs at his direction, such as, "hit 40 meters north of my smoke". We then hit an area at very low level with our 20 MM. Someone in our flight reported ground fire, but I was too busy to see it. The FAC seemed pleased with our work and I was greatly relieved that my bombs had hit where they were supposed to have done. Except for one live fire mission on the tactical gunnery range at Luke, during which I dropped napalm on a tank, I had never before dropped a bomb in anger. Our flight leader called for a rejoin, which was different only in that we did a battle damage check on each other just as we joined up in close formation. We flew home, landed, de--briefed and went to the bar for a cold beer. So, combat flying was not so much different from all the other flying I had been doing over the years-- except that the next morning I found that one of our aircraft had taken a small arms hit in the stabilator. It was too small a hole to have been seen on the airborne battle damage check, but the crew chief caught it on post-flight. So, combat flying was not so much different except that people were trying to kill you!

A few days later I was introduced to the difference between being on alert in Vietnam and being on alert in Air Defense Command. Rather than having two birds on alert as in ADC, we had eight; and by the end of the day all eight had scrambled at least once. I was also introduced to the night flying mission during my first few weeks. There were two other squadrons of F-100s on Bien Hoa besides our 90th "Pair O' Dice" squadron. Normally, one squadron flew nights for a week while the others flew in daylight. It was probably a good system since it was hard to sleep in the heat of the day and the fewer times the biological clock had to be re-set, the better. Night flying was usually more interesting than the scheduled daytime missions because the Viet Cong usually attacked at night and we were frequently diverted to "troops in contact" situations, The TIC strikes allowed us to ignore the so-called safety parameters imposed by staff officers at higher headquarters and put our ordnance exactly where the FAC wanted it--usually very close to the beleaguered ground troops. These missions nearly always elicited a heartfelt thank you from the grunts on the ground for whom our arrival on the scene often made the difference in whether they lived or died. Fighter pilots all have the little boys' yearning to be the cavalry coming to the rescue, so we all loved the TIC missions. At night the adrenalin level was further stimulated because of tracers lighting up the sky and the twinkling of our own 20MM rounds hitting the target.

F-100 Over The Mekong

One of our frequent daytime jobs was to fly escort for the "Ranch Hand" aircraft which were C-123 cargo planes converted to crop sprayers. Their unenviable job was to spray "agent orange" on the jungle or sometimes on VC crops to reduce their hiding places or their food supplies. The C-123s flew at low speed and were very tempting targets for the VC. Our job was to fly past them at high speed and respond with 20MM or Cluster Bomb Units (CBU) if they drew any ground fire. Sometimes we put down suppressing fire while they sprayed an area, usually crops, where they were in open areas and very vulnerable to ground fire. On one such mission while I was dropping CBU at 450 knots (a little over 500 mph) I saw ahead of me some children on a dike watching the show. I stopped releasing my bomblets to keep from hurting these "kids". As I streaked by I realized that they weren't kids at all, but were three VC firing away at me with AK-47s. I warned my following wingmen to forget about being compassionate. We had great respect for the "Ranch Hands" who were protected to some degree with armor plate, but nevertheless took heavy doses of battle damage, sometimes landing with 150 holes in their aircraft. They always wanted us to drop our ordnance closer to them than we thought was safe, and inevitably one of our new pilots blew several CBU holes in a C-123. We apologized for the mishap, but they weren't at all upset, saying that the kid had it just about right, but maybe he could move it out "just a tad."

I had flown several Ranch Hand missions by the latter part of December, and on Christmas Eve I had an unexpected midnight visitation. I had abandoned the Christmas party going on in one of the other "hootches" (barracks) and was at my desk writing a letter. A group of Ranch Hands, wearing their distinctive purple scarves, came into the hootch singing very off-key Christmas carols. Their leader, a hulking major with a really bad singing voice, signaled the choir to cease caroling while he announced, "Ranch Hands want to buy the fighter pilots a drink". I replied, politely, that I thanked them but that I had had enough to drink for one night. This was a breach of etiquette on my part and I should have known better. The hulking major placed a very large hand on my shoulder and squeezing tightly repeated, "Ranch Hands want to buy the fighter pilots a drink!" Realizing my error and not eager to provoke the hulking major further, I said, smiling, "How about some scotch?". This pleased the Ranch Hands greatly. They poured me a drink, thanked me for flying escort and to my great relief resumed caroling and went to the next fighter pilot hootch. I got to know many of the Ranch Hands during the rest of my tour and I still have the purple scarf they presented me at my farewell party 11 months later. They were good people.

By the time I had been with the squadron five weeks I had accumulated 50 hours of combat flying. Since it looked like I wasn't going to be the type who might drop a bomb on our own people, I was designated a flight leader and started leading most of my scheduled missions. I confess that, as strange as it seems, I was enjoying my new job with the "Dice" squadron. I was certainly not the "war lover" personality (there were a few), but flying in support of the troops was the most rewarding thing I had done in my entire

Returning From A Mission. Note Empty Bomb Racks.

life, and I was thoroughly enjoying it. Night flying introduced another bit of craziness into our fighter pilot's existence. Typically we'd fly two missions, landing from the second one just before dawn. After de-briefing we'd go to the club around 7 AM and order drinks. All the support people were there having breakfast and probably thought these nutty, noisy fighter pilots had been partying all night. We didn't care what they thought. To us it was cocktail hour, and it helped us get to sleep during the day.

Our impromptu parties were a release from the stress we all were under, during night missions especially, and the support types had enough good sense not to interfere. I noted in a letter a mission I led in February that was fairly typical. We were scrambled for a TIC target down south and were briefed on the way that our people were under heavy fire from a VC force on a hillside. When we arrived the FAC was also taking fire and a C-47 flare ship was trying to float flares somewhere near the target area without getting shot down himself. It was hard work because the hilly terrain left us unsure of our proper release and pull-out altitudes. Lighting from the flares was barely adequate, but we did good work and the FAC gleefully reported that all firing had stopped after we dropped our bombs. On my last pass I looked back over my shoulder to see where my bomb had hit just as the last flare burned out. My world turned from brilliant flare-light to inky blackness instantaneously. As I rolled out on downwind leg things didn't seem quite normal. Whenever things don't seem normal, you trust your instruments, as all the years of training had taught me. I scanned my instruments and discovered that I was flying perfectly straight and level and perfectly upside down! I rolled the world to the right side up position and joined up my wingman for the flight home. The mission didn't earn us any medals, since it was all in a day's work, but I surely felt it had earned me my breakfast cocktail!

By mid-February things had fallen into a routine, if combat flying can ever be considered routine. I had been appointed as Commander of "A" Flight and had volunteered to be squadron historian and Information Officer. Sam Shealy had recovered from his appendectomy and was flying from Phan Rang. I met him on a short R&R at Clark Air Base and later he visited me for an overnight at Bien Hoa. Sam was waiting to take command of one of the Phan Rang squadrons and he did so a few months later.

As for me, I had been "A" Flight Commander for only a few weeks when the boss, Lieutenant Colonel Don Hooten, informed me that I was now the Assistant Operations Officer of the squadron. I would be working for Major Dale Rook, the Operations Officer. I was delighted with the new arrangement because I liked Dale, we got along well together, and it made it very unlikely that my name would be thrown into the hat when one of the frequent levies came up for a fighter pilot to go to headquarters or to forward air controlling. Dale warned me that he didn't like paper work and he'd be shoving much of it my way. While I had no great love of paper work, I had done a lot of it and found it easy. It kept me busy, and I liked it that way. Dale and I had a good partnership and ran a good operations office until we rotated together in November.

The 90th Squadron's Operations Staff - Dale Rook, Left

Somewhat more ominous was my selection to be accident investigation officer on an F-5 crash that occurred in February. Normally the investigating officer must be current in the aircraft involved in the accident. This stipulation was waived in my case because I had experience in accident investigation, most notably the "Black Friday" affair at Thule. I describe the assignment as ominous because it re-connected me with the Safety career field which I was determined to avoid. The Safety Officer at Bien Hoa was attached to our squadron for flying. I led him on several combat missions. His name was Ray Walden and he was a good pilot and a nice guy. Unfortunately, once he discovered that I had

Safety experience he seemed determined to get me back in the career field. It was he who recommended me as the Investigating Officer on the F-5 accident.

In truth, accident investigation was the one function in the Safety business that I found interesting, and I really had no objection to investigating the F-5 accident. I became engrossed in the investigation after examining the wreckage. I had gone to the Air Force's Jet Engine Accident Analysis Course while I was the Safety Officer at Suffolk County, and I immediately saw irregularities with the engines. The pilot had been on a go-around when he suddenly ejected. He was too low and didn't survive. As with any accident there were "experts" at every headquarters level who immediately pronounced their theory about the accident, ranging from fuel exhaustion to enemy action. It appeared to me from engine rotational damage that the engines were both operating at low RPM even though the power levers were wide open. I went to the Engine Shop to find an experienced engine maintenance man who had also been to the Jet Engine Accident Analysis Course. I found an intelligent-sounding sergeant who fit my qualifications and I asked him to look at the wreckage without telling him my opinion. He took one look and said, "Those engines were operating at low RPM when he crashed, Major". His estimate of the RPM was very close to mine.

After checking many other possibilities, like fuel gauge inaccuracy and pilot incapacitation, I wrote the accident report listing the most probable cause as RPM rollback of both engines at a critical point in the flight. The Wing Commander was reluctant to sign the report fearing that the Teardown Deficiency Report, which was to be done when the engines were disassembled in the U.S., would prove me wrong. To make a long story short, the TDR confirmed my findings and I felt great satisfaction in having found a problem which could be corrected and possibly save lives in the future. What I didn't know was that some people in the local Safety Office were telling the Personnel people that this guy was being wasted outside the Safety business. But that problem would not arise until later.

I was thoroughly enjoying my assistant ops job, and additional projects like the F-5 investigation just helped to pass the time until I could rejoin my family. I even got to play Squadron Commander for a short time when Don Hooten got sick while Dale Rook happened to be on R&R out of the country. I enjoyed my brief moment in the sun but discovered that squadron commanders were very busy people.

Our routine was broken from time to time by trips to Taiwan where we dropped off F-100s for major maintenance. I went on one such trip in late April and got to spend a day or two in a nice, air conditioned hotel and enjoyed dining in the downtown Officers' Club. I also visited with the Laird family, close friends from Suffolk County days. Barbara Laird took me on a shopping tour where I was able to buy Marion fabrics, clothing and other treasures under Barbara's much needed supervision. After picking up my F-100 I flew it to the Philippines, the jumping off point for the flight back to Vietnam. Since safety policies did not allow single engine aircraft to make the trip alone across the South China Sea, I teamed up with an F-4 and flew his wing back to Vietnam where he headed for Cam Ranh Bay and I went to Bien Hoa. My old F-100 couldn't climb with the modern F-4, but I stayed with him as much as 10,000 feet low until he leveled off. After that I had no trouble staying with him.

I was glad to be back at Bien Hoa and quickly fell back into my routine of flying and paperwork. On May 11th I went to bed early having scheduled myself for an early morning takeoff. Unfortunately the VC decided to interrupt my deep slumber at around 0100. We were accustomed to sporadic mortar attacks on the base and everyone pretty much ignored them after the first few weeks in country. But this was different. They launched about 125 rounds of mortar and 122mm rockets. The rockets were fairly potent and would dig craters about eight feet deep. I had long ago learned to sleep through outgoing artillery which the Army fired all night, every night and was annoyed to be awakened. It took me some time to realize that this was incoming and for some reason I decided that it was more important to don my boots and carefully lace them up before proceeding to the sand bag bunker. I finally went to the bunker looking quite debonair in my underwear and neatly laced boots, whereupon I transferred my anger from the Army to the VC. After about 15 minutes the barrage ended and we went back into the hootch. I was taken aback by the sight of John Schulz, a newly arrived pilot, stretched out on his cot. I immediately thought he had been hit by shrapnel and began looking for a wound. This caused the "corpse" to arise, sleepy eyed, asking what was going on. It seems that despite being in country for only a few days John had acclimated so well to the noise of artillery that he slept through the entire barrage with its earthquake-like impacts all around. I decided that in the future I would knock John out of bed on my way out the door. I also resolved to skip the footwear next time.

Direct Hit On F-100 Revetment

I pedaled my bicycle (the primary means of ground locomotion for supersonic pilots at Bien Hoa) to the flight line and discovered that my operations office had taken a direct hit with my swivel chair having suffered mortal damage from shrapnel. We had several aircraft damaged and two mechanics wounded, but we were back in business by afternoon. Some of the other squadrons were not so lucky, having lost several airplanes and vehicles to direct hits. We were very fortunate not to be flying on the night schedule since the direct hit on our building would probably have killed many people if they had not evacuated to the bunker. The attack had one positive effect that I covered in a letter to Marion, who had been worried by sensationalized accounts of the attack in the news media:

I think that Charlie's mortar attack was the biggest morale builder we've had around here. All our maintenance troops feel like combat veterans now and they all want to carry guns around with them. We're not giving them any because I'm sure they'd start shooting at each other at the first sound of an artillery round.... They're all good soldiers and it's too bad we can't turn them loose on the VC. We need them too badly to fix airplanes. I guess they were like college boys at a football game when the alert birds scrambled just after the last mortar round hit. They finally got to see the airplanes they load and refuel every day go out and fight.

Mortar Round Direct Hit On Ops Building (Right), My Office (Left), Fortunately Unoccupied, Showing Shrapnel Holes In Wall

Our mortar survival champion was a young pilot named George Riddle. Everything happened to George. Shortly after his arrival he was bitten by a rat and had to undergo the anti-rabies series of shots. He was from that time forward known as "Rats Riddle". But his real adventure involved one of the sporadic mortar attacks which the VC launched frequently. George had just pedaled his bike down to the Squadron ops building to take care of some routine business. As he stepped off his bike a random mortar round hit next to him, imbedding itself under a concrete sidewalk. Miraculously, it failed to detonate. George walked away without a scratch and EOD defused the live round.

Live ordnance was, of course, a part of daily life at Bien Hoa. We almost never flew without a full load of bombs and 20MM cannon ammunition. Familiarity bred a blasé attitude toward armament among the munitions people as well as the pilots. We tried very hard to eliminate this attitude with only partial success. In the back of our minds was the knowledge that a major, deadly accident had occurred the previous year when an explosion rocked the flight line killing many and destroying several aircraft.

In-flight incidents occurred often enough to most pilots that the hazards were well respected. I had my share. On one of my first combat missions I was flying as number two in a flight of three. All three aircraft were armed with 750 pound bombs but the bombs were fitted with a type of fuse that was designed to detonate the bomb just before impact. I watched the lead aircraft, flown by Bobbie Blaylock, a very experienced and very good pilot, roll into his dive bomb pass. I rolled in slightly behind him. As he pulled out of his dive a huge explosion erupted ahead of me. My first thought was that the VC had somehow brought in the granddaddy of all anti aircraft guns to fire at me. But we all, including the FAC who was also too close to the explosion for his liking, quickly realized that it was one of Bobbie's bombs that had detonated prematurely. We aborted the mission and had a discussion with the armament officer after landing. It seems that the fuses were left over from WWII and some staff officer decided that they should be used. We never used them again.

Some months later I was flying wing on a so-called "Skyspot" mission. These were night missions whereby a flight of two F-100s flew straight and level at approximately 25,000 feet and dropped their full load of bombs on a signal from the ground radar station. We fighter pilots hated these missions for a number of reasons. First and foremost we thought they were ineffective. If the weather was clear we could watch our bombs impact and we, more often than not, saw them detonate harmlessly in a rice paddy or forest. Secondly, they were boring if the weather was good. Third, the weather was rarely good and we were nevertheless required to fly close formation through any and all of that weather, including thunderstorms. On this particular mission I was hanging on the leader's left wing as we bounced through the fringes of a thunderstorm complete with lightning. As we approached the countdown point to bomb release, I was, shall we say, disconcerted to observe a streak of "Saint Elmo's Fire" several feet long attach itself precisely on the fuse of lead's outboard bomb! Saint Elmo's Fire is a static electricity phenomenon that is known for unpredictable behavior. We went into the countdown and I elected to stay in formation to bomb drop, hoping that lead's bomb wouldn't instantly vaporize both of us. Needless to say, bomb release was normal and lead never knew about the electricity on his bomb fuse until I told him about it at the bar. The armament officer assured us that the fuse was mechanical and not subject to electrical disturbances, but he wasn't there.

A final mishap occurred to me late in my tour. I was leading a flight of two on a low level mission with high drag bombs and napalm. On my napalm release I saw a bright flash that disappeared instantly. Somebody, probably the FAC, said, "Holy----!", and my wingman gasped something like "Lead, are you OK?" I checked my aircraft and it seemed fine. My wingman did a standard battle damage check also finding nothing. Discussing it back on the ground, my wingman told me that when I dropped my napalm my aircraft disappeared in a ball of fire, then immediately flew out of it. I had obviously had a premature detonation of the napalm, but my 450 knot airspeed rocketed my F-100 out of danger. My wingman, seeing the fireball thought at first that I had crashed, but post flight inspection found nothing, not even scorch marks on the paint job. It was an interesting event, but not something I would like to try again.

When a tour of combat flying extends to roughly 300 missions, there are bound to be quite a few clunkers. We flew what seemed to be an inordinate number of missions attacking "suspected VC concentration" or "suspected VC bunker complex". These missions were based on old intelligence and rarely yielded results. We complained about these missions to the point that we sometimes forgot the "good" missions, especially the ones where we got the heartfelt gratitude of the grunts on the ground. We all had our share of these:

On July 22nd, 1967 I had settled down for the night on the alert pad when, to no one's surprise, the scramble phone rang. My wingman was John Schulz, well known for exhibiting narcoleptic tendencies during the May 11th artillery attack on Bien Hoa. John, by now, had lived down his sleepy eyed reputation and had developed into a competent and dependable fighter pilot. We were vectored to the target area, located the FAC and were briefed on the battle situation. It seems that a Special Forces camp at a place called Binh Dai was under heavy attack and in apparent danger of being over run. Nothing, I thought, that we couldn't handle. The FAC then broke the bad news to us, that is, sorry, guys, but there's no flare ship and the grunts need you right now! That left no decision to be made. I told the FAC to mark the target and I would be putting my napalm in first to try to get some illumination on the area. I put the nape on target and although it provided surprisingly little illumination, it did provide a good reference point for our bombs. John dropped his high drag bombs adjacent to my nape and I had him deliver his napalm to provide some light for my subsequent high drag pass. This tactic worked well and seemingly delighted the FAC, the Special Forces grunts and everyone else except the attacking VC who immediately lost their enthusiasm for the fight. We picked up a little ground fire indicating that the VC had diverted their attention from the Special Forces camp to us. We returned their fire with our 20MM which seemed to convince the attackers that they were on the losing end of the shoot-out. We then bid the FAC goodnight and returned to Bien Hoa for dinner and kudos from the Binh Dai residents.

October 31st was not only Halloween, but also the 15th anniversary of my enlistment in the Air Force. I was scheduled for a routine "Skyspot" mission wih Jack Doub on my wing. We had just dropped our bombs on what appeared to be a nondescript piece of the Vietnamese countryside when Control diverted us to a troops in contact situation. I advised the FAC that we had nothing but 20MM, silently cursing the timing that had just deprived us of our bomb load. The FAC was happy to have anything, especially strafe, since it was already a close-in target situation. As we approached the target, which turned out to be the Loch Ninh Special Forces outpost, it was obvious that no mark from the FAC would be needed. There was a dirt runway running along the camp perimeter, and the VC were attacking across the runway seemingly determined to overrun the outpost with frontal attacks regardless of casualties. A C-47 flare ship was circling upwind, drifting flares over the camp. The flares, smoke and heavy tracer fire across the runway in either direction created a hellish scene, but one in which we could easily identify the attackers. The FAC cleared us for multiple passes down the runway. I made the first pass using just two guns to save ammunition. Jack followed and we soon established a gunnery range pattern. With our lights out we called our positions in the pattern and were able to keep cannon fire on the runway and the adjacent area opposite the base camp almost continuously. The FAC spoke encouragingly to us while our high explosive incendiary rounds sparkling on the ground added to the unreal display of deadly fireworks. My top two guns soon ran out of ammo and I switched to the lower pair. After several more passes I was startled by the sound of only one gun firing. The other either jammed or was out of ammo. I had never before heard the popping sound of a single cannon when firing from the cockpit.

Since one gun was obviously better than none, I continued making passes until it ran out of ammo in a few seconds. Since no other fighters had arrived to relieve us we continued to make passes lighting the afterburner, hoping the explosive sound of the burner would disrupt their plans. This, of course, drew an immediate barrage of ground fire. Fortunately, reinforcements arrived with full loads of ordnance and we were able to fly home.

The battle of Loch Ninh went on for two more days with tactical air scoring heavily. The defenders of the outpost called to express their gratitude, making our day. While we were not the most effective aircraft because of our having nothing but cannon fire, I believe we were the first on the scene and were able to get the battle headed in the right direction. I read a very inaccurate report of the battle in one of the leading news magazines two weeks later and began to realize for the first time that the news media were not on our side in this war and, in fact, seemed to be actively seeking our defeat. But that's the subject for another long and detailed study.

With "My" F-100 S.N. 710

Large scale battles like Loch Ninh, where air power does much to save the day, usually generated recommendations from ground force commanders for awards. Most of the time certain parameters had to be met before an award was approved. Normally a troops in contact situation involving night or bad weather and ground fire had to be part of the mission. Fighter pilots were, or professed to be, somewhat indifferent toward medals. Napolean's famous dictum that men would die for a "piece of ribbon" was not operative. More likely to be heard was the bar room ballad stating that, "...distinguished flying crosses do not compensate for losses".

Sometimes we got awards for missions that we thought were all in a day's work while other missions that were really stressful went unrecognized. While I think I earned most of the awards I received, others fell into the "all in a day's work" category. On the other hand, the most demanding and most dangerous mission I flew was completed without so much as a thank you. I think every fighter pilot had one or two missions like that.

In this case, I was leading a flight of two, my wingman being relatively new, on a routine, pre-planned mission. It was a beautiful day and I was feeling almost bored when I contacted the FAC. His briefing ended my boredom and got my undivided attention. He advised that he had been watching the VC build a large storage facility, which he suspected housed munitions, for several months. He had not put it on anybody's target list because he didn't want his discovery compromised by the normal intelligence network. Next, he described the target. It was located at the apex of a "V" shaped canyon with sheltering rocks and vegetation. I located the target area easily, although I couldn't see the structure at all. The FAC did not want to alert the VC with a smoke rocket, so he cleared me to attack when ready. We were carrying high drag bombs which are delivered at low altitude and were probably the only munitions type that could be used on this target. The only possible approach to bomb release was up the box canyon directly toward the overhanging cliff face. As I dived toward release point, airspeed increasing to 450 knots, it became obvious that pulling out without hitting the overhanging cliff face was going to be difficult. I decided that I could make it and pressed on to bomb release, pulling out with as many "Gs" as I thought my trusty F-100 could stand. The FAC was pleased with the hit and I suggested we call it a day. He was disappointed and requested that we hit it with the rest of our bombs, since he was sure we could trigger a secondary explosion. I reluctantly cleared my wingman in telling him to drop everything on one pass, with the admonition, "watch your butt on pull-out, two--it's very close". He took me at my word and dropped his bombs short of the target. I was then obligated to make another pass and did so with the same hair-raising pull-out. The FAC didn't get his secondary but recorded that we had totally destroyed the target. "Nice working with you, Dice", was the FAC's only comment. I had a couple of thoughts on the way home, the first being that I had never been closer to getting myself killed over there and nobody even said "thank you". The other was a gnawing feeling of déjà vu--I had been there before. I finally decided that I had seen it all before in a movie!

A Cliff Robertson movie I had seen a few years before, "633 Squadron", depicted British light bombers going after a German installation by flying toward a cliff and barely making the pull-out. That was the source of my déjà vu. I resolved to stop watching air war movies. My wingman, who thought I was nuts, resolved, I think, to fly with somebody else.

While I was experiencing déjà vu, Marion, back in Pennsylvania, was having an encounter with ESP. Late in my tour, the Wing Information Services Officer was looking for someone to interview. I always made it a point to be too busy for that sort of nonsense, but this time I was trapped since I had just landed and nobody else was around. I described our mission, which involved strafing VC sampans in the Delta and it was his job to make that sound interesting. He recorded the interview and I promptly forgot about it. I never mentioned it in my letters home to Marion.

At her apartment a few days later, Marion arose very early, something she rarely did, because she couldn't sleep. She also turned on a small radio, something she never did, and tuned to a station she never listened to. The first thing she heard was the announcer saying, "We have a recorded interview from Vietnam with a fighter pilot from the area, Major DeGroote". Now, the number of coincidences that would have to have occurred at exactly the right moment for Marion to hear that forgotten interview is beyond calculation. So, we've chalked it up to ESP, which we don't understand either.

I had one further close encounter with the media that furthered my inherent dislike and distrust of people in that business. My tour in Vietnam and subsequent assignment to Laos solidified my suspicion that the American people were being lied to. So, when we had a request from one of the major network news corporations through our Information Office, for a correspondent to fly a hot mission, I decided to take him myself--if for no other reason than that I could control what was said. We had two F-100Fs, the two-seat version of the Hun, in the squadron. We normally flew them single pilot except to check out new arrivals or to supervise any pilot that we thought might need extra training. They were also useful for jobs like this.

I picked a simple mission, one that would probably not expose our "guest" to significant ground fire or other hazards. I would lead a flight of two with Bobby Mahoney, one of our better dive bombers, on my wing. I conducted a standard mission briefing and carefully explained ejection procedures to the newsman. He was, incidentally, fairly well known--not by any means in the Cronkite class, but a familiar enough face on major network television. When I covered procedures to be followed in the event that one of us were to be shot down, I noticed that our guest was turning slightly green. I took him aside after the briefing and explained to him that we were required to cover things like being shot down in all briefings, and that I didn't anticipate anything but a routine mission. I hoped to get him to relax, but it was apparent to me that the poor guy was terrified.

We flew the mission and it was, as expected, routine almost to the point of boredom. I was grateful that our newsman said virtually nothing and managed to retain his breakfast. After we climbed out of the airplanes I was amazed to witness a virtual metamorphosis in my passenger. Before my eyes this quivering Milquetoast turned into Steve Canyon! He began shouting orders to underlings who appeared from nowhere, had make-up applied by one and cameras positioned by others so as to show him, in flight suit, next to the formidable guns of the warplane. He conducted an interview with the negative questions I expected but with the confidence of a man who was now in his element. Bobby and I were, on the other hand, out of ours. We did our best to deflect the anti-war bias of the questions, and I must have succeeded because Marion wrote me that she watched me on television, but I didn't say anything. Evidently what little I did say was edited out. The entire unpleasant episode brought me closer to my conviction over the war years that our most dangerous enemy was not the VC but the American news media. After all these years I have not changed that conviction at all.

We occasionally took some real people in the back seat of the "F" as well. The ground troops sometimes asked to go along with us on a strike, and we were glad to oblige. I talked at some length to an Australian officer who had gone on a mission that day, and it was to me a revelation. I considered the ground troops to be heroes, knowing that I would be scared to death walking through the jungle knowing there might be a VC right behind the next tree. I was, therefore, quite surprised when my Aussie friend confided to me that he had been terrified during his flight with us. He said it was not only the strangeness of being in a fighter with "G" forces, diving at the ground, flying in close formation and the rest. It was also the fact, he said, that when he was in the dive on target he knew that every gun down there was pointed at him and only him. In his war people shot at groups and to him this seemed safer. To each his own, I suppose, but I told him I'd take my war over his anytime.

While we were on duty twenty-four seven we tried hard to get everyone off the base as much as possible for R&R. The big one was a ten day official R&R that usually took the "vacationer" to Hawaii. But there were other opportunities that took people to Clark in the Philippines, Taiwan to ferry aircraft or to Hong Kong on mini-R&Rs. While the trips complicated scheduling somewhat, I thought they were well worth it--and since the schedule was my problem the R&R program took priority in the 90th Squadron. I had my share, including a trip to Taiwan, discussed earlier, one to Clark and one to Hong Kong, managing to meet Sam Shealy on the latter two trips. Sam and I lived the good life, dining at the best restaurants, seeing the sights and purchasing the obligatory tailor-made suit in Hong Kong.

A month or so past the half way point in my tour I took my official R&R to Hawaii, having arranged to meet Marion there some weeks earlier. Simply stated, it was the best vacation of my life, a second honeymoon that was infinitely better than the first. We rented a little sports car which I almost wrecked pulling out of the rental agency parking lot. Accustomed to my jeep at Bien Hoa, I missed the brake pedal on the sports car and almost hit another car. Fortunately no damage was done and we proceeded to drive around the island of Oahu. Most evenings we dined at the Kahala Hilton, at that time a lovely new facility. After the months of subsisting at the Officers' Club or the Mess Hall at Bien Hoa, I felt as if I had stepped into a dream. The only down side was that 10 days went by at the speed of light and we were soon facing yet another gut-wrenching farewell. We consoled ourselves with the knowledge that the tour was well past the half-way point.

When Marion arrived home her twin, Ruth with husband Don met her at the airport. Ruth had been looking after the three boys and

Marion And "The Boys" New Year's Eve 1966

Marion was surprised that only Steven and David were with her. When Marion's first question was, "Where's Douglas?", Ruth, teary-eyed, announced that Doug was in the hospital. He had developed a childhood respiratory problem and was soon fine after Marion picked him up, feeling somewhat guilty about not being there when her youngest needed her.

I didn't find out about this until later because of an unstated policy Marion and I adhered to while I was away. I avoided telling her about my combat missions and VC mortar attacks unless I knew they were significant enough to be in the media, in which case I preferred to mail her my more low key version of the action. Marion, for her part, thought I shouldn't be burdened with her home-front problems, so she seldom recounted to me the many difficulties she had to deal with in raising three kids unaided. While I disliked being kept in the dark about the kids, in retrospect our mutual policy of selective concealment was probably best for both of us.

When I arrived back at Bien Hoa I was eager to get back to work, get my tour behind me and hopefully win the war while I was at it. I was pleased but a little disappointed to note how well things had gone without me. The truth was that the squadron practically ran itself because we had so many talented people, almost all of whom were ready and eager to pick up the ball and run with it. I had written to Marion several times that I had been in many squadrons but never one with such a surfeit of talent. The vast majority of our young officers were Air Force Academy graduates, but they were, in general, indistinguishable from the ROTC graduates. They were, almost without exception, top notch people. The few who were not didn't last long in the squadron. We had in our group of roughly 25 pilots a Rhodes Scholar and a Fulbright Scholar, one an Academy grad and the other from the University of Montana. Another young captain had a PhD in Astrophysics, a degree he acquired after graduating from the Air Force Academy. He came into my office one day with a new method of dive bombing that he was convinced would improve our accuracy. It involved working with trigonometric functions while in the dive. He was perfectly capable, himself, of solving equations while diving on a target, but I had to explain to him that the average fighter jock didn't know what a trigonometric function was, let alone how to use one during an attack run. Of that same group of "average" line pilots, seven were eventually promoted to general.

The leadership at Wing Headquarters, often a weak spot, was also outstanding. The Wing Commander was a former leader of the Thunderbirds Aerial Demonstration Team and an Olympic competitor in high diving. I was delighted to hear that a new, young captain, also on the Wing Staff, would be attached to us for flying. He was very experienced in the Hun and, in fact, had recently been a member of the Thunderbirds as well. I welcomed "Chet" to the squadron and put him on my wing for his first combat mission. The mission was a flight of four, each aircraft carrying four M-117 bombs. The flight went normally with each aircraft making three dive bomb runs, dropping the outboard bombs in pairs and the inboards singly. Unfortunately, all four of Chet's bombs were duds. Duds in our line of work were almost always caused by the pilot pressing to too low an altitude, not giving the fuse time enough to arm. It was a safety feature which kept pilots from shooting themselves down by flying through the debris of their own bomb. Now, on the gunnery ranges in the States it was common practice for fighter pilots to press below normal release altitude in order to get better scores. You could get away with this since the tiny practice bombs used on the range presented no danger to the aircraft. Fighter pilots, being competitive creatures, used every trick in the book to outscore their wingmen, even though it involved poor technique and some danger of flying into the ground. Back in Vietnam, I was angry on the flight home because it seemed obvious to me that Chet, in order to make an impression on his first mission, tried to beat the system by pressing. The crime of this kind of show boating was that the VC were experts at retrieving dud bombs and turning them into deadly land mines for the purpose of killing our kids in the jungle.

I took Chet aside after landing and, controlling my temper as best I could, explained to him that we could not tolerate that kind of gamesmanship in combat. He began by claiming that the bombs must have been improperly fused. Trying really hard now to control my temper, I pointed out that all sixteen bombs were hung by the same armament crew and the likelihood of all four of his being singled out for malfunction was infinitesimal. I also pointed out that we had not had a dud dropped by a squadron pilot for several months. Still angry, I dismissed Chet knowing I was dealing with a proud man whose pride had been wounded. I hoped, for his own good that I had got through to him.

A few days later I scheduled Chet to lead me on a two-ship dive bombing mission. I had by now calmed down, but I wanted to be personally assured that I had made my point. I had. Chet led the flight very professionally, made three excellent dive bomb runs and, most importantly, had no duds.

Flying home, I was in spread formation when Chet signaled me into close formation. He then gave me the wind-up signal for in-trail formation, the beginning of a good, old fashioned rat race. It instantly became clear to me that Chet, still smarting from my lecture, was going to take me down a peg by demonstrating his strong suit. We virtually never practiced air combat maneuvering because there was no threat of enemy fighters in the south. I thought about telling him to stick to business but we had enough fuel and, let's face it, my fighter pilot's juices started flowing. I knew that Chet, as an ex-Thunderbird, was an expert at pulling the Hun to the very limits of its performance envelope. But my unsaid attitude was "Give me your best shot, Son". I think he did just that. I never before or since pushed an F-100 so hard. We went round and round until we had to quit because of low fuel. Chet's objective was, obviously, to shake me, quickly if possible, get on my tail and stay there. My objective was to make sure that he didn't do that and to stay on his tail forever. Neither of us succeeded completely. He certainly never got on my tail, but he was good, and I never had a good tracking solution on him either. I would have had some snapshots of him on my gun-camera film but never a sustained burst. After landing, I played it low key and simply said "Good mission". But I noticed that the back of his flight suit was as sweat-soaked as was mine. Afterward, Chet demonstrated that he was a top-notch Hun pilot without the gimmickry and we became good friends.

Our primary mission was, of course, providing close air support to our nearby ground forces, primarily Army troops from the 25th Division and the 1st Division, the fabled "Big Red One". There were several informal programs set up to establish some kind of rapport between fighter pilots and troops we were assigned to support. As much as I disliked slogging through the mud, I felt an obligation to visit with the grunts, if for no other reason than to let them know that we cared. I arranged to visit the 25th at Cu Chi fairly early in my tour and flew several FAC missions in the back seat of an O-1. It was very educational for me and gave me a new respect for the dangerous and complicated work the FACs did in coordinating air strikes between us and the ground troops. Late in my tour I spent several days with the 1st Division at Lae Kay.

The Army's Division Commander at Big Red One was very much in favor of these liaison visits between the fighter pilots and his people. He expressed his support by sending a helicopter to transport us (there were representatives from each of the three F-100 squadrons) to Lae Kay. The helo arrived to pick us up and I immediately noticed that the warrant officer pilots looked to be about 15 years old. And they proceeded to fly like teen-agers turned loose with Dad's car. In an apparent effort to impress the fighter jocks, they flew at or below tree-top level all the way. They also decided to show us the results of a strike we had put in the previous day. It was a bunker complex which had obviously taken several direct hits. I'll have to admit that it was interesting to observe the results of our work, something that we never saw from our F-100s moving at 450 knots. But the chopper pilots circled the area time and again which struck me as being not very smart. I kept thinking there might be one last VC down there, really ticked off by our bombing and right now aiming his AK-47 at my body which did not have so much as a flak jacket for protection. After three circles around the bombed-out bunkers I tapped our boy pilot on the shoulder and told him we had seen enough and I thought it prudent to get the hell out of there. He reluctantly complied. I had only a few months left on my tour and had no desire to become a casualty at this late date flying in a helicopter with a teen-ager at the controls. (I may have been a bit uncharitable in light of my own years in Alaska playing the role of boy fighter pilot!)

I made good use of my time in Lae Kay and was especially impressed during a visit to an artillery fire base. It seemed to me that the fire base was in the middle of nowhere, up on a hill with a few men and a few artillery pieces and terribly vulnerable to attack. The officer in charge told me that they had indeed been attacked a few days earlier and defended themselves by lowering the guns' elevation as much as possible and firing anti-personnel rounds. They seemed to feel perfectly secure in their position, but I felt a lot more secure in the helicopter on the way back to Lae Kay.

I was also impressed with the Army's eating arrangements. The three fighter pilots were treated as guests and we were invited to dine at the general's mess. This was in a tent as befits an Army combat unit, but it was equipped with--so help me-- a chandelier!

If the Army was trying to impress us with the quality of their food, they succeeded. Their mess sergeant apologized to me because they were out of eggs Benedict at breakfast. I invited him to join us for powdered eggs sometime at Bien Hoa.

My relationship with the Army was always good and was especially so with the 1st Division people since we did most of our work with them. I discovered many years later that our good friend and lawyer, Howard Kalis, was an Infantry officer with the 1st at the exact time that I was at Bien Hoa, and there is no doubt that I put in air strikes during some of the operations he was involved in. We have a special bond with the Kalis' because of those days, but I didn't know Howard at the time. Much more complex was my relationship with Bobby, my sister Doris' son. Bob was one of the thousands of kids who were drafted into the Army and suddenly found themselves in the middle of a war that they didn't understand. I and all the other fighter pilots were professional soldiers, but we all had one overpowering, if unexpressed, fear in flying combat. That was the fear of making a mistake and dropping explosives on our own troops. It happened from time to time and often it didn't take an egregious error to create a tragedy. The pressure I felt was suddenly magnified a hundredfold when without warning my nephew, Bob, showed up at Bien Hoa. Once I knew that Doris' son might be among the troops we were supporting, the war suddenly became very personal.

To make a long story short, Bob survived the war and I survived the stress of knowing he was down there; but, tragically, he died just past the age of fifty from a heart attack. I wrote a eulogy for his memorial service, which I include because it pretty well sums up the special bond that we developed in those days. Bob, after leaving the Army, had a career in law enforcement and later became a successful businessman, but I called the eulogy:

TRIBUTE TO A SOLDIER

I'm Bob's uncle-perhaps not a distinction that makes anything I have to say special at a time like this. But Bob and I shared something that bonds us forever, and I cannot allow his unexpected crossing of the river ahead of me to pass without comment. I very much wanted to speak at his memorial, but a faulty vocal cord, which I'm sure would fail me under stress of the emotions I feel made me reluctant to try.

Bob and I spent most of a year together in a terrible place at a terrible time. The year was 1967, the place was Vietnam, and the United States was in the midst of a huge buildup of forces in an effort to win a victory that was never to be. Bob was a teenager suddenly caught up in the maelstrom of a war that he could barely comprehend. I, on the other hand, was the stereotypical professional soldier, relatively ancient at thirty-five, and supposedly wise to the vagaries of air-to-ground combat in a mad war.

One day, as I was walking from my aircraft to the operations building, I heard, incongruously, someone call, "Uncle Al!". Certain there was some mistake, I approached the skinny infantry private who had called and was shocked to discover that it was indeed my nephew, Bob. I had heard that Bob had been drafted just months before, but I simply could not believe that he was already in Vietnam. He had just arrived, and knowing where I was based, had found a way to finagle transportation- a talent of his at which I constantly marveled during our tour. My first shocked thought was "My God, what is this child doing here?". I was to discover quickly that he was no longer a child. He was, however, still idealistic, informing me that he had done well in basic training and was anxious to "help these people". I felt ashamed of my own budding cynicism.

Bob departed for his unit, and I was left to ponder the very dangerous year that he had ahead of him as an infantryman, the toughest job in Vietnam. My own private apprehensions soared when I found that Bob was assigned to the 1st Division, a unit for which we as a fighter wing had primary close air support responsibility. I had grown accustomed to delivering devastating firepower within yards of 1st Division troops, but never with the thought that someone in my immediate family might be vaporized if I made a mistake. I told Bob of my fears on his next visit, and the grizzled, middle aged major found himself being lectured by the teen-aged private on the need for controlling stress and being professional in combat. I listened, and slept better that night.

Bob visited often. At the art of scrounging transportation, he was a virtuoso, making it easy for him to sneak away to the relative luxury of our air base. I always made sure he had the comfort of a shower and a decent meal before he left, but I worried about his rapidly vanishing youth. He still looked like a kid, but the eyes had changed. They had seen some hideous things, and the imprint was indelible. To be confronted at nineteen by your own mortality must be a terrifying thing. Bob confided his fears to me after seeing a friend killed. I could do little but offer platitudes about the unlikelihood of being hit and conversation about better times. For his part, he would reassure me that he always felt secure in the field when air support was coming from the "Dice", (our call sign), squadron, since he knew we'd get it right. I prayed that his confidence was not misplaced. He always seemed to feel better after his visits, and would part with his lopsided kid's smile, no matter how stressed out he may have been. I hoped I had made him feel better. I knew for a fact that he had made me feel better. I left Vietnam a few months before Bob, and breathed a huge sigh of relief when I heard he had made it home safely. In later years when we met, all too infrequently, at family gatherings, we seldom mentioned Vietnam. We knew we had helped each other through a hellish time, we knew the bond was there, but it was a private thing, not something that needed words. I wish now that I had said more to him about a lot of things, but there always seemed to be time in the future. In any case, Bob would probably have been embarrassed. So I can only offer this small tribute to his all too short life.

I call it a tribute to a soldier, but that's probably inaccurate. Bob wasn't really a soldier. He was a civilian thrust into a uniform and a political conflict he didn't pretend to understand. But he became a soldier because he was there and because somebody had to do this distasteful job. And Bob, being Bob, decided if there was work to be done he'd jump in and do it. He did that work with a resourcefulness and courage that I, the professional soldier, could only stand in awe of.

Vietnam was a generation ago and has become irrelevant. But it was a watershed in Bob's life that deserves to be remembered as we say goodbye. He was my nephew, but he was also my comrade-in-arms, and I will never forget him or that terrible, special time we shared. I think that he, too, never forgot. Despite all his accomplishments in the later, more important, part of his life, my memory will always be of the teen aged infantryman I came to know so well. So, I bid you farewell, Bob. And I salute the boy-soldier who taught me much. Your light burned briefly, but with exceeding brilliance. You will not be forgotten.

Albert J. DeGroote
Colonel, USAF (ret)

So, my combat tour drew to a close with Doris' son still in mortal danger, but with the family connection still strong. I was glad to have it behind me without a family tragedy having occurred, but I was also grateful to have been able to support and perhaps to save the lives of countless kids like Bob. The family collectively stopped worrying when Bob came home in one piece a few months later, with nobody suspecting the tragedy to come. Meanwhile, I went on with my Air Force career.

On Thanksgiving day, 1967, I flew my last combat mission. Dale Rook and I had the same rotation date, and since we had gotten along so well running Operations, it seemed appropriate that we should go out as a team. The mission was a simple landing zone preparation flattening an area for the Army to land its choppers on and discouraging any bad guys from hanging around. We dropped 500 pound high-drag bombs at low altitude, and I must confess that for the only time I flew in Vietnam I carefully observed minimum altitudes for bomb release. I thought that for once it might be more important to get home in one piece than to have the most accurate bomb on record. When your priorities get to that point, it's time to go home. We did just that and thoroughly enjoyed Thanksgiving turkey at the mess hall. The squadron put on quite a party for Dale and me during our last week. We expected the usual patio party with a few discrete speeches, drinks and dinner. Instead, we were escorted outside where a flatbed truck awaited with a linen-set table in the center, and a waiter to pour the wine by candle light. We were then driven all around the base escorted by the Air Police with sirens blaring along with rotating beacons. The Wing Commander came racing out to see what was going on, but relaxed when told it was only the 90th having a little get together. We ended up at the usual spot for dinner and speeches. We heard afterward that someone commented that it was unfortunate that Dale and I were leaving at the same time. Someone else then said, "yeah, the 90th is leaving." As nice and as flattering as that was to our ears, Dale and I both knew it wasn't true. The squadron was awash in talent, and we'd be forgotten in days. That's the way it should be.

I finished my letter writing to Marion and a few of my thoughts may be relevant. One of my final missives was an apologia for my actions of the previous year:

> *...I guess I should talk about my volunteering for this tour and what I've put you through for a year. I don't know if you ever understood what I went through making the decision to come here. Having gone through it once before I was torn between the knowledge that I'd be miserable for a year without you and knowing that I couldn't live with myself unless I came. I suppose it was all a matter of personal pride and what it amounts to is that I traded one of the best years of our young lives for my own self respect. I'm not sure that having come here will do a great deal for me, but I'm pretty sure that if I hadn't come I'd have gradually deteriorated into a real loser. I can't ever give you that year back, honey, but maybe you'll get a better man out of the deal...*

I guess I felt guilty about abandoning my family, albeit for unselfish motives, and writing the letter helped. But the guilt was also there because in the back of my mind I knew that I had done something fulfilling and useful. I was certain that some kids in Army fatigues were alive because I was there. The guilt came from the fact that I thoroughly enjoyed the work!

After Final Combat Mission

So, a few days after Thanksgiving I boarded a commercial charter flight headed for the USA. I had been fighting with Personnel for weeks about my assignment, but I lost the battle. I was going to England, which was exactly where I wanted to go. But I was going as a Flying Safety Officer which I vehemently resisted. When I had been chosen to investigate the F-5 accident at Bien Hoa it was evident that my Safety background was still in my records, but I had hoped to escape from it. Finally I rationalized that I was going to London and would probably be in a cushy staff job where I could at last devote some time to my family. My letter to Marion acknowledged: "Maybe I should accept the fact that I'm 35 and not the boy fighter pilot any more. Who knows? I might even like it. I know I'll like having a family again."

I had a glorious homecoming, welcoming the winter weather along with the holiday season, and took advantage of the time to get re-acquainted with the boys, especially Doug who had not the faintest idea who I was. I had one more combat-like experience on my first night at home. Marion arose at her usual hour and decided to let me sleep in to recover from jet lag. She went downstairs in the apartment, after washing up in the bathroom, to make a nice breakfast for me. Unfortunately, while in the bathroom she had turned on the electric heater that was on the wall, something she had never done before. The heater was near the floor and there was a plastic towel rack above it. After Marion left the room the rising heat evidently began to melt the plastic, allowing a towel to come in contact with the hot electric grid. The towel caught fire as did the bathroom door. A large mirror mounted on the door then shattered from the heat--and that's when my slumber ended. My first reaction was -- MORTAR ATTACK-- and I rolled onto the floor. I immediately noted that I was on wall-to-wall carpeting and obviously not in Vietnam. But the smoke and flames were real and I found myself beating out the fire with a towel. I succeeded in my fire-fighting role and we were able to resume normal life without calling the fire department. The heater-towel rack set up, incidentally, was a design hazard and the apartment management made no attempt to charge us for damages. Some years later the entire apartment complex burned to the ground and I understand that the bathroom set up was to blame.

I had successfully applied for surface transportation to England which meant we would cross the Atlantic on the S.S. United States. We had never been near an ocean liner so we were quite excited, especially the boys. I was also permitted to ship my car on the same vessel, so I drove our Volkswagen to New York several days before our boarding, dropped it off at the dock and returned home by train.

In early January, having enjoyed a wonderful family holiday season, we embarked on our next adventure, this time in a magical place known as the United Kingdom.

London

Our Atlantic crossing, as could be expected was not exactly tranquil. The Atlantic in January is not the Caribbean. Sailing out of New York Harbor we were served lunch and the dining area was full. Once we hit open ocean, however, the diners diminished in number until, a few days out, we had the dining room almost to ourselves. Fortunately all five in our family had no trouble with sea sickness and we thoroughly enjoyed the voyage. Some of the crew told us that it was their roughest crossing ever. At times the ship pitched so badly that it vibrated violently when the stern was up, presumably from the propellors leaving the water. For Steven and David it was all part of the grand adventure, and while Marion and I would have liked a little more smooth sailing, we still thought it a great vacation.

On arrival at Southampton we were greeted with a rare English snowstorm. Since I had to collect my VW from the hold of the ship I had no choice but to drive to the hotel where our sponsor, Warren Hunt, had made reservations. Warren and his wife, Jinny, had originally planned to meet us, but were unable to do so because of the storm. Fortunately, the hotel was not very far from the docks, since driving on the wrong side of the road for the first time, with a left-hand steering wheel, in the snow was a bit sporty. We spent the night in a charming British hotel where we were introduced to the very civilized ways of British dining and hospitality. I was suitably impressed but not so impressed to discover that our room had a large bath tub but no shower. I turned on the radio for a weather report and chuckled as a distinguished British announcer intoned, "Once again nature has shown the British that England is a sub-Arctic island, and once again the British were surprised!". I hoped that the traffic snarls we hit on the way to the hotel would be cleared before I had to drive to London in the morning.

As it turned out the drive to London was not a problem. The main roads had been cleared of snow, aided by some brilliant sunshine, and the snow-covered countryside looked like a Currier and Ives Christmas card. On the way, I worked at convincing myself, with some difficulty, that it was OK to drive on the left. On arrival, we moved into the Barn Hotel, a small, very British establishment. It had nicely appointed rooms with adequate plumbing and a sumptuous English breakfast that went with the room tab. It was also within 10 minutes driving time of my new office.

I went to that office the first day in town, somewhat apprehensive because I was pretty certain that I wasn't going to like being a Flight Safety Officer at 3rd Air Force Headquarters. The headquarters was located in an old shoe factory which looked exactly like--an old shoe factory. I introduced myself to the office staff, observing that the boss was a Lieutenant Colonel who didn't have much on his desk. I also noticed a Major with a desk full of papers and not a lot of time to sit and chat with the new arrival, although he made it clear that he was certainly glad to have the help. The Major turned out to be Warren Hunt who, along with his wife, Jinny, became our lifelong friends. Warren passed away a few years ago and Jinny asked me to write a few words to be read at his memorial service. I decided to include it in this narrative because it sums up Warren's considerable influence on my career and provides a concise thumbnail sketch of my four-year tour at Third Air Force:

Thoughts about Warren

In November of 1967 I rotated from Vietnam after a year flying combat in the F-100. I was generally pleased because I had requested and received a consecutive overseas tour to Europe. After a year of separation from my family, I was looking forward to three years with Marion and our three boys in a nice place.

Only one thing clouded my optimism about the future. I had hoped to go to Europe flying fighters at the squadron level where I was always happiest. As it turned out, I was going to the Third Air Force Headquarters staff, and even worse, going as a Flying Safety Officer.

The flying safety career field had not been kind to me in the past. I had been a happy and respected young fighter pilot in the 2nd FIS at Suffolk County Air Force Base in New York. My squadron commander, Mike Culwell, called me in one day to ask me if I would mind filling in *"temporarily" at group headquarters as the group safety officer. Being an eager young captain, I agreed to help out the boss. Big mistake! While I was filling in "temporarily", I was given the entry level flight safety officer AFSC. A few months later, Air Division levied a requirement for a flight safety officer to go to Thule for a year. Guess who was the only guy on base with the AFSC, albeit entry level?*

So, I did my year in Thule, the longest year of my life, then went to Colorado Springs for three pleasant years as a fighter operations inspector. Next I volunteered for fighters in Vietnam and until rotation forgot all about my nasty experience in the flight safety business.

So, I was on my way to London, a great place, but with a serious attitude problem about my new job and a real determination to get out of it and back into operations. That's when my career path ran headlong into one of the most unforgettable characters I'd ever met.

My sponsor was a guy named Warren Hunt. I fully expected my new office to be manned with typical headquarters weanies, and I assumed that this Hunt guy would be one of them. I was mildly surprised to discover that he took his sponsorship job seriously, having made hotel reservations for us in both London and Southampton where we had been delayed by a snowstorm. Grateful for his assistance, I was nevertheless still skeptical about what I'd find when I reported for duty. I was never more surprised.

Warren was a major, as was I, but he was senior to me and we both worked for a laid-back Lt. Col. It took me only a day or two to figure out that Warren was the guy who made everything happen. We hit it off immediately, since our common favorite subject was airplanes, especially fighter airplanes. I discovered that he had flown a combat tour in Korea in F-94s, was current in the F-4, and had time in all kinds of fighters, including the F-104, at the time the hottest thing in the inventory. I remember thinking to myself, "hey, this guy's no headquarters weanie, he's a damn fighter pilot!"

From that time on, my attitude began a gradual transformation. I knew I was a real neophyte in the safety business, with only a year and a half of experience several years back and never having been to the formal safety officers' school in California. But I was astute enough to observe that I had the world's greatest mentor working right next to me-and, fortunately, I was bright enough to take advantage of that situation. Warren sensed that I was not thrilled to be a flying safety officer, and I in turn sensed that he didn't really give a damn. It became evident to me, although he never said as much, that Warren's attitude was that the Air Force wasn't paying us to do what we wanted to do, it was paying us to do what needed to be done.

I suddenly found myself being caught up in Warren's-not enthusiasm, but sense of responsibility. Third Air Force was suddenly having a string of fighter accidents, and there was work to be done. The accidents had to be investigated and somehow brought under control. I began to comprehend that losing an airplane to a stupid accident was as catastrophic as losing one in a dogfight with a Mig. We were very busy people and, fortunately, Warren was promoted to Lt. Col. and put in charge of the shop. With his new power, things began to happen.

Warren observed that while the safety shop was working long hours and weekends, nobody else at the headquarters was doing much of anything. He used his considerable powers of persuasion to convince the two-star general in command to get the rest of the staff involved in solving the aircraft accident problem. And we did have a problem with some 25 fighter accidents in one year-i.e., a full squadron lost to accidents-worse than combat losses.

Warren assembled a team of the best operations and maintenance people at the headquarters to run safety surveys of all five bases under Third Air Force. If we knew of a hotshot operations officer or maintenance man at one of the bases we'd attach him to the team looking at another base. This led to a great exchange of ideas on things that were being done well and things that were being done poorly. In one case we found the engine shop at an F-100 base that had lost a half-dozen airplanes because of engine failure to be grossly mishandling critical-tolerance parts. We changed supervisors and procedures at the base and almost miraculously the engine failures stopped.

By the time Warren left England the accident rate had gone from 25 a year to near zero. While Warren would scoff at the idea that he was *responsible for that turnaround, those of us who participated knew that it wouldn't have happened without his common sense and leadership. There's no doubt in my mind that some fighter pilots stayed alive because of Warren's efforts.*

Aside from the job, which by now seemed very important to me, Warren and I became very close friends. Jinny and the three girls complemented Marion and our three boys beautifully, and some of our family's fondest memories revolve around the ski vacations and cruises down the Thames organized, of course, by Warren.

Warren was a man's man, a leader and a loyal friend. In my case, he worked patiently with an attitude case, leading by example, to convert me from a guy looking for the exit to a true believer who ended up in the Director of Safety job. I haven't met many people in my life who could have pulled off such a conversion.

I think Warren would like to be remembered first as a good husband and father, but right behind that as a good fighter pilot. No matter how busy we were at work Warren always found time to go fly the F-4, and he made sure to find a way for me to go flying in the F-100. I can think of no greater tribute than to say I'd fly his wing anytime, anywhere. Who knows?-maybe I'll get to do it one of these days.

Al DeGroote, Col, USAF (ret)

Under Warren's influence I began to change, reluctantly to be sure, from the boy fighter pilot into somebody with a broader outlook on service and responsibility--but I was still a fighter pilot. Warren, somewhat to my surprise, wanted me, before anything else, to get re-current in the F-100. So, as soon as I completed the first steps in getting Marion and the boys settled, I found myself on the way to RAF Woodbridge to become attached to the 79th Tactical Fighter Squadron for flying.

Getting Marion and the boys settled was easier said than done, but in the end it worked out beautifully. We were talking to the housing officer, a British civilian, about what was available when his phone rang. It was a local Brit who had just decided to rent his house and thought he might get a better price from an American. To make a long story short, we called on the local Brit, loved the house, agreed on a price, and planned our move into what became known as "Marion's Mansion". A mansion it was not, but it was a very large, very nice house, and we were to spend four happy years residing at Norfolk Lodge in Uxbridge. After spending two of the last five years away from my family I was determined to spend more time with them and seeing Europe seemed the way to do it.

Warren And Jinny Hunt On Post-Retirement Visit.

Warren tossed a few easy administrative tasks my way and I think he was greatly relieved to discover that paper work did not overwhelm me. I mentioned that I had done an accident investigation while in Vietnam and Warren, obviously pleased, gave me a few recent accident reports to review and to prepare position papers and endorsements for the General's signature. After I had passed my first trial at being a headquarters bureaucrat I said I was ready any time to get myself recurrent in the Hun. Warren, as I said, considered it a top priority and a few days later I checked in at Woodbridge feeling greatly relieved to find myself airborne again.

The 79th was a good squadron, people were friendly and made me feel part of the group. They were probably happy to have a "headquarters weanie" competing with them on the gunnery range, with the usual stakes of "nickel a hole, quarter a bomb" for strafe and bombing scores. But my year in Vietnam bombing and strafing every day had made a marksman out of me, a change from the initial mediocrity I had displayed on my first encounter with air to ground work on the range at Luke. I felt right at home on the ranges in the U.K. and usually ended up collecting my share of quarters after a range mission. On a deployment to Wheelus Air Base in Libya, at the time the premier gunnery base in Europe, I got to fly every day, like all the line pilots, and I won money on every mission I flew. It's always a great feeling for a headquarters weanie when he can outshoot the full time jocks. I was probably just lucky, but I never had to prove my prowess again on a Wheelus deployment because Ghadaffi closed the base shortly after my first trip over there.

Refueling Over Germany

I had promised myself that I would make up for my absences from the family on my next tour after Vietnam, and I sincerely tried to do so. But fate and my own depression-era insecurity stepped in to make my reformed parenthood plans go awry. First, while I had been anticipating an undemanding staff job in London, I suddenly found myself caught up in a record-setting number of fighter accidents throughout 3ʳᵈ Air Force. Nearly all of them were F-100 accidents, and I was the designated F-100 expert on accident prevention! This transformed my undemanding staff job into a six and sometimes seven day a week backbreaker of a job.

The F-100 was, by 1968, an old airplane. It was well beyond its design service life, but was still the workhorse in the fighter inventory. Structural problems began to surface while I was still in Vietnam. Those of us who flew it every day in combat were hearing rumblings from FACs that fatal aircraft losses attributed to enemy ground fire looked suspicious. Several FACs claimed that they saw no ground fire during crashes they witnessed but that it appeared a wing failed during the pilot's pull out. This happened during low altitude deliveries where the pilot had no chance to eject.

Taking On Fuel

The problem came to a head in September, 1967. The 3ʳᵈ Tac Fighter Wing lost six aircraft and six pilots in a nine day period. One of the losses hit close to home because the pilot was Clyde

Carter, one of my good friends and a member of our tennis playing group. The other crashes we had experienced occurred in the jungle or in enemy territory where the wreckage was not recoverable. Clyde, however, had been making a high speed pass over the base, undoubtedly in celebration of his last mission, which it was. The wreckage fell on the base and was quickly examined. We found fatigue cracks in the wing center box section, supposedly the strongest part of the wing assembly. After we notified higher headquarters not much happened except for some precautions taken locally that fell more or less into the wishful thinking category of accident prevention. We were instructed to limit our pull outs to 4 Gs if at all possible. We tried to do that but when the situation demanded it--such as troops in contact-- we put the ordnance on target and pulled as many Gs as necessary to get an accurate delivery. It was an apprehensive period for F-100 pilots although nobody in my memory complained about the situation. We were all accustomed to risk taking. It was part of the occupation. What set this apart, however, was that it had nothing to do with skill or proficiency. If a wing came off during a low altitude delivery, you were dead and there was nothing you could do about it.

While higher headquarters showed no sense of urgency about our problem an accident far, far away put a huge spotlight on the situation and suddenly the sense of urgency was palpable throughout the F-100 community. It happened in Del Rio Texas where the Air Force's Thunderbirds demonstration team was doing a show. One of the solo pilots was Captain Tony McPeak who would rise in his Air Force career to eventually become the Chief of Staff. But today he was just starting his "routine" job of doing vertical rolls through the famous "Bomb Burst" finale of the show. As he applied G force in the entry his F-100 seemed to explode! What actually happened was that the wings came off and the subsequent cloud of fuel ignited causing a real explosion. Tony ejected successfully and no one was hurt on the ground. So the high profile Thunderbird team suddenly made the center box section of the F-100 wing a subject of great interest in the Air Force as well as in the civilian community. Wings coming off the airplanes flown by our aerial demonstration team do not make for good recruiting or publicity!

So, by the time I arrived in London the corrective action on the wing center box section was well in hand, and our job was principally one of monitoring. Unfortunately, the Hun began to show its age again with a different component, making my life more stressful and busy for a long time. The old, reliable Pratt & Whitney J-57 engine began failing at an alarming rate. I had flown J-57s from my initial checkout in the F-102 at Suffolk County in 1957. In all those years I had had only one catastrophic failure, and that was during the start of takeoff roll in an F-101 which has two engines. I had only to abort the takeoff and turn the aircraft over to maintenance. I followed up on that failure with the engine shop and it turned out to be an isolated case caused by a pump failure in the oil system.

The problem that surfaced in the early 70s was far more serious and widespread. The compressor cases which housed the two stages of compression were physically cracking causing instantaneous and catastrophic failure. Airplanes like the Hun and the F-102 which had only one engine were at great risk. At 3rd Air Force the toll of F-100s lost climbed over twenty in my first year. Most of the accidents were caused by engine failure.

During this siege of failures I continued to fly whenever I could, not only because I liked to fly but also because I had the latest information about the failures and the steps being taken to mitigate the problem. I actually became an eye witness to one of the accidents while trying to establish better rapport with the Flight Surgeon, of all things. The story still brings a smile to my face despite the threat to life and limb that it involved.

At 3rd Air Force Headquarters we had a base dispensary and one of the doctors was a feisty little Flight Surgeon with the unfortunate name, for a doctor, of Jon Plummer. Jon was required, like all flight surgeons, to log a minimum amount of flight time each month. He normally did so by flying in one of the administrative T-29s based at nearby RAF Northolt. But Jon, being conscientious and adventuresome, thought that since he administered to fighter pilots like me at the headquarters, he should sometimes fly with one of them. He asked me several times to arrange a flight and I finally relented, asking RAF Lakenheath, where I was at the time attached for flying, to schedule me in the two-seat F-100F model with Jon in the back seat. I explained to him that we were fighting a huge safety problem in the Hun because of compressor failures and there was some risk involved. Being a gutsy guy, Jon insisted on going anyway.

I briefed him extensively with the aid of an ejection seat simulator, reminding him once again of the possibility of compressor failure that might make use of the seat mandatory. Jon was very attentive and seemed relaxed even though he had never before flown in a fighter. We drew an excellent mission to the over water gunnery range in the Northern U. K. The weather was perfect and I flew number four in the flight which would allow Jon to take nice close formation pictures as well as to experience the thrills of high-G work in the gunnery pattern.

All went well on the flight to the range with Jon commenting on the beauty of the view from our tight formation. At the range we set up a holding pattern awaiting our turn to use the targets. The mission routine was suddenly interrupted by a terse radio transmission from one of the aircraft working in the gunnery pattern. The pilot said, almost routinely, "Mayday, I just lost my engine--bailing out." We watched him eject, saw him separate from the seat and watched his chute deploy. His F-100 hit the water, exploding in a great cloud of black smoke. We immediately went from a gunnery training mission into a rescue monitoring role. The downed pilot climbed into his raft and informed us with his survival radio that he was OK. Several small boats were headed his way and we headed for home once he was taken aboard.

Through all this excitement Jon had been completely silent, realizing that we were busy coping with the emergency. He remained silent until our flight of four, in spread formation, leveled off, headed for home. Jon then asked in a slightly tremulous voice, "Do you think our compressor will hold together until we land?" "I think so, Jon", I said. "I think so". I apologized to him for not being able to show him our work on the gunnery range but he didn't seem to mind at all, saying that he had experienced quite enough excitement for one day. He never asked me to take him flying again!

In addition to the F-100 problems, another impediment, this one self imposed, kept me from fulfilling my promise to myself to spend more time with my family and to be a better father to my boys. I was worried, probably with good reason, that my Air Force career would suffer because I was competing against officers with college degrees while I had none. My old depression era insecurity took over and I resolved to complete my degree program while in England. I had taken a few courses at Suffolk County, a few more at Thule, more still at Colorado Springs, but many of the credits were not transferable from one university to the next. With a stable three-year tour I thought I would be able to complete the requirements of a single university, in this case the University of Maryland which had an extensive overseas program.

I completed the degree requirements for my undergraduate degree and decided, since I was back into studying, to go on to get my master's degree with the University of Southern California. USC, like Maryland, had an excellent program for overseas military people. They frequently employed local instructors to supplement their teaching staffs and I found myself studying under professors from such prestigious establishments as Oxford, Cambridge and The London School of Economics. I still had my knack for divining what questions would be asked on the exams and the professors, mistaking this for brilliance, anointed me with distinguished graduate laurels upon graduation from both programs. I never believed my own publicity, but I was very glad to have the squares filled on my service records. I felt I could now compete for promotion with all of my degree-holding contemporaries. I also knew that I had paid a high price in fulfilling my family responsibilities. I usually took two courses at once in order to complete the degree programs before leaving England. This meant that I literally didn't have a spare minute. My normal schedule was: work at the office until time for class, go to class and then home for a 10 PM dinner, study until midnight and get up early to repeat the cycle. It was a rat race, but insecurity can be a great motivator, and I'm sure my academic credentials helped me to get promoted.

Whether it was worth it to my family is something I still wonder about.

With Marion, Mom, Steve & Dave at London Graduation From USC

In the short term my efforts seemed to pay off. I was promoted to lieutenant colonel and after Warren Hunt rotated I found myself, after a short stint working for an interim Chief, appointed as the Director of Safety for Headquarters Third Air Force. It was ironic that a guy who moved mountains trying to get away from the Safety career field ultimately found himself in charge of the whole program. As I indicated in my earlier tribute to Warren Hunt, my transformation into a true believer could be credited directly to his leadership. The Safety career field did, however, beat me down one more time before I left it for good. My boss, Major General John Bell, called me into his office one afternoon and asked me if I would like to take command of one of our F-100 squadrons at Lakenheath. My resounding "Yes, Sir" could be heard in the next building. It was my dream assignment as it was for any fighter pilot. I was walking on air for several weeks anticipating my move to Lakenheath until our personnel director informed me with a sad face that I couldn't take the assignment. It seems that the Safety career field was critically undermanned while F-100 qualified lieutenant colonels were a dime a dozen. I was bitterly disappointed but on reflection in later years it probably was a good thing for Marion and the boys. I had not yet finished my graduate studies in London and would not have been able to do so at Lakenheath. My chances of being promoted to full colonel would probably have been greatly diminished without the degree. So, it probably all worked out for the best--but to this day I think I would have made a helluva fighter squadron commander.

Life in London was busy but we did manage to enjoy ourselves. We made trips down the Thames River in cabin cruisers supplied by Air Force Special Services. Warren and I appointed ourselves ships' captains and sailed merrily down the river navigating through locks and enjoying cook-outs on the river banks with our families. Mom visited us several times while we were in London and she went along on one of the boat trips, thoroughly enjoying herself. We also took advantage of British cultural attractions, especially the London stage shows. Over the Christmas holidays we usually managed to fly as a group of families to Germany where we exercised our very limited skiing skills.

I asked for and received a six month extension of my three year tour in order to get the boys back to the States in the summer time so they could begin school in September. That was good planning, but unfortunately the personnel people later decided that my still critical Safety AFSC could not be easily replaced and I was involuntarily extended another six months, putting the boys back on the mid-term back to school schedule. We, as a family, decided that four years was enough and we accepted our latest rotation date of January, 1972.

Thus, our time in London came to a close. We had lived there for four years, longer than anywhere else until I retired from the Air Force. Douglas was enamored of the place and, as an adult, took a job in London and spent an additional eight years there, acquiring dual citizenship in the process. For me it was a hard working but productive time, having earned a promotion and two college degrees. Somewhat to my surprise I did not ship out in the Safety career field. Some one in the mysterious corridors of Officer Assignments at Air Force Personnel evidently decided that I needed to be assigned, for career development, to a joint staff. So off we went to CINCLANT Headquarters in Norfolk, Virginia where the family became re-Americanized, but as it turned out, for only a brief period.

Virginia Beach

My new office was at the Norfolk Naval Base in the city of Norfolk, but we looked for and found a house in nearby Virginia Beach. Becoming Americans again meant spending lots of money on lots of things that weren't easily available in England. These "things" included our house, a modern, air conditioned rancher, a new light green Oldsmobile, and the inevitable color television set. So, broke but contented, we settled into an easy going suburban life style with many of our neighbors being military. Steven and David enrolled in the local school but we found that they were none too pleased with the sprawling suburban school campus. They didn't complain a lot, but I sensed that I had placed them into an environment that didn't fit the life style they had been used to and that it might eventually lead to trouble.

I had never before been part of a joint staff so my job was a new experience. I was assigned to the Plans Directorate and my job title was "Joint War Plans Officer". Whereas my job in London had kept me busy seven days a week, I soon discovered that my job as a war planner was anything but demanding. It was strictly eight to five and the idea of coming in on weekends, as I frequently did in London, was simply not done. I suspect that the CINCLANT leaders had intentionally over manned the headquarters because they knew that the extra people would be needed badly if a shooting war started. This may have been a prudent policy, but I found it oppressive. I was bored!

I was equally bored with my flying activities. I had expected to be attached to Base Operations at nearby Langley Air Force Base flying the venerable T-bird--not an F-100, but at least a jet! Langley had other plans for me.

During my final months in London, the support aircraft stationed at the various bases in England began to have accidents or incidents. This was unusual since support aircraft had a very hazard-free mission of flying straight and level from point A to point B. My boss, General Bell, asked me to get checked out in one of the support aircraft to see if I could trouble shoot the safety problem. I chose to check out in the Convair T-29. The T-29 is a piston engine transport that was a short-haul airliner in its civilian version. The airliner version was very common and was known as the Convair 240. I found the T-29 to be easy to fly although I was surprised at the amount of control pressure required after spending most of my career flying fighters with hydraulically boosted controls. I also had to become accustomed to using the autopilot. Most fighters were equipped with autopilots but since they were useless in formation flying they were never used and were, consequently, not maintained. The T-29s were based at nearby RAF Northolt and were configured as VIP transports. I quickly became spoiled by being served gourmet lunches by the assigned flight attendant. Since we also carried a flight engineer I rarely had to start the engines. In my trouble-shooting role the experience I had gained as an Operations Inspector on the ADC ORI Team proved useful and I was able to make some suggestions for improving training for the behind-the - lines pilots who usually crewed the aircraft. I inspected the other U.K. bases that had support aircraft as well and hopefully did some good. In any event, whether by coincidence or not, the accident/incident rate for support aircraft returned to its normal rate of zero.

All of this leads up to my situation at Norfolk where the Operations people discovered that a much needed T-29 qualified pilot had fallen into their hands. Over my objections about being a fighter pilot, I found myself taking the necessary exams and flight checks making me an aircraft commander in the T-29. I didn't know it at the time, but my fighter pilot days were over.

The flying I did from Norfolk was routine. The aircraft were configured as high density passenger carriers and were normally flown on pre-arranged shuttle routes up and down the east coast. Gone were the flight attendants and fancy meals as were the flight engineers. I quickly became proficient again in starting the Convair's engines--something that was not as simple as it sounds, since they were notoriously hard to start when hot.

My day job consisted of maintaining and keeping up to date a single war plan in a strategically important part of the world. Upon reading "my" plan -- and it took some reading since it was about six inches thick--I decided it needed a complete rewrite. This entailed briefings and memos to all the other staff agencies involved. It was a necessary but tedious exercise. I had of necessity over the years become a fairly efficient bureaucrat and my boss was favorably impressed. My boss, by the way, was a Marine colonel straight out of central casting. When I had arrived at CINCLANT my sponsor, a Navy commander, said as he was leading me toward my new boss' office, "You won't have any trouble calling him 'Sir'". He was right. Colonel Ralph looked like a professional football player. There was good reason for that since he had once been a professional football player. He also sported a broken nose and was missing part of a thumb, all of which made him look like the fierce warrior that he was. But first impressions were deceiving since he turned out to be a laid back, thoughtful leader and a nice guy besides.

My job also involved a considerable amount of public speaking, not only to brief aspects of my war plan, but also because the Navy liked to use Air Force and Army officers as briefers to "Visiting Firemen". This was to make the headquarters, which was basically a Navy show, look more like the "joint" operation it purported to be. I never liked public speaking and didn't think I was very good at it, but it was part of the job and sometimes the "Dog and Pony Shows" provided unexpected entertainment.

For example, I was tasked on one occasion to brief the incoming Undersecretary of the Navy. The briefing was to address the CINCLANT mission and the basic organization of the command. There were perhaps 50 officers in the briefing room including a dozen or so admirals sitting nervously in the rear seats poised and ready to correct this misplaced Air Force fighter pilot in the event he made an error that might embarrass the command. I had done this briefing before and was comfortable with it. Early in the pitch I always commented on the prolific use of acronyms, such as COMSUBLANT, CINCLANTFLT, etc. which many people find confusing. All military units use acronyms but the Navy has raised their use to a fine art. I always told my audience to stop me for a translation should an unfamiliar acronym appear. The new undersecretary, a political appointee, nodded wisely at this and I continued the briefing. It was a slide presentation and shortly a slide came up labeled "Antilles Defense Command". The new Undersecretary of the Navy raised his hand and asked, "An-till-es, what does that acronym stand for?" Obviously, this guy, who had tremendous power and influence over the United States' fleet, had never heard of the Antilles Islands. The admirals in the rear stiffened, one or two looking skyward, in anticipation of how the Air Force guy would dodge this curve ball. I cleared my throat briefly to consider a reply and quickly blurted "It's not really an acronym, sir, it just looks like one. It refers to the Antilles chain of Islands, Cuba, as you know, being the largest." I had said, "as you know", knowing full well that he had no idea what I was talking about. I then brought up a new slide and shifted off the subject of the Antilles. Afterward, one of the admirals said, "Nice job Colonel," shaking his head and rolling his eyes. We both were thinking that maybe, just maybe we could find better qualified civilians to be placed in charge of the military. A few years hence I was to find myself handling an embarrassing situation with another undersecretarial appointee, this one an Air Force designee. More about that later.

My bureaucratic routine was interrupted twice during my tour at CINCLANT by an amphibious exercise incongruously named "Exotic Dancer". The exercise basically tested the military's ability to invade North Carolina, with all branches of the service cooperating in a single effort. I was assigned to be the Air Operations Liaison Officer aboard the invasion force's flagship, a cruiser, the USS Little Rock. I was appalled at the lack of sophisticated communications equipment. I expected that we would be able to communicate with anyone. What I found was that not only could we not communicate Navy to Air Force, we couldn't even talk reliably Navy to Navy or Air Force to Air Force.

On several occasions I had to request a Marine helicopter take me to Langley AFB, the Air Force's Command Center for the exercise, so I could hand carry documents requesting Air Force support. I, like everyone else involved, complained loudly about this shortcoming in after-action reports, but the following year brought more of the same. I'm sure that poor equipment was the direct result of budgetary constraints, but Exotic Dancer shook my confidence in our ability to run joint operations. It made me wonder about how we managed to come out ahead on D-Day during WWII.

I continued to be assigned as a briefer on subjects that really should have been assigned to Naval officers. The Air Force blue uniform displayed "jointness" and usually was the deciding factor in who did the briefing rather than who had the most experience with subject matter that involved, for example, ships. I very nearly rebelled when one day I was told that I was now the CINCLANT mine warfare officer and would be briefing the Commander-in-Chief of the Atlantic Command on the mine warfare plan. I not only did not write the plan, I had never even read it! Furthermore, I had never so much as seen a mine and I refused to brief anybody, let alone a four star admiral, about a piece of munitions that I had never seen! I was then given a set of orders sending me to the Navy's Mine Warfare school in Charleston, S.C. where I could take a familiarization course and observe mines to my heart's content. It was a pretty good school and I decided to include myself in the military definition of an expert as a guy who just went to a four day school which nobody else had attended. I reluctantly accepted my fate and prepared my briefing for the admiral, having by now been able to read the plan.

The admiral arrived and I swept through my briefing as if I knew what I was talking about. I did, however, have a precautionary ace in the hole, having placed a Naval Aviator friend in a rear seat in the audience. He had actually been in the mine warfare business and I planned to use him as a consultant if I found myself unable to field one of the admiral's questions. My trepidation proved to be unfounded since the admiral sat attentively through my pitch, asked no questions, thanked me and left. I noticed that he wore aviator's wings, so he probably felt sorry for this misplaced Air Force guy briefing the Navy on its own business.

Virginia Beach was a pleasant enough assignment, and I was able to spend more than the usual amount of time with the family. Steve was now old enough to drive and I was reminded of the rapid passing of time when I was teaching him how to handle a Volkswagen. I had never had so much time on my hands, which was probably a good thing, but I could not escape the fact that I was bored. The Navy's Oceana Naval Air Station was close by and I spent much time looking enviously at the young men flying the sleek F-14s.

A few things happened to break the pattern of boredom I was experiencing--from the endless briefings to flying the East Coast shuttle in the T-29. The first event triggered a celebration. I was sitting at home watching television when the phone rang. It was my old friend from ORI Team days, Hoot Gibson. Hoot had advanced access to the findings of promotion boards and had discovered that my name was on the list for advancement to full colonel. We verified things like serial numbers to make certain that it really was my name on the list and Hoot gave me a little congratulatory speech. While I never was obsessed with promotion, as some officers clearly were, it was nice to know that all the hard work had paid off and that the Air Force had enough confidence in me to trust me with the greater responsibilities that came along with the colonels' eagles.

The second event was a partial offshoot of the first, since I was about to become a full colonel filling a lieutenant colonel's billet. I knew that I would get an assignment sooner rather than later and I forewarned the family to expect a move. The boys, strangely enough, voiced no objection. This included Steve who would be leaving just as his high school senior year was starting. It seemed that they had developed a certain wanderlust and sense of adventure as a result of our constant relocations and actually looked forward to the new life at a new place. They were about to find adventure enough to last a lifetime.

I was once again sitting at home on a Friday night when, once again, the phone rang. This time it was a major in the Colonel's Assignments Branch in the Pentagon. A jovial type, he informed me pleasantly that I had been selected for consideration to be the U.S. Air Attaché to Laos. He seemed hurt at my immediate reaction which was, "What else are you guys selling tonight, cancer?" I pressed him for more information, asking first if it was another damned remote tour away from my family. Knowing Laos simply as a place where we had dropped an enormous number of bombs, I could not conceive of it as a location where families could be sent. The jovial major advised me that I was misinformed and that Vientiane where I would be stationed was quite secure and that the Embassy was fully staffed for housing and schooling children. Wives were not only welcomed to accompany their husbands but were expected to participate in entertainment and social functions. It sounded like it was right up Marion's alley and the jovial major seemed pleased when he detected that my interest in the assignment was piqued. He informed me that the assignment called for a French-speaking colonel with a background in fighters and that thus far he had been able to locate only two, me and one other. I told him that I had hardly spoken a word of French since taking the Air Force Academy's course in Colorado Springs. He seemed only interested in the fact that my records said that I was fluent as a result of my taking the AF Language Proficiency Test eight years ago. I didn't press the issue farther.

I was soon scheduled for an interview at the Pentagon where, presumably, the competition between me and the other French-speaking fighter pilot was to take place. Marion was expected to attend and she voiced no objections.

So, after making arrangements for the boys, Marion and I departed for Washington and after being welcomed by some people from the Defense Intelligence Agency (DIA) we were ushered into a conference room where we sat in chairs facing a semi-circle of other chairs occupied by colonels and a brigadier general. As Marion observed later it was a situation that should have made us nervous but was nothing of the sort. Laos was not exactly Paris and we were not really lusting after the assignment. We, in fact, were interviewing them, not the other way around.

Whatever we said in the interview was apparently what they wanted to hear because I was notified a week or so later that I had been selected for the job. I never did find out who the other French-speaking fighter pilot was and I wondered whether he really existed or had been dreamed up to use my competitive instincts against me. In any case I was informed that I would have six weeks to complete what was normally a two year attaché training course. Half of that two year period was normally devoted to language training, so DIA reasoned that I was already half prepared. I later found that the person originally chosen for the job was discovered, almost at the completion of his training, to be an alcoholic--thus the haste to find a last minute replacement.

I closed out my desk at CINCLANT and began to attend classes set up for me in Washington. I rejoined the family in Virginia Beach on weekends and Marion made several trips with me to D.C. where she attended briefings that supposedly would prepare her for life in the diplomatic circles of Vientiane. The briefings were mostly a waste of time as were the classes I was attending. After two weeks of enlightening courses on things like how to operate a camera, I went to the DIA decision makers and told them that I was wasting time and needed to get my badly rusted French up to speed since I wouldn't be able to gather much intelligence if I couldn't talk to anyone. They reluctantly agreed and the following Monday I found myself speaking French with a very attractive native French speaking instructor. I'll readily admit that I had no objections about DIA's choice of tutors and I thoroughly enjoyed her company and the language training course she had prepared. On my final day of class I invited her to lunch at the Bolling Officers' Club. She accepted and we had a pleasant farewell lunch. As we were about to leave we were approached by an old friend from Suffolk County days who had been one of the chaplains there. In a voice dripping with sarcasm he said, "Hello, Al. How is Marion?" The chaplain, on seeing me away from home with an attractive woman had jumped to the conclusion that I was guilty of something. I replied, "Hello, John, Marion's fine. I'd like you to meet Mrs Blanc, my French tutor", stressing the word, "Mrs." I explained what was happening with Marion and me and the chaplain departed, relieved and, I hope, suitably chagrined. That completed the preparations for my new job in Laos and we planned as best we could our departure from Virginia Beach. It appeared that we had little chance of selling our house which we had owned for only a year and a half so we decided to keep it as a rental property. We were not happy about that, but in the end we kept the property for many years and it turned out to be a very good investment.

I was very interested in what sort of airplane I'd have available to fly. The DIA people seemed to think I should be more concerned with things like embassy protocol than with a simple thing like an airplane, but I had my own priorities. I was advised that a C-47 was assigned to the Air Attaché in Vientiane, that I would have a mechanic assigned and that the three assistant Air Attachés were trained in the aircraft. Normally pilots assigned to attaché duties went to Hurlburt Field, Florida to get checked out in the C-47 if a C-47 was in place at his end assignment. But, once again, there was no time and I would have to be checked out once on station.

While in Washington I was contacted by Major Bob (RK) Taylor who had just completed his training and was to precede us, with his family, to Laos. We were delighted to accept a dinner invitation to their home where they filled us in on many details that they had picked up during two years of training. RK confessed that languages were not his strong suit and that his French was marginal. I thought mine was coming along nicely so I wasn't concerned about it. I was, however, happy to learn that he had been a gunship pilot flying C-47s in Vietnam, so we would have one experienced C-47 driver on the staff, and I would have a qualified instructor pilot to check me out in country.

Things began to fall into place and in September, 1973 we began, as a family, our long flight to the fascinating and mysterious Kingdom of Laos.

Laos

The flight to Laos was long and tiring and was to be via Bangkok where we would be met by the C-47 from Vientiane for the last leg of the trip. But before embarking on that final leg we spent a day in Bangkok recovering from jet lag. I had been in the Far East, of course, in Vietnam and had spent a few days in Bangkok during my tour there. I was not, therefore, affected by culture shock. But Marion was! I had tried to prepare her for the sights and sounds of the Orient, but I evidently did a poor job. We wandered around the streets of Bangkok and Marion couldn't wait to get back to the relative luxury of our hotel room. I thought, "Good Grief--Wait'll she sees Vientiane!"

She didn't have long to wait. The C-47 arrived and presented a startling contrast to the ultra-modern, brand new 747 airliners we had been traveling in. The takeoff, with props struggling to achieve some semblance of synchronization, stirred memories from sounds of old WWII Humphrey Bogart movies. The interior décor of the 1943 model "Gooney Bird" did little to dispel that impression.

I watched the by now familiar landscape of Southeast Asia pass below and wondered how my family would adjust to this part of the world which looked lush and beautiful from the air, but looked primitive and often treacherous from the ground. Marion's morale suffered another blow when we were informed by one of the C-47's pilots that the comfortable house reserved for the Air Attaché had been taken over by the new Defense Attaché, an Army Brigadier General. This later proved to be accurate but very incomplete information. When we arrived at the airport in Vientiane we were greeted by a small entourage of the Defense Attaché staff along with some of the wives. Barbara Taylor, who had arrived a few weeks earlier was a familiar face for Marion because of our dinner party in Washington. She was typically upbeat, telling Marion that she would "Love it!"

We were escorted into a Ford "limousine" driven by a uniformed Lao "chauffeur" named "Bing" who was, I was told, my assigned driver. Not being accustomed to chauffeured travel of any sort, I could see immediately that this job might take some getting used to. We drove from the airport to the local hotel with me riding up front and Marion in back with the boys. As we drove through the city the boys and Marion were introduced to the chaotic traffic sounds and open sewer smells of Asian cities. It was very quiet in the back seat until eight year old Douglas piped up with, "Is this where all the poor people live?" He had yet to discover that compared to Americans almost all people were poor.

The following day I was briefed on the fly by an Air Force lieutenant colonel who was filling in for the last Air Attaché who had already departed. It seems that while we were en route a disgruntled Lao Air Force colonel had taken over the detachment of armed T-28s based in Vientiane and launched an unsuccessful coup d'état. This had involved some rather inaccurate bombing and strafing of portions of the city leaving a few casualties and some slight damage. Unfortunately, some of the attacks came close to the hotel where the Taylors were in temporary residence, scaring their three girls but causing no other damage. I tried to downplay the story but couldn't help feeling that my family was looking at me wondering secretly what exactly the old man had got them into this time. It made me more appreciative of Barb's upbeat attitude with Marion but made her welcoming exclamation of "You'll love it!" somewhat less believable. In any case, the coup was defeated and the Lao military slipped back into its customary torpor, leaving us to make a more or less normal adjustment.

I went to work the next day, anxious to discover exactly what an Air Attaché did for a living in a country that was still deeply involved, at least peripherally, in the Southeast Asian War. My escorting lieutenant colonel seemed competent enough as did the other members of the staff that I met. But it seemed disturbingly obvious that there was a great deal of animosity between the Air Force and Army people assigned to the Defense Attaché Office (DAO). The points of disagreement seemed petty, almost childish to me while I was gathering my first impressions. I began to lose patience when my escort informed me that the Army had taken over my parking space at the DAO office entrance. This would require me to walk an additional 10 feet or so or so from another parking space and did not therefore, impress me as a major problem. My cumulative first impression left me thinking that maybe there were too many people here without enough to do.

My first visit was to the embassy to meet the Chargé d' affaires, John Dean. I had spoken by phone to the incoming Ambassador, Charles G. Whitehouse, while in Washington where he was being briefed on his new job, but John Dean was the overall boss in Laos until the Ambassador arrived. The visit with Dean confirmed my initial impressions. He informed me, without the trace of a smile, that he had more trouble with the U.S. Army fighting with the U.S. Air Force than he had with the Communist Pathet Lao fighting with the Royalists. He said that he hoped my arrival would help to alleviate that situation. I assured him that I would do my best to take care of the problem quickly. I left his office privately fuming that the U.S. Military had a reputation among State Department people and other local bureaucrats for being part of the problem rather than part of the solution. I had, after all, just left a joint headquarters where I worked quite amicably for a Marine colonel who in turn worked successfully for a Navy admiral. This did not impress me as something that couldn't be solved quickly.

As luck would have it I was about to meet a kindred spirit. He was the newly arrived Defense Attaché, Brigadier General Richard G. Trefry. Dick Trefry was the ogre who had supposedly taken over the Air Attaché dwelling, leaving me and my family out in the cold. In truth, when the embassy housing officer took us to see our assigned quarters, asking us if they were adequate, I replied that the house looked like a bloody hotel! It was large, brand new and comfortable to the point of ostentation. I later discovered that General Trefry, who had no children, decided to take the existing Air Attaché's quarters, which were significantly smaller than those assigned to the DATT, because he knew I would be arriving with three children. I was then given the DATT's quarters although I didn't know it at the time. Marion, of course, was delighted with the arrangement. She knew that she would be expected to entertain frequently and the house was ideal for anything from a cocktail party to a large formal dinner. I was happy that the great housing crisis was behind me and I would be able to go to work.

On my first day at the office I heard rumblings that the new general was not getting cooperation from some Air Force people in setting up his new office. Thoroughly fed up by now, I went to investigate and discovered that the general had responded to the affront by ordering that the most beat-up metal G.I. desk in the warehouse and an equally beat-up G.I. chair be installed, along with his flags, in the office and nothing else! I remember smiling inwardly and thinking that I just might get to like this guy.

My expectations proved to be correct. General Trefry was a tall, slender West Pointer with an obvious intellect and a vocabulary worthy of George Patton. I liked him immediately. I made an appointment for an extended conversation at the first opportunity and immediately brought up the subject of the local war between the Air Force and Army. I suggested some immediate steps including getting rid of the excess people who seemed to be wandering around creating problems. I also informed him that the chief of Air Force Intelligence in Washington had told me that Vientiane was a "cesspool" and he wanted me to clean it up. He agreed with everything I said and let me know that he was already doing something about it. For starters he had already been directed to reduce the American presence in Laos drastically and people would be leaving in droves shortly. We also took immediate steps to get the slot machines and prostitutes out of the bachelor quarters for those who would remain.

I observed early on that the primary mission of the DAO was overseeing the logistic system for the Royal Lao Army and Air Force, not the more traditional attaché role of collecting overt intelligence. General Trefry was an expert on the logistics mission, having come from running the semi-covert logistics headquarters at Udorn Air Base in Thailand. I, on the other hand, had no experience in running a logistics operation and in fact had very little training in the traditional attaché intelligence role. The Defense Intelligence Agency (DIA) seemed perfectly content for me and my three assistant attachés to spend our time collecting tid-bits of information at cocktail parties and at athletic events. But Laos was still very much involved in a shooting war and I was not at all content to play DIA's game.

I set up another meeting with General Trefry to inform him that I was not satisfied to be the Air Force's resident tennis player in Laos and that if there were no more important needs for my services then I would just as soon get a ticket home to re-join the fighter Air Force. General Trefry smiled and said he thought he could solve my problem.

The next day there magically appeared a complete organizational chart showing the DAO set up along the lines of a traditional joint staff. I suspect General Trefry had the plan in his desk drawer for weeks and was just waiting for me to make the first move. I was pleased with the arrangement since I was to be his deputy. I could think of no faster way to learn the logistics system for the Lao military than by following this guy around. The transition was far from smooth, however, since the new organization was against all of DIA's guidelines. Those guidelines kept the attachés separated by service. Not only did DIA object but I had a minor rebellion among my assistant attachés. One in particular was a handsome West Point graduate, a major, who was the ranking assistant and, as such, my deputy. Under the new organization he reported instead to an Army colonel. He was very much worried that his career might suffer as a result. I tried to reassure him with little success, but by the time he rotated he came to not only accept the organization but praised it to high heaven in his end of tour report.

With the administrative work and the endless cocktail parties taking up most of my days and evenings, I was hard pressed to get checked out in the C-47. Finally, at Bob Taylor's urging I set aside some time each day for "flight training". The old "Gooney Bird" was no great beauty and, produced in WWII, was showing signs of her age. But the sound of her radial engines starting up was enough to make me remember why I had joined the Air Force in the first place. Bob Taylor was a good instructor and my T-6 tail-dragger experience came in handy. In a few days I felt comfortable enough to be designated as pilot-in-command. One of my early flights was into Long Tieng, known to the media as the "CIA's secret base in Laos". It was no longer much of a secret, but flying into its single runway was an adventure. The approach was in one direction only since there was a large mountain at the far end. Takeoff was, of course, in the opposite direction. To make it even more interesting, there was a large hill on final approach to the runway. Landing meant clearing the hill by a few feet, lowering full flaps and reducing power to sink down to some semblance of a normal glide slope. It was fun as was landing at various "Lima Sites" around Laos some of which had dirt runways, usually carved into the side of a mountain. After all my years flying supersonic fighters I thoroughly enjoyed stepping back in time to fly a venerable, old classic, the C-47. The old bird was destined to be very useful to us before our tour in Laos was finished.

Although the Southeast Asia War was still going full tilt, it was proceeding at a snail's pace in Laos. It did not seem to be in the Lao people's make up to hurry anything, let alone something like combat. The United States had embarked on a policy of disengagement from the war and much of our mission was to prod the Lao military to take charge of their assets and operations with our people fading away to a supporting role. The results of this policy were mixed at best but while it lasted Laos was a pleasant, albeit primitive, place to be stationed. Marion was the perfect Attaché wife. She loved to entertain and was very good at it. After a short period when her confidence suffered at the prospect of having to compete with the typically highly educated embassy females, she found that common sense was all that was needed and became one of the most popular hostesses in Vientiane society. Mostly, she was successful because everyone loved Marion just being Marion.

The boys, for their part, adjusted amazingly well to their new, exotic surroundings. The American School of Vientiane had small classes with good instructors. It was easy to find native speakers to teach foreign languages and the boys became interested in French, something that Steve cultivated in later years as an airline pilot on the New York to Paris run. In a little side adventure, Steve and I made our way to a seaport in southern Thailand to pick up the family Oldsmobile. We then proceeded to drive the length of Thailand to the Mekong River where a ferry took our car into Laos, looking very much out of place on the mostly unpaved roads. Dave was interested in photography and it was easy and cheap to build him a dark room in our basement. Doug was still very young but had many friends and many interests. All in all life for the DeGroote family was good.

Somewhere along the way we even acquired a dog, something I had always opposed because dogs were such a nuisance for a much traveled family. But the story of "Tiki" is worth telling. We found ourselves, one evening, attending the American School's senior student play in which Steve had a major part. At a serious moment in the play a cocker spaniel walked quietly up the stairs leading to the stage, crossed behind the actors so they were unable to see him, lifted his leg on a piece of furniture and walked slowly off the other side of the stage. This, of course, broke up the audience much to

Tiki, The Wonder Dog

the dismay of the actors who couldn't fathom why the audience was laughing heartily at their dead serious dialogue. The dog was Tiki, a stray who had been abandoned by some family who probably didn't want to pay the considerable fee to ship the dog home when they rotated, so Tiki became the school bum, scrounging food from the students--his favorite dish was pizza--and sleeping anywhere he chose on the school grounds.

One evening a few days after the play I noticed a pretty cocker spaniel wandering around in our front yard. A few more days went by and I saw the dog again. I hadn't made the connection of the cocker in the school play and this apparent stray at my house. At dinner I commented that I had noticed a dog hanging around the house and I wondered where he had come from. The boys looked at each other sheepishly, Doug unable to suppress a grin, and I knew that I had been had. Protestations were made that the household staff would feed and take care of Tiki and that my replacement would inherit a dog along with the property--no problem. Somehow I knew it wouldn't end up that way but I went along with the setup. Besides, I had to agree with the boys that Tiki was much too good looking a dog to be a stray.

Not long afterward the first rumblings of catastrophe began to be heard in Laos. The so-called Peace Accords were being routinely violated as all of us in the military knew they would be. The United States' liberal establishment in Congress as always chose appeasement over honor and I knew it was only a matter of time until our idyllic Asian lifestyle would come to an end.

The nuts and bolts of my job involved keeping the Royal Lao Air Force (RLAF) flying through training and logistics support. The RLAF was a little hard to take after years of being part of the most professional fighting force in the world. But patience and understanding were required. Most of the pilots were, after all, just a year or two removed from operating a water buffalo rather than an armed T-28. In an all too typical incident a Lao pilot took off from Udorn, Thailand to ferry a T-28 to Vientiane, a flight of about 20 minutes. He tuned the low frequency radio to Vientiane, put the directional indicator on the nose and proceeded straight ahead. Several hours later he was still proceeding straight ahead until, seeing an airport and being almost out of fuel, he landed. Unfortunately, the airport where he landed was in China. He had over flown part of Thailand, the entire country of Laos and parts of North Vietnam and China on his planned 20 minute trip. It never occurred to him that the low frequency beacon, to which he had entrusted his entire navigational planning, might not have been working. I was called by a very annoyed Chinese attaché who asked that we be a bit more circumspect with respect to our war planes, even those flown by Lao pilots.

I had an opportunity to test the product of our training of Lao pilots during a routine visit to several RLAF bases. The commander of the RLAF was, at the time, General Sourith, a gruff muscular man whose background was as a paratroop commander. Apparently jumping out of airplanes was close enough to flying them to qualify him for the top job. I went on many excursions with Sourith and the trips were usually fruitful in finding problem areas with the RLAF's training or logistics operations. I always offered to fly our C-47 myself with Sourith as a passenger. This worked fine until one day when he insisted that we take an RLAF C-47 flown by a Lao crew. I was nervous about this but I could hardly refuse to fly with pilots whom we had trained and with whom he flew all the time. I also think that Sourith felt more comfortable with me in the cockpit so I was puzzled by his insistence on the change. I was shortly to find the answer.

After inspecting an RLAF training base, we returned to the C-47 and Sourith announced that we would stop at Sayaboury for lunch. We did so and I was treated to a meal at a restaurant with a dirt floor and several dogs wandering around the tables. We all had some sort of stew, ordered by Sourith, from which I surreptitiously extracted a small duck's foot, slipping it to one of the dogs who also rejected the morsel. Having finished our delightful repast, we returned to our aircraft and I discovered the real reason for our flying in a Lao C-47. Lao ground crew had just finished loading the aircraft with large, white painted rocks. It seems that Sourith wanted to decorate his home with an extensive rock garden and Sayaboury had just the size rocks he needed. Knowing full well that I would never have allowed our VIP configured C-47 to be loaded with rocks, he had insisted that we take one of his cargo carriers. I objected loudly anyway since the Lao crew fully intended to take off with the heavy rocks rolling about the aircraft floor. I did a quick mental weight and balance calculation and insisted that the rocks be somehow secured in the forward part of the cabin. A large board was found which was secured at one end to a bulkhead and at the other end by a large Lao airman holding the board with an attached rope. Knowing that I would never get Sourith to abandon his rocks I briefed the Lao crew that if the rocks broke loose and rolled to the tail on take off, we were all going to die. That seemed preferable to them to incurring the wrath of General Sourith. I sat next to the cockpit, prepared to leap forward and chop the power at the first sign of the large Lao losing his grip on the rock collection during takeoff roll.

Happily, the rocks stayed put and we returned uneventfully to Vientiane. Afterward, I always found a reason to insist on flying my aircraft on excursions with the general. He was content with that since I'm sure he thought I was a worry wart.

During the evenings we went to social functions and played the more traditional role of overt intelligence collectors, which is what attachés are supposed to do. While being a professional cookie pusher was a little out of my line, I'll readily admit that I thoroughly enjoyed meeting some of the characters who made up the population of the Asian "Casablanca" we were living in. One of my favorites was Soviet Colonel Tzarkov who was right out of central casting for a James Bond movie. He was rude, arrogant, a die hard communist, and completely delightful because he was also stupid. Any time we wanted to spread disinformation, Colonel Tzarkov was available to soak it up. On the other end of the spectrum was George Vorobiev, a slick, intelligent KGB operative who spoke English like a native of Dayton, Ohio. I was warned about him and shown his photograph on the day I arrived since George's M.O. was to introduce himself to any new arrival as "George", hoping that the new arrival would assume he was American and give him some useful information. Sure enough, at my first cocktail party George came up to me, introducing himself as "George". I smiled and said, "That's George Vorobiev with the Soviet embassy, isn't it?" He returned my smile and, giving me a "Well, I gave it a shot" look, proceeded with a normal conversation. I think he was pleased that I had done my homework and would be a worthy adversary.

Another Russian, also KGB, and also named George, was very pleasant and was, I think, none too proud of his country's political system. He never said so, of course, but he always had a skeptical demeanor when the subject arose. We spoke at the "Détente" tennis matches that we frequently engaged in and I invited him to a dinner party. He surprised me by accepting, bringing his "wife" who I think was just another agent playing his wife. She turned out to be ill-suited for the job and arrived with George in a very nervous, chain smoking state. I tried to calm her down, but I think she was convinced by her previous training that she might be abducted by these evil Americans. We got into a discussion of literature and she asked me about a book which I knew to be an anti-American diatribe written by a far left American author. She had obviously been programmed to embarrass me and waited for my response, fully expecting me to deny having read or even having heard of the book. Instead, I produced a copy of the book and offered to lend it to her with the admonition that it wasn't very good or very accurate. Totally taken aback by my offer, she shot a panicky look toward George and declined my proposal. We never saw her again. I suspect she was declared unsuitable for the job and sent back to Russia for reassignment. I actually felt sorry for her.

My association, bordering on friendship, with George led, a few months later, to a bizarre series of events that never quite reached fruition. My phone rang at 3 AM and I was shocked to hear George at the other end. He said, "Albert, this is George. I need help." My immediate thought was that I might have a defector on my hands, but George quickly dispelled that notion. He went on to explain that a delegation of Soviet VIPs had departed earlier in the Soviet AN-2 and the airplane was missing and presumably down somewhere between Vientiane and Sam Neua, the Communist Pathet Lao headquarters. George wanted me to use our C-47 to search for the missing AN-2, a very large, single engine biplane. Such a search would have us fly over Communist controlled territory and under normal circumstances would surely have resulted in our getting shot down. I told George that I would have to have absolute assurance that Pathet Lao gunners would be informed and would hold their fire. I also would insist that an officer from the Soviet embassy go along. George immediately agreed and said he would go along himself. He had obviously cleared this ahead of time with Moscow and whoever was missing in the AN-2 must have been important. I told George that I would have to clear it with my Ambassador but I would make arrangements for the flight immediately if the Ambassador approved. I called my boss and then Ambassador Whitehouse who was skeptical at first but saw a great opportunity for another move toward détente. Besides, Charlie Whitehouse had been a dive bomber (SBD) pilot in WWII and I think it appealed to his sense of adventure. As I was making final preparations to leave, however, the phone rang again. It was George. Another AN-2 had located the wreckage of the first and our assistance was no longer required. I was unable to get any details from George as to casualties or who the passengers were. He thanked me profusely for my willingness to help, and I expressed my condolences for any loss of his countrymen. So ended our search and rescue of the Soviets' mission. I was a little disappointed that we couldn't pull it off, but it was probably all for the best. There's always some S.O.B. who doesn't get the word and in this case it might have been one of the Communist gunners.

Things began to get a lot less friendly a short time later. It was 1975 and the United States' policy of disengagement began to be tested by the Communists. This time, with Congressional edicts forbidding our use of air power, the North Vietnamese finally found that they could succeed with blatant aggression. We looked at air reconnaissance photos of the Ho Chi Minh trail and observed that it had become in spots a 4-lane highway. These photos were clear proof that the Peace Accords were being violated, but I never saw a single one published in a U. S. newspaper. It was clear that our policy of disengagement had become a policy of abandonment. We were getting out and our allies were on their own. The Vietnamese attaché, a friend, approached me at a social function. He asked, "What is the U.S. doing to us? We agreed to take over combat operations but your President promised to give us the weapons we needed to do the job. Now our soldiers are going into combat with six bullets each. That's all we can give them. Our artillery pieces have two rounds a day to fire. What are you doing to us?" I could only mumble apologies for our policy and offer to help him and his family to escape from Laos if necessary. It was the only time in my life that I was ashamed of my country.

Once the North Vietnamese had field tested our resolve and found it lacking, they launched their full-scale, final offensive, secure in the knowledge that this time American air power would not intervene. The fall of Saigon left me profoundly depressed, but there was nothing I could do. Phnom Penh was the next domino to fall and it was clear that Vientiane would be next. With that in mind, I scheduled a meeting with the Search and Rescue people in Nakhon Phanom, Thailand to arrange for an emergency evacuation operation should one become necessary. The SAR forces were very helpful and I felt quite confident after our meeting that we would be able to pull off the operation if necessary. There would be no roof top helicopter evacuations, Saigon style, if we had to leave quickly. We supplied recent photos of landing sites and approach routes. A small disagreement over time of day to best launch an operation was settled and we left for home feeling prepared. Fortunately we never had to launch the operation.

While preparing for the worst we tried to keep other parts of our existence as normal as possible. This included the inevitable social gatherings. Our DAO people, along with a few chosen embassy civilians, were invited by a Lao general named Soutchai to visit his turf in Pakse, southern Laos. The occasion would include a tennis tournament, visits to local attractions and the usual sumptuous dining. We flew down in the C-47 and all went well, General Soutchai being a most gracious host. The following day, when I had expected to leave right after breakfast, General Soutchai announced a surprise for his guests. He would take us to visit the ruins of Wat Po, a Lao national treasure that was similar to the more famous Ankhor Wat ruins in Cambodia. The wives were delighted. I was worried. My first concern was how we were going to get there. Not to worry! Several helicopters suddenly appeared and we were instructed to board. Unfortunately the helicopters were ancient piston powered H-34s in combat configuration. Marion was seated on a canvas seat opposite the H-34's yawning open door. While this afforded an outstanding view of the terrain, I could see from Marion's expression that flying in combat helicopters was not her thing. I wondered how far the Lao pilots were removed from their last job as rice farmers and I hoped we had trained them well.

After we landed the wives happily inspected the ruins while I was observing that our area had M-16 equipped troops posted in what looked to me like a perimeter defense formation. I found General Soutchai and asked point blank, "General, is this a secure area?" He smiled the typically engaging Lao smile that informed me, without words, that the answer to my question was, "Hell, no!" I immediately began lobbying for a quick departure. The thought of getting Marion and the other wives engaged in a fire fight seemed a little more adventuresome an outing than we needed. We returned to the airport without incident and the Lao pilots did a fine job of terrain-hugging flying. The wives talked about their excursion for weeks and the trip to Pakse was deemed a success. I was glad we had done it but was even more glad that General Soutchai, who was one of the Royal Lao Army's best commanders, had supervised the planning. He was confident that the risks were minimal and I guess, as it turned out, he was right.

As time went on the Communists became more aggressive and brazen. Laos had been ruled for many years under a coalition government which was always one step away from anarchy. The Royalist faction in the coalition was preeminent while it had U.S. backing, but after Saigon and Phnom Penh fell, and American largesse was obviously in decline, the Lao recognized what they described as the "New Realities". That meant that the new big dog in town was the Communist Pathet Lao backed by the Soviet Union. It wasn't long before the American community began to feel the results. First came the inevitable demonstrations. It seems that no Communist takeover can ever begin without a demonstration by "students". We were no exception. On one occasion I went to the usual "Country Team" meeting at the embassy and found myself cornered there, along with the rest of the embassy staff, by a raucous mob shouting anti-American slogans. After a few hours the demonstrators, who were probably imported from out of town, grew tired of demonstrating and, in typical Lao fashion, just went home for a nap.

Unfortunately, the rabble-rousing soon took a more serious turn. In May of 1975 armed Pathet Lao troops took over the American compound which contained much highly classified information belonging to the DAO and the CIA. A lone Marine who happened to be in the DAO locked himself in the vaults and spent several days shredding documents while existing on a case of C-rations and a case of tuna that someone had left behind. Semper Fi!

Perhaps potentially more serious was the Pathet Lao decision to surround the American housing compound known as km6. The compound housed mostly U.S. Government civilian families and most of the occupants were women and children. It also was the location of the American School of Vientiane. The incarceration of American civilians was serious and made the front page of most U.S. newspapers. The communists probably got nervous, not wanting to twist the tiger's tail too much, and negotiated the civilians' release. The Americans were allowed to leave with only one suitcase, and all expensive articles, like cars, had to be abandoned to the communists who proved to be talented thieves. A few of our enterprising DAO officers managed to get into the compound, found some sugar and poured it into most gas tanks, leaving a very large junkyard for the Pathet Lao instead of a used car lot. Most of the school's records were left behind, creating some difficulty for David when we had to enroll him in school at our next assignment with no record of his 11th grade work.

While all this was going on the DAO was under new leadership. General Trefry had rotated and was replaced by General Roswell Round. General Trefry had introduced General Round at a party at our house. He had known General Round since their days at West Point and finished his introduction stating that we had "lucked out" in getting Ros Round as our new boss. He was right. When things got nasty just after General Round's arrival I silently worried that the new boss would be in over his head, not having had time to get his feet on the ground. Added to General Trefry's departure was Ambassador Whitehouse's appointment as Ambassador to Thailand, leaving the Lao embassy to a Chargé d' affaires. We had lost our two prime leaders at the same time, in a period of serious crisis, and I was concerned. I need not have worried. Ros Round was a complete change in personality from the George Patton replica that was Dick Trefry. Ros was more the George Marshall type and was completely unflappable in the Lao pressure cooker he had been thrown into. While much of the State Department staff was in a state of panic, Ros, who had cut his teeth with rioters years ago during the Washington D.C. racial riots, where he was the officer in charge, seemed quietly underwhelmed by the crisis. The Secretary of State, apparently displeased with the train of events in Laos, sent out his well known trouble-shooter, Phillip Habib, to examine the situation. I noticed that, after getting acclimated, Habib began dealing with General Round and the DAO to get things done.

As the situation in Laos grew uglier, it became obvious, painful as it was, that the Southeast Asian war was lost, that my many friends lost in combat had died in vain, and that my country was disgracing itself by abandoning its allies. I had a heavy heart, but there was much work to be done. Most of my daily effort was directed toward evacuation of Americans and a few endangered foreign U.S. employees. Most were evacuated on Royal Air Lao aircraft, primarily C-46s. The CIA Station Chief called for help in evacuating his people from locations in Laos that no longer had any kind of air service. Our ancient C-47 suddenly became indispensable. My first evacuation flight went to Ban Houei Sai, a city in northern Laos. Navigational aids in Laos had been managed by Air America, the CIA's private air force. But as the situation began to spiral out of control, Air America departed without a word, at least without a word to me. Since I was supposed to represent the U.S. in matters of air navigation, this left a decidedly bitter taste in my mouth. The navigational aid facilities were looted and within a few days were worthless. In any case, my flight to Ban Houei Sai and all subsequent flights were accomplished the old fashioned way--by reading VFR charts and navigating by pilotage and dead reckoning. It was ironic that the agency that most needed help from the Air Force was the CIA, whose people had left us without navigational aids. But there was no time for recriminations and we pressed on as best we could.

One of the largest contingents of Americans was in the panhandle city of Savannaket. The CIA Station Chief called, somewhat upset because of the large number of people involved. After some quick planning I decided that two C-47s would be needed. I was also concerned by the lack of current intelligence coming out of Savannaket. I did not expect that we would be welcomed with open arms by whomever was in charge at the Savannaket airport, but we had to give it a shot. I called on Bob Taylor to fly co-pilot since he was probably more familiar with the RLAF people at Savannaket than any of us. For the second aircraft we enlisted the support of a C-47 from our logistics base, DEPCHIEF at Udorn, Thailand.

It was late afternoon before we could get things organized, but we arrived in the Savannaket area at the same time as the second aircraft. As expected, we got no response when we tried to call the Savannaket control tower, so I told the second aircraft to hold while we landed to check out the situation. We landed without incident and taxied to the RLAF ramp to park. As we parked one of the RLAF pilots looked up at us, shaking his head in disbelief, as if to say, "What in the hell are you guys doing here?" I decided that things were quiet enough to risk landing the second aircraft and we did so.

Since the CIA had lost contact with their people, it was up to us to somehow find their leader and get the evacuees out to the airport as quickly as possible. The DEPCHIEF aircraft would take off as soon as they had a full load of people and we would collect the stragglers. The phones were out so our immediate problem was to borrow a vehicle from the RLAF to get into town and contact the CIA's leader at his home. The RLAF T-28 pilots knew us and were still friendly, but their vehicles were all out of gas since no supplies had reached them for some time.

The ever resourceful Bob Taylor noticed a fire engine parked at the fire station and we asked if it still had fuel. Our RLAF friends said that it probably did since it was rarely driven. So, with the RLAF pilots and our own DEPCHIEF people looking at us as if we had lost our marbles, we headed for the Pathet Lao controlled city in a bright red fire engine, dressed in our brightly colored flight suits adorned with American flag patches. Bob drove while I greeted passerby, including a few AK-47 armed Pathet Lao soldiers, by waving and ringing the bell. They all looked somewhat puzzled, but they all waved back.

We found the CIA's resident chief at home and he immediately started a recall to get everyone to the airport. I impressed on him the urgency of the situation since it would soon be dark and there would be no runway lights. He readily agreed to use their own vehicles rather than attempt to load people into our "camouflaged" fire engine. When Bob and I returned to the fire engine we noticed a group of young Lao civilians a block away looking suspiciously at the fire truck. Ominously, they didn't return my wave. Bob and I decided it was time to get out of town.

Back at the airport, relieved Americans were arriving in groups and we soon had the DEPCHIEF C-47 airborne, fully loaded, on its way to Udorn. We took a head count for our aircraft and there was one person missing, the inevitable straggler, who was supposedly on his way. It was now getting dark and I waited until the last possible minute before saying that I was sorry, but if we didn't leave now none of us might get off. As I was starting the engines we noticed a cloud of dust coming up the dirt road toward the airplane. Sure enough, it was our straggler who had finally got his wife and possessions together. By the time we got him on board it was pitch dark. We were familiar enough with the airport that I could taxi and take off just using the landing lights, so we pressed on. As I started to taxi, one of the two landing lights burned out! If the other decided to burn out as well, we would have been out of business. Fortunately it did its job and after a somewhat shaky takeoff, keeping the offset landing light on the runway centerline, we were safely on our way to Udorn.

Once at Udorn we unloaded our passengers and prepared to fly back to Vientiane. Just before I was able to start the engines, a Royal Thai Air Force jeep parked in front of us and trained its quad .50 caliber machine guns on us. Now, for many years past we had operated our C-47s across the Thai border as if the border didn't exist. Now our good friends, the Thais, suddenly wanted all kinds of country clearances and documents that we didn't have and never had. It seems the Thais had figured out that we would soon be abandoning them also and decided to put their relationship with the U.S. on a more formal basis. I was furious because I thought that our airplane might be sorely needed if order continued to break down in Laos. But my verbal eruption had little effect on the Thai captain who was detaining us--and he had the .50 calibers. We were escorted to quarters, and though it was all basically friendly, we were, in effect, under house arrest. I called Marion, who was quite concerned about our absence, and assured her we would be home the next day. Bob and I adjourned to the club and had several drinks before dinner.

The next day I put on my formal Air Attaché personality and went after the Thai captain who had apparently been assigned as our watch dog. I demanded, in my best full colonel shout, to speak to the Thai Air Force Chief of Staff. I then flashed my black diplomatic passport, informed the captain that detaining a diplomatic vehicle was technically an act of war, and that I would press my Ambassador to forward a formal diplomatic protest from the U.S. Government to the Government of Thailand over this very serious international incident which he, the captain, was helping to perpetuate. The captain, by this time was on the verge of tears and made several phone calls in the Thai language while I waited impatiently pacing the room. Within minutes I was driven to our aircraft, the machine gun-bearing jeep was gone, and we were cleared to fly to Vientiane, leaving a very worried Thai captain on the ramp.

When we returned to Vientiane we found widespread chaos. The Pathet Lao had taken over the governmental ministries and were attempting to assert themselves by arresting key Royalist leaders. The RLAF Chief of Staff was now General Bouathong who had earlier replaced General Sourith. Bouathong was far more affable than Sourith. He was cooperative and generally easy for us to work with. I felt that we had an obligation to him and invited him to my office to suggest that he leave the country because I was sure he was in danger. He demurred, saying that he believed there would be a "Lao Solution" to the current difficulties and that he was in no danger. We shook hands and I told him to call me if he changed his mind.

Within a few days he did indeed change his mind. I was sitting in our living room late at night during a driving rainstorm when Bouathong appeared at my front door, having driven a motorcycle through the storm to contact me. He said that he was being threatened and feared for himself and his family. I suggested that he leave everything and get across the Mekong into Thailand as soon as possible. He did so the following day, impersonating a fisherman taking his family to a wedding in order to get through the Pathet Lao guards. I made arrangements with the CIA, who owed me a few, to meet the family and find them shelter in Thailand. This was taken care of and Bob Taylor and I performed a late night burglary of the Bouathong residence, collecting anything we could find of value. We brought the stolen objects to my house, loaded them on the C-47 and flew them to Udorn the next day. Our loot included two elephant tusks which proved to be very heavy but very valuable. Bouathong told me that his family lived off the proceeds of the ivory for months. Complicating our "Asian Wetback" operation was Mrs. Bouathong's health. Whether brought about by stress or something else, she became very ill. Because of her illegal status we were reluctant to take her to a Thai hospital so I had to resort to the old fighter pilot network. An old buddy from Vietnam, Bill Mol, was now the F-4 Wing Commander at Udorn. He listened to my story about the cross-river escape, the burglary and the rest, chuckled and said, "Damn, Al, this sounds like Terry and the Pirates!" He then picked up the phone, called his base hospital commander and told him to treat a Lao lady patient who would be arriving, and treat her with no questions asked. Since Bill had no authority to treat a Lao civilian, especially one who was part of a politically sensitive cross border escape, I was very grateful to him. In fact, I had no authority to arrange for the escape of a Lao general either. But knowing full well that the State Department would dither until it was too late, I just did it. We later got the Bouathong family into the Southeast Asia refugee program and, sponsored by Marion's sister's church, had them settled safely in the U.S.

While on the subject of refugees, our cook, Giu, came to me one evening in tears. While he had spent his entire life in Laos, he was actually ethnic Vietnamese and was now in danger of being drafted into the North Vietnamese army! To make a long story short, I helped Giu get his family across the Mekong where they kept a low profile until we could get the family into the Vietnamese refugee program. Giu's family was an immigrants' success story. Giu got a sponsor with a little help from us, worked two jobs, and put his five kids through college. They are all very productive members of American society today, the kind of immigrants that the country needs and wants. General Bouathong, on the other hand, had difficulty adjusting to his loss of status in coming to the U.S. He eventually moved to the West Coast where I lost touch with him. There is little doubt, however, that we saved his life. As Ambassador Whitehouse recounts in his Memoir (page 157), "It is particularly poignant that these senior officials and officers who chose to remain in an effort to ameliorate the lot of the Lao people were dispatched to the notorious 'seminars' in the jungle from which few returned. As is well known, the King and Crown Prince and every Lao General were all killed by the Communists."

My primary refugee concern was, of course, my family. Steve had gone off to college, Mary Round and the army attachés wife, Jackie Wilson, had no accompanying children, so we had only five to worry about. We had previously evacuated many others using the C-47. It had been decided that the families of higher ranking people would be last to leave in order to avoid possible panic. That was well and good, but the streets of Vientiane were now crowded with Pathet Lao soldiers, all of whom looked to be 14 years old. Since there are few things more dangerous than a teen-ager with an automatic weapon, I decided that it was time for the high ranking families to leave. General Round agreed and we decided that the next day would be appropriate. Marion had been oblivious to the near anarchy going on around her and seemed to think that her life in the diplomatic community would resume shortly. Far from being panicked, she seemed only annoyed that she could no longer get cocktail party snacks at the commissary, which had been looted by the Communists. In fact, on the day we had decided on her departure, she was happily planning a farewell party for two assistant attachés. But I had to call her to announce that the guests of honor had just left the country on our aircraft. Undeterred, Marion simply changed the affair from a dinner party to a cocktail party to which anyone remaining was invited. I informed Marion during the cocktail party that she would be leaving in the morning. She was upset by the short notice to pack, but the party continued, attended by nearly all males since almost all wives had already gone.

A peculiarity of the "Fall of Vientiane" was the Lao propensity for observing routine. Part of the routine at the Vientiane Airport was the daily C-47 courier run to Udorn. It arrived and departed the same time every day, using either our aircraft or one from DEPCHIEF. We were apprehensive when the Pathet Lao installed .23 MM anti-aircraft guns at the ends of the runway, but we decided to run the courier anyway to see what would happen. As we expected, nothing happened. The courier was part of Lao life, so it was allowed to continue. This went on for months.

The day after our last cocktail party we packed a borrowed van with the boys' and Marion's treasured possessions. I briefed Marion, David and Douglas that we might be stopped by Pathet Lao guards, and they might decide to confiscate, i.e. steal, everything in the van. There had been incidents of this kind of behavior in the past. The family was to let me do the talking and no arguments with the guards. If they confiscated the van, so be it. As luck would have it, the single guard we encountered simply waved us through to the C-47, despite some attractive items like Steven's radio-controlled model airplanes which Dave tossed in the van at the last minute. I flew the C-47 to Udorn where Bill Mol had promised to take care of the evacuated wives. He was as good as his word, putting the ladies up in vacant aircrew trailers which were air conditioned and each provisioned with a bottle of scotch. Once the families were settled I flew back to Vientiane. Bob Taylor, having evacuated his family, moved into my quarters which were now missing a cook since Giu and his family were also across the Mekong. We still had our houseboy who was a lousy cook but considerably better than Bob or I.

We went back to work with the understanding that we, the DAO staff, would preside over the departure of any remaining Americans and provide any intelligence that we could. We expected that the U.S. would break diplomatic relations with Laos and that we would all be unceremoniously kicked out of the country. It never happened. Apparently the Lao Communists decided that it was in their best interest to maintain some sort of relationship with the U.S. Similarly, our leaders in Washington decided that it was also in our best interests to keep a presence there for intelligence purposes. It led to some interesting events.

One of those events involved the Lao Air Force changing sides. General Round came into my office one morning and announced that the new Lao Minister of Defense, a hard line Communist, had requested a meeting with us. We were puzzled, but could hardly turn down this opportunity to meet with one of the new government's most influential leaders. After the standard exchange of pleasantries, not always a given when dealing with Communists, we got down to business. The Defense Minister had astutely observed that he had just inherited an Air Force. Now he had to find a source of supply for spare parts and a pathway for changing over the existing Air Force to Communist command. I suspect he was saying to himself, "The Americans are suckers. They just might go for it." Anyway, he spent considerable time acting as though there would be a simple change of command ceremony and, VOILA!, the U.S. continues to foot the bill for an Air Force that just happens to be under new management. The conversation reached the height of inanity when he complained that some of his fleet was getting up in years and we might begin to think about shipping him some new models

Already stifling laughter, I was tempted to ask him in my most sincere voice whether he would prefer F-15s or F-16s, our two most modern aircraft at the time. I restrained myself and eventually we took our leave, Ros Round having assured the Defense Minister that we would pass on his requests to our higher headquarters. Outside in our car we reviewed what had just transpired. The Defense Minister spoke no English, or so we had been told, so the entire session had been in French. Ros and I agreed that nothing had been lost to us in translation and that this character was seriously suggesting that the U.S. might support the operation of a Communist Air Force. We chuckled most of the way back to the office, but dutifully produced an Intelligence Report on the interview. In fact, while the meeting had all the attributes of a farce, it was one of the first indications that Laos, unlike the other Southeast Asian "Dominoes", would maintain friendly, if frigid, relations with the U.S. in the future. That, in fact, is how it worked out.

Our military contingent in Laos was rapidly shrinking. General Round was forced by administrative demands to work primarily at DEPCHIEF at Udorn. The few military officers remaining moved into the vacated CIA compound near the embassy. The CIA's building was concrete, windowless and generally much more secure than any other office space in town. The "student" rioters beat on the door occasionally but were easily discouraged by the building's fortress-like construction.

Sitting at my desk one morning, I was amazed to hear the phone ring. The U.S. switchboard had been taken over weeks ago by the rioters and our phones had not worked since. I picked up the receiver cautiously, answering, "Colonel DeGroote". From the other end came, "Colonel DeGroote, this is Colonel Harwood from Headquarters Command in Washington. I see that you're rotating soon, and I was wondering if you'd be interested in becoming the Vice Commander of Bolling AFB." Still amazed by the operating telephone, I replied, "My friend, if you can get me out of here in one piece, I'll take any assignment you can find. And by the way, how in the world did you get through on the phone?" Colonel Harwood had been unaware of the unpleasantness going on in Laos and had simply dialed the "Autovon" number for Vientiane. The rioters, being unfamiliar with the equipment, had evidently overlooked the automatic circuits and those automated lines were working just fine. It was thus that I learned of my next assignment and serendipitously discovered that we could still, for a while at least, communicate with the outside world.

We were extremely busy trying to monitor and perhaps influence what was literally the loss of a country from the ranks of the free world. I had no time for personal problems, including the shipping of my household goods to somewhere outside the country. I somehow arranged for an itinerant Frenchman who claimed to be in the household goods shipping business to pick up our things. He arrived, unannounced, early one morning as I was leaving for work. I told him that I had no time to help him and that he was on his own. He seemed to appreciate that I spoke to him in French, especially since he seemed to have no knowledge of English. But later in the day, I happened to drive by the Embassy's storage area and noticed my possessions strewn about on a dirt field out in the open. I decided that I would never see our things again and got back to work. I was later to be quite surprised at the fate of our shipment.

Our shrinking group of military people continued to get smaller and I found at the Country Team meeting one morning that my own departure was imminent. "Roger", one of the last members of the CIA's once extensive empire in Laos greeted me with a knowing smile.

"Have you read the morning paper, Sunshine?", he asked brightly, tossing the local English language journal across the table to me.

"You're front page news". Sure enough, there on the front page was an old photo of me and General Bouathong with an accompanying article about the General's hair-breadth escape from Laos and what a great help his friend Colonel DeGroote had been in making that escape possible. After watching me squirm as I read the article, Roger asked, "When are you leaving?" I opined that this afternoon seemed appropriate to me. And so, after gathering a few personal items from my house, I paid off what was left of our household staff and flew south to Udorn.

That was not quite to be my last day in Laos. General Round decided that it might be amusing to tweak the Soviets' nose one more time before we left for good. The Russians had, after all, pretty much called the shots in forcing us down to a single military attaché in country. For a time we had only a young Captain named Don Loranger in Laos. Don, observing that all U.S. military had departed from Vietnam, Cambodia and now Laos, began signing his teletyped messages as "CINCSEA", i.e. Commander -in-Chief Southeast Asia. We told Don that we found the affectation unbecoming so he desisted. But July 4th was coming and the American Chargé had elected to have the traditional national day party at the Residence despite the atmosphere of defeat that hung over the small American group that remained in Laos. The politicians may have lost the war for us, but we were still the United States of America! General Round told me of his plan and I thought it was a great idea. We'd fly in on the courier schedule, stay over on the 4th and fly back on the 5th after surprising the Russians at the party. It worked like a charm! Ros and I stood in the reception line, resplendent in our formal white uniforms, smiling confidently at the dumbfounded Russians, who all had the same comment, a stammering, "We didn't expect to see you here". My retort was, "Why not, it's our national day, isn't it?"

We spent the night at the Residence and headed for the airport in the morning. On the way we had a radio report from one of our friendly agents that a group of rioters was gathering at the airport and might have evil designs on our trusty C-47. We told the driver to speed it up and I jumped into the cockpit of the airplane which my co-pilot had already pre-flighted. We were airborne in record time and my co-pilot opined that since I was probably not the most popular colonel in Laos among the rioters it might have been smarter for me not to have re-entered the country. He was, of course, correct, but if I had it to do over again, I'd do the same thing. The expression on Colonel Tzarkov's face had made it all worthwhile.

General Round must have had a few second thoughts about our little adventure since he said he didn't want any more flights into Laos without his specific approval. I thought that reasonable since I had no further desire to push my luck anyway. Fate, however, had other ideas. I was called by one of the Foreign Service Officers who was still on duty at the Embassy. It seems that an American merchant of some sort had chosen not to be evacuated. He had a

Lao wife and planned to stay indefinitely. Unfortunately he was shot in the stomach, perhaps in a simple robbery by a common criminal. Whatever the circumstances, his wound became infected and the embassy people told me it that unless he received proper medical treatment he would die.

General Round was taking care of business in Bangkok and even though we had arranged for communications beforehand I was unable to contact him. I found myself in the position of either countermanding his direct order or letting the man die. Obviously there was no choice. The Embassy people assured me that the Pathet Lao had approved the humanitarian flight with the restriction, for some unknown reason, that we not use a helicopter. So, with a volunteer doctor and nurse on board, I flew for my last time into Vientiane. We flew the patient, who looked to be at death's door, to Udorn where he was transferred to a C-130 bound for Clark Air Base in the Philippines where a modern hospital was available. Sadly, despite our efforts, he died en route to Clark.

That was my last C-47 flight and it turned out to be my last flight ever as pilot in command of an Air Force aircraft. Ros Round agreed with my overriding decision to make the mercy flight and we both returned to our job of winding down our business with the Southeast Asia war. There was some irony in the fact that, having spent so much of my life as a fighter pilot, I would end my Air Force flying career on a humanitarian mission piloting a WWII transport. But maybe it was a good thing--if I hadn't been able to fly the venerable "Gooney Bird", I would have missed something in the aviator's world that I could never have replaced. And the attempt to save a man's life on my final flight, albeit a failed attempt, made that last flight more meaningful.

Bolling Air Force Base

We left Udorn almost reluctantly because, although we looked forward to seeing the U.S.A. again, Laos had been perhaps the most interesting of my Air Force Assignments, aside from Vietnam in which the family didn't directly participate. As we flew toward the U.S. I looked at Marion and the two boys and decided that Laos may have been a little too interesting. It all worked out well and it was for David and Douglas a grand adventure that would last them a lifetime. But things could have gone seriously wrong and I could have put my family in danger. I quietly resolved to be smarter in the future.

We elected to fly home by way of Europe since Laos is about the same distance from the East Coast either direction. Besides, we could arrange a short layover in London allowing us to get re-acquainted with some of our old British friends, especially Tim and Malise Chaney, our erstwhile next door neighbors. We enjoyed wandering about our old neighborhood, had a short but pleasant visit with the Chaneys, and reminisced about what had been a very pleasant four year period of our lives.

As pleasant as London was, we were understandably anxious to return to our families in the U.S. and get on with our new life in Washington. We wanted to catch up on Steven's activities as well. Steve had planned to return to Laos between semesters at Wilkes College, but his entry back into the country had been disallowed by the State Department because of the tense political situation there. We had a pleasant 747 flight back to the U.S., made all the more pleasant by the airline's placing us in first class because of an overbooked cabin class section.

We stayed at Marion's twin sister's home when we arrived. Ruth and her husband, Don, had graciously provided a second home for Steve while we were in Laos, and even provided our newest family member, Tiki, with kennel space. Tiki was the more troublesome guest since he didn't get along with the Dickson's two schnauzers.

Speaking of trouble, Tiki's story was trouble itself! My contribution to the care and feeding of a dog was supposed to have been zero. It was Steve's dog, but it would be cared for by the household staff, and would be passed on to my replacement as part of the house. So, as events transpired, Steve left for college, the servants disappeared into the refugee program, Marion, David and Douglas were evacuated to Udorn and guess who became, by default, the proud owner of a cocker spaniel? I took care of him as best I could, but had very few hours to devote to his well-being. Meanwhile, Steve's letters to Marion pleaded that we somehow get Tiki out of Laos if we could rescue nothing else. I noted, with some minor resentment, that there were no pleadings to make sure that dear old Dad got out in one piece. Steve feared, with some justification, that Tiki, left to his own devices, might end up in a Lao stew-pot. That didn't seem a likely fate for Dad--too tough.

Anyway, while we were still operating the C-47 out of Vientiane, I scheduled myself for a trip to Bangkok with a cargo stop at Udorn. As I opened the door to load the piece of cargo a sharp-eyed Air Force loadmaster noticed Tiki on his leash tied in the rear of the airplane. The loadmaster lectured me officiously saying, "Colonel, you can't transport a dog in an Air Force aircraft". After what we had been going through in Vientiane I was in no mood for lectures about regulations from behind-the-lines bureaucrats. I smiled and said, "Sarge, that's not a dog--it's a Lao pig and they're authorized" The sergeant looked puzzled as I closed the door, but he didn't argue. We continued on to Bangkok where I put Tiki in the hands of a trusted employee there to be sent via PanAm to Philadelphia. I don't remember how much Pan Am charged to ship a cocker spaniel half-way around the world, but it was considerable. My "free" dog by now had the price tag of a pedigreed show dog.

Steve was notified of Tiki's arrival by people at Philadelphia Airport and my sister Dolores volunteered to take him to pick up the dog. Dolores, who had also arranged for a summer job for Steve, went way beyond her obligations to family in this case. For starters, she was driving her spotless new Cadillac to pick up a dog that had been in a cage for days, was filthy and smelled more like a skunk than a dog. But Dolores graciously said that seeing the reunion of

Steve and Tiki, who hadn't seen Steve for over a year, made it all worthwhile. By the time Marion and I arrived Tiki had pretty much established himself as the dominant dog in Ruth and Don's household and Steve had taught him, old dog that he was, a series of new tricks. The Tiki story would continue into our days in Washington and beyond.

More important than our dog problems were those concerning the people whom we had helped to escape from Laos. Ruth and Don had put forth an enormous effort to have their church act as sponsor for General Bouathong and his family. They also sponsored a luncheon with some of my family attending. Since Bouathong felt more comfortable speaking French, the French speakers in my family helped put him at ease. I conversed with him in French, but I tried to steer him toward English since it was vital that he improve his English in order to get a decent job. I had only limited success with his re-settlement. We established contact with an Army friend from Laos who had retired and was running a construction company in Virginia and was interested in hiring Lao refugees. Bouathong worked for him for a while but eventually moved to a Lao community on the West Coast where I finally lost contact with him. Before he departed for the West Coast, I was called by a contact at the Unconventional Warfare Center at Hurlburt Field, Florida. They wanted to have General Bouathong speak to a class about the unconventional air war in Laos. He was delighted to do so, and the trip to Hurlburt was quite successful. But there was a major downside. When Bouathong returned he called to thank me for arranging the trip. He said that it "made him feel like a general again". I had been endeavoring to make him stop feeling like a general so he could compete in the American labor market where commanding generals of unconventional air forces weren't in great demand. In retrospect, while I thought the trip to Hurlburt would be good for his self-esteem, it undoubtedly set back his adjustment period and was probably a mistake.

We had the opposite experience with our Lao cook, Giu. Giu called on the very day we arrived at Ruth's home to tell us that he was at the refugee re-settlement center in Indiantown Gap and that he already had a sponsor in Texas. I've already discussed the American success story that was Giu and his family. To this day we still get a phone call from Giu every Christmas to thank us once again for getting him out of Laos and into the U.S.

It was time to head south for our new life in the nation's capitol. We bought a new dark green Plymouth to replace our light green Oldsmobile that I had sold in Bangkok and set out for Bolling. We were assigned base quarters that were Spartan but adequate. Our household goods, which I had last seen on the vacant lot in Vientiane, and which I fully expected would be lost or destroyed, arrived on time and without a scratch. I mouthed a silent thank you to the itinerant Frenchman who had done the last-minute packing and shipping job in Vientiane.

We had some personal adjustments to make, first among them being the task of getting the boys in school. Steve had done well in his first year at Wilkes College in Pennsylvania, but he was less than thrilled with the liberal arts courses he had taken. That probably was my fault, and inevitably was related to flying airplanes.

Steve's last year of high school was at the American School of Vientiane, and his choice of Wilkes was mostly because the school would be close to family. While he was still in Laos I gave him a Christmas gift of flying lessons through first solo. It happened that the embassy in Vientiane had a one-airplane flying club with a Cessna 150, so I updated my flight instructor's certificate and taught Steve to fly. His first solo was made memorable by being in an exotic location, but also by his being cut out of the pattern by a Russian airliner.

In any case, when the subject of college and future employment again arose, Steve opined that he thought he would like to fly for a living. I suggested that he go to Florida to check out Embry-Riddle Aeronautical University. He did so and returned with a big smile on his face. So Steve was off to begin a new college curriculum and to lay the ground work for his future as a professional pilot.

Dave had a different problem. His 11th grade scholastic records had been left in the American School, Vientiane when the Pathet Lao took over the compound at km6. As far as the school authorities were concerned Dave had not completed 11th grade.

The school system we were dealing with was a private institution, well known in Washington, Saint Stephen's School for Boys. We had been warned early that the Washington D.C. schools were irredeemably bad and that virtually everyone at Bolling sent their children to private schools. Saint Steven's was impressive. Unfortunately, it was also very expensive. To illustrate just how expensive: when Dave later went to college at Penn State, my tuition bills for him actually went down.

But the immediate problem was getting Dave's 11th grade work recognized. While I had no patience with private school administrators, Marion did and successfully charmed them into allowing Dave to take an equivalency exam to cover his 11th grade work. Doug had a similar problem, but the administrators didn't seem to be worried about the younger grade school kids. I worried about putting food on the table since we had one son in an expensive Air University which included flight training, and two others going to a school that cost more than college. The problem for all military people in Washington with kids stemmed from the D.C. school system, which we supported with our taxes but was totally useless. I understood at the time that the system cost more in terms of dollars per student than any other school system in the nation, but had the worst scholastic achievement record in the country. I understand it is the same today--a national disgrace!

Despite these little problems, I managed to go to work in my new capacity as Vice Wing Commander of Bolling AFB. My boss was Colonel Arch Murphy, a slightly rotund, cheerful guy with a very good mind and a penchant for hands-on management. I liked him immediately. Arch had until recently held my job and was now the Base and Wing Commander. It was evident that I would be groomed to follow the same path. While I should have been flattered, I wasn't sure that I was totally thrilled with my new career path. This was my first non-flying Air Force assignment and I was certain of one thing--I would miss not being in an Air Force cockpit--ever again! I had flown, as a passenger, into Bolling many years before in a C-124 while a young aviation cadet. Now the runways were gone and in their place were 1,350 family housing units, filled with 1,350 families, all with problems that would be, at least partially, mine to solve. But I soon got caught up in Arch's enthusiasm as we raced from one crisis to another. I had to admit to myself that there was never a dull moment and that no two days were alike. I had been reminded many times during my recent career that bird colonels are paid too much to do nothing but drive airplanes, so I had to accept that fact of life. But since my entire salary seemed to be going to educational institutions, I wasn't sure I accepted the main premise that I was being paid too much

One of my early tasks was to act as escort for a newly appointed Undersecretary of the Air Force. Having briefed a newly appointed Undersecretary of the Navy during my CINCLANT tour I felt well qualified to take on this job. At least I wouldn't have to explain what the Antilles were! The new Undersecretary was a very nice guy who seemed very appreciative of my showing him a little of Air Force life. He was a technocrat with a PHD in some exotic science and, surprisingly, no military experience at all. Marion and I escorted him and his wife, also very pleasant, around the base and its facilities. I decided to take them to dinner at the base dining hall to give him a feel for how the troops were fed. We had an excellent dining facility and I would be proud to show it to them. I'm sure he was expecting dinner served on a metal tray with ice cream piled on top of mashed potatoes. He and I were both in for a shock.

It so happened, purely by accident, that a special occasion was scheduled at the dining hall. The United States Air Force Band, a highly professional unit that played for White House functions and many other prestigious affairs in Washington was a tenant on Bolling. As a treat for the Airmen the band's violin group, the "Strolling Strings" would, from time to time, play beautiful music while strolling among the dining hall tables. Not to be outdone, the dining hall cooks put linens on the candle-lit tables and served the very best cuts, like prime rib, from their larders. Needless to say, the new Undersecretary was impressed. I was impressed! I was left with two tasks: First I had to explain to the new Undersecretary that we didn't do this every day, and second I had to convince him that I had not set this up solely for his benefit.

We had a few laughs about the coincidences of dinner and adjourned to my quarters for coffee. There, he somewhat sheepishly advised me that he was going to work for the first time in the Pentagon on Monday without the faintest idea of what the military ranks were. He literally did not know how to differentiate a sergeant from a general. I told him that, yes, that could be embarrassing and I gave him my old dog-eared copy of "The Air Officer's Guide" which had full color pictures of all uniforms for him to study. He was very appreciative and promised to study it carefully over the weekend. He must have learned his new job well since he later became Air Force Secretary and was well thought of during his tenure. Thus ended, thankfully, my duties as mentor to various Undersecretary appointees of the various Services.

My encounter with the Undersecretary had political implications, of course, but that was to be expected. Bolling was one of the oldest bases in the Air Force, and probably the most politically sensitive. Jimmie Carter, for example, liked to use the Officers' Club for social events and was a frequent caller. We had Senators and Congressmen on the base, usually to make use of the Officers' Club dining facilities, on a daily basis. Fortunately, I had a gem of a Club Officer in place to ease the burden. Arch Murphy had told me when I arrived that the Officers' Club was one thing I would never have to worry about because it was being run by a fast-moving Major named Chuck Walter. Arch was right! Chuck had an amazing ability to anticipate problems and he almost always told me about a problem he had just solved rather than one that I needed to solve. He was also a master at schmoozing the politicians including a few with monumental egos. Chuck eventually was promoted to full colonel, a rarity among club officers, and the advancement was richly deserved.

Internal Air Force politics were also in play mainly because tenants in our base family quarters included forty generals. The generals usually stayed out of my way since many of them had been Base Commanders themselves and understood the problems. The forty generals' wives, however, had no such inhibitions and were not the least bit hesitant to call the Base Commander to solve the smallest of problems. Fortunately, I had time to learn from Arch Murphy before, inevitably, I became the Base Commander myself.

I had never considered myself much of a diplomat when in the role of Air Attaché at the Embassy in Laos, and I likewise didn't think I was much of a politician in the Washington milieu. Fortunately, I had Marion. She had been the best of the diplomatic wives in Vientiane and she quickly became recognized as the best Commander's wife in the D.C. area. She not only did outstanding work on volunteer jobs like running Family Services, but she also attracted other volunteers by always seeming to love the work. In fact, she did love it! To sum up Marion's contribution as "Mrs. Base Commander" I'll relate one short story. I was in the Officers' Club one evening making certain that an art show we had sponsored was going o.k. when I struck up a conversation with one of the attendees. She eventually asked, "What do you do here at Bolling, colonel?" Puffing up my chest ever so slightly, I replied, "Why, I'm the Base Commander here." She brightened up immediately, saying with a broad smile, "Well, you must be Marion DeGroote's husband!" I exhaled my puffed up pomposity and mumbled, "Yeah, that's right." It became clear to me where the power lay in the governance of Bolling Air Force Base.

One of the things that kept life at Bolling interesting was that we met interesting, accomplished people almost daily. I've never been a celebrity watcher, but the job at Bolling and my subsequent years in corporate aviation forced me into contact with them whether I liked it or not. I not only was unimpressed by celebrity status, I made a conscious effort to avoid famous people because I found their need for security and other special treatment a bore. But there was one notable exception.

One afternoon I received a call from my boss, Major General Fred Starr. General Starr and I got along well. We had a mutual trust and I never hesitated to discuss my problems with him. So I was happy to accept his invitation to discuss one of those problems with a general at the Pentagon. He picked me up in his staff car and told me we'd be discussing planned renovations to senior officer housing at Bolling with a General Stafford. I was very familiar with the project and happy to discuss it with anyone. But the general's name rang a bell. "That's not Tom Stafford the astronaut is it, boss?" I asked. General Starr confirmed that it was indeed. And from the time that I was introduced to Tom Stafford in his office until we left an hour or so later, I felt, for the only time in my life like a star-struck teen-ager. All I could think of was, "This guy's flown to the moon!" I covered the details of the housing project but I kept wanting to say, "I'll take care of this stuff--let's talk about flying to the moon and back!" Fortunately, I maintained my decorum but I've always regretted not finding a way to steer the conversation, for a while at least, to space flight.

Meanwhile, life went on at a hectic pace, and while I sometimes felt like a prisoner on my own base, I did enjoy the job. A Base Commander has a lot of power and the authority to spend money to fix problems. It was very satisfying to see projects completed that made life easier, especially for the enlisted troops whose meager pay didn't allow for much high living off base in Washington.

Our family life was mostly excellent. Steve was happy at Embry-Riddle, Dave graduated from Saint Steven's and enrolled at Penn State, and Doug was doing well also at Saint Steven's. We were broke, but the boys were getting educated.

In the category of "The Air Force takes care of its own", was an incident involving Dave and his move to Penn State. Dave borrowed the family car to transport some things from Bolling to his Penn State dormitory. The car was registered in Pennsylvania but had not had a current state inspection since we had not been in the state recently. A sharp-eyed Pennsylvania policeman ticketed the car and we had to pay a fairly substantial fine. I was ready to pay the fine, but Marion was indignant and composed a letter in which she railed against the unfairness of fining people who were serving their country just because their car was out of state. I chuckled and wished her luck in appealing to a state judge. But a few weeks later we received a letter with our check enclosed. The letter excused our violation and was signed:

The Air Force does indeed take care of its own.

No description of our adventures would be complete without the inevitable close call involving Tiki. Well established as the family pet by now, Tiki still had the stray's instincts for freedom. One day, completely unnoticed, he slipped out the door, made his way to the main gate, and proceeded to stroll down the speedway that was Interstate 295. It so happened that the Chief of Security for the Air Force, Major General Tom Sadler, was driving on I-295 and noticed a handsome cocker spaniel nonchalantly walking ahead with cars and trucks narrowly missing him. General Sadler was one of my 40 general officer tenants on Bolling and he liked dogs. He stopped on the interstate, scooped up Tiki and returned to Bolling where he left the dog with the Security Police who in turn placed him in a kennel. Tiki was wearing his dog tag and the S. P.s were able to trace his owner. Marion was still unaware that Tiki was out of the house and had to be convinced by the police that they had her dog. She retrieved a guilty looking Tiki who had once again been saved by his good looks.

Steve had been enjoying his work at Embry-Riddle where he had landed a part time job in the weather station. It didn't pay much but he learned a lot about weather. While his flight training was going generally well, he called just before summer break to complain that he was having some minor problems with instrument flying. That provided the excuse I needed to go to the local private airport, Woodbridge, and get checked out in a Piper Cherokee. I planned to give Steve some dual instruction on instrument flying while he was home on summer break. We flew together whenever I could break loose from the problems of Bolling Air Force Base, and I also worked with Steve on his academics. This required me to re-familiarize myself with basic aerodynamics, weather, and some of the more mundane subjects like Federal Air Regulations. As I dug deeper into my airmanship training memory bank, I slowly came to a realization that was to mark a major turning point in my life. It occurred to me that I was enjoying this re-exposure to my previous life and that I very much missed my first professional love, flying airplanes. I quietly sent away for a study guide for the FAA Airline Transport Pilot rating and looked into the rules for in-service G.I. Bill flight training for the ATP rating. For the first time in a quarter century I was seriously considering leaving the Air Force.

Time went by, Steve returned to Embry-Riddle, having pretty well mastered the art of flying basic instruments I thought, and I began to spend many hours mastering the ATP study guide. I took and passed the written exam and entered the ATP flight training course offered by the operator at Woodbridge. After my years flying Air Force equipment, flying the exercises required for the ATP in a light twin, a Piper Aztec, presented no serious challenge, but I <u>was</u> rusty. The old cliché about it being just like riding a bike doesn't apply to airplanes. To fly an airplane at a professional level requires constant practice. In any case, I enjoyed the course and took my check ride with an FAA examiner. I got a taste of how things had changed in civil aviation when the examiner turned out to be a young lady. Once I recovered from my culture shock we flew my check ride and I enjoyed the experience.

With my new ATP in hand I had a decision to make. My tour as Base Commander would soon end and it seemed to me that the Air Force would probably look at me as a prime candidate to fill a staff job at the Pentagon. It would, after all, make a great deal of economic sense since there would be no moving expenses involved. I was already living in base quarters and would simply move to a new office. The prospect left me completely cold. My last pure staff job was at CINCLANT and I remembered well that I was very often bored to tears. A Pentagon tour would probably be good for my career, but it would also separate me from flying again, this time probably forever.

Once again in my life the call of the wild blue tugged me in a direction that pure logic would have dictated that I probably should not have followed. I decided to retire. My boss, General Starr, was upset when I called him since he, naturally, didn't want to lose one of his experienced base commanders. He happened to be at the brigadier general promotion board when I called and he told me that I was his best hope of getting one of his people promoted. I was flattered but unconvinced. Besides, the thought of roaming the corridors of the Pentagon wearing stars instead of eagles didn't make me any more thrilled with the prospect. In any case I thought my chances of being promoted further were slim to none and possible advancement in rank just didn't enter into my calculations.

I had sent out a few tentative feelers for possible employment in corporate aviation during the past two or three months and had been somewhat surprised to get a phone call, very shortly thereafter, from the president of a small energy company in New Jersey. He was a businessman pilot and was interested in having his Beech Kingair professionally operated. He invited Marion and me to fly to Florida with him and his wife for a weekend. We did so, and I was hooked! While Marion had reservations, I was delighted by the prospect of operating a shiny, new Kingair and made the final decision, culminating in my phone call to General Starr the following morning.

My retirement ceremony at Bolling was spectacular. It began with a full blown parade put on by the Air Force Honor Guard itself. The Honor Guard was technically under my command but responded to tasking, frequently for Presidential functions, from the Pentagon. Each of the Services had spit-and-polish drill teams and honor guards to perform and represent the United States at ceremonial functions. They were all good, but I thought our guys were the best. They were led by a sharp, young captain named Charlie Spriggs. Charlie and I got along well and his highly disciplined guardsmen never gave me any trouble. As a result, I let them do their own thing, stopping at their barracks only occasionally for a perfunctory inspection where I never found anything wrong. But I always pretended to find a little dust somewhere so their first sergeant could tell them that they were a disgrace. The guardsmen were on to my game and played along with it, humoring the old man. In any case, they put on a parade that made this old aviation cadet shake his head in wonderment. Its precision was at the point of perfection. General Starr was in attendance and I was pleasantly surprised to see that General Trefry, my old boss from Laos, now an Army three-star, had taken off from his busy Pentagon duties to attend the ceremony.

Charlie's guardsmen, by the way, were also instrumental in my "legacy" to Bolling Air Force Base. About a year before I decided to retire, a young guardsman made an appointment to see me in my office. It seems that the young man had discovered, through a friend at nearby Andrews Air Force Base, that the Air Guard unit at Andrews was planning to fly one of its F-105s to the "bone yard" at Davis-Monthan AFB in Arizona for destruction. This seemed to the young guardsman like a terrible waste. He thought the airplane would look "cool" on a pedestal at Bolling's main gate. I told him that since the base had just recently come under the control of Military Airlift Command that the cargo plane specialists at MAC might object to having a fighter on display at the main gate of their most visible base in Washington. But I promised the young man that I'd think about it. I did, and the more I thought about it the better I thought the idea was. While I had never flown the F-105, affectionately known as "the Thud", it had carried the load of the air war over North Vietnam and had a proud record. Why not recognize that record at one of the oldest bases in the Air Force, right in Washington? I was now <u>sure</u> that it was a good idea and I was equally sure that the cargo specialists at MAC would disapprove any requests for a fighter plane display, especially a request made by a fighter pilot! I made a fighter pilot decision--when in doubt, check with no one--just do it! Dave Ferree, our very talented base civil engineer designed a pedestal while I was arranging to "buy" the Thud from Andrews. We arranged to tow the aircraft from Andrews to Bolling on Interstate 295 in the wee hours where it wouldn't interfere with traffic and would not be noticed by people who might not approve of the transfer.

The plan was working to perfection when fate stepped in, in the form of a high-speed chase. A bandit of some sort and several pursuing police cars passed literally under the wing of our towed F-105 at very high speed. Reporters where chasing the chase and naturally wondered what a fighter plane was doing on Interstate 295 at two in the morning. The whole thing ended up on the front page of the Washington Post definitively ending the secrecy of our secret operation. I knew that many curious people from the Pentagon and MAC headquarters would soon overcome their shyness and start asking questions, and who better to ask than the Commander of Bolling AFB? I decided to go on the offensive. I asked our Personnel folks to find me a general at the Pentagon who had flown the Thud in Vietnam. They found one quickly and I phoned him. I told him about our F-105 on a pedestal and he told me that he had heard about it and thought it was a great idea. Good start! I then asked him if he would be the speaker at a dedication ceremony we planned with the Air Force Honor Guard performing ceremonial duties. I could sense the pride in his voice as he graciously accepted my invitation. I now had a priceless ally-- a fellow fighter pilot who flew the Thud in combat, was wearing stars, and thought the display was a great idea. We were home free! Instead of detractors we now had people talking about how good it looked. I thanked the young Guardsman who had started it all and the dedication went off without a hitch. Years later the cargo specialists from MAC were gone, MAC itself was gone, but the F-105 was still in its place of honor. And it still looks good.

The evening after the Honor Guard's outstanding parade, we had a farewell banquet where many nice speeches were made and I had a chance to voice my appreciation for the outstanding support I had received from the people at Bolling who made things happen for me when I was in charge. Making the evening perfect were the Air Force Band's Strolling Strings who circulated among the tables playing romantic music on their violins. I doubt that the Chief of Staff had a better send off when he retired.

Pittstown to Pottstown

With all of the retirement formalities over, we headed north, depleted bank account in hand, to our new life as civilians. We bought a house near my office in a rural New Jersey town called Pittstown. Things were OK, but I began to have some second thoughts about leaving the Air Force when it dawned on me that my world had suddenly become a pretty small place. I had just come from a job running a base with a population of 10,000, a budget of $21 million and $1.3 million in construction and maintenance projects. I was now the assistant to the President of a company with one administrator and one clerk. While I had adjustment problems, my family really had adjustment problems. Marion went from being Mrs. Base Commander where large organizations, like Family Services, depended on her, to being a housewife living across the road from a dairy farm. She was lonely and unhappy. Douglas was also unhappy. He had gone from an elite private school in the nation's capitol to a rural school filled with farmers' kids who found Douglas a bit too sophisticated for their liking.

Adding to my own disillusionment was the fact that I wasn't flying nearly enough to keep me contented. The airplane was used essentially to carry buyers on short vacations, usually to Florida. It was a long, dull flight in a Kingair, but that wasn't the real source of my discontent. After having flown so many clearly defined missions in the Air Force, I never felt comfortable flying for the sole purpose of influencing someone to buy our product rather than another. Later, when helping the tax attorney go through records to justify business use of the aircraft, I did not agree with some of the decisions and assumptions made. The tax expert laughed at me for being too much the military by-the-book stereotype about tax rules, but I thought the whole business a bit tawdry and outside my ethical parameters. I began quietly looking for another job.

The boss unknowingly helped me along by tasking me with a project to prepare a study justifying the aircraft as a business tool. I'm sure he assumed that I wouldn't study myself out of a job. He was wrong. Using hard operating cost figures I proved beyond a doubt that the airplane not only was not essential to the business but was, in fact, a detriment. While I half expected that he would burn my report, he surprised me a few weeks later by announcing that he wanted to sell the airplane. I took on the job of airplane salesman and simultaneously began looking for a new job in earnest. The boss told me that I was under absolutely no pressure to get a new job, but I put myself under pressure since I had no real function once the airplane was gone

My employment problem worked itself out when the chairman of a utility company in Valley Forge PA called expressing interest in the Kingair. The company was expanding rapidly into the energy business and the chairman, also a private pilot, wanted to acquire a corporate airplane to make their executives more mobile. I gave him my résumé and he offered me the job of setting up a flight department on the spot. I accepted on the spot. Unfortunately, negotiations over price of the Kingair dragged on and the airplane ended up being bought by someone else.

I was assured by the chairman of the utility company that he still wanted me to set up their flight department, but before I had an opportunity to come aboard, he bought an airplane on his own. It was a Rockwell Turbo Commander, a good airplane, but this particular airplane had engines that were coming due for overhaul. I wished that my new chief had let me study the problem before making his somewhat impetuous purchase.

Be that as it may, I found myself after just one year out of uniform in an office at the UGI corporate headquarters at Valley Forge. Before the hiring process was complete I was required to spend a day with an "Industrial Psychiatrist" who sent me to various interviews and to classrooms for written examinations. The final interview was with the psychiatrist himself who informed me that I had done very well with all phases of the intelligence and knowledge tests. But he was concerned, he said, with results of interviews that indicated a tendency toward perfectionism. He warned me, darkly, that perfectionists were frequently very difficult to work for. I looked him squarely in the eyes and said, "The next time you're in the back of an airliner, and the weather is lousy, say, a snowstorm with a 200 foot ceiling and a half mile visibility, think about whether you'd rather have a perfectionist or a laid-back good ol' boy up front." He stared back at me for a few seconds, laughed, and said, "That's a very good point!" My hiring process was thus complete.

Retired Colonel, Now Corporate Chief Pilot With Ever-Smiling Marion..

While it looked to me that this was a company that could really use an airplane, the executives had no previous experience with and no knowledge of corporate aviation. So I had a selling job on my hands. My first task was to somehow break the news to an ultra conservative staff that we had just bought an airplane with run-out engines and that it was going to cost a small fortune to get them overhauled. I assured them that I was working feverishly on a budget and that in the future we would accumulate engine overhaul reserve funds. I briefed the company staff several times on the advantages of flying on their own time schedule and after a few months of trial flights I had a small group of executives using the airplane on a regular basis.

I was pleased with early operations, but the best thing that developed during my stay with UGI was hiring Steve as my co-pilot. I had been hiring part time co-pilots from the local airport but they were never expert enough in the airplane to suit me. This wasn't really their fault--they simply didn't fly with me often enough to be proficient in my airplane. I lobbied for clearance to hire a full time pilot and talked my way around anti-nepotism rules to allow me to hire Steve. Steve had been flight instructing at the local airport after having spent time post--graduation as an instructor at Embry-Riddle. He was delighted to escape the dull, but sometimes stressful, life of a flight instructor. I worked hard on his training in the Turbo Commander and he worked even harder. In a few months he was able to pass the written and flight check requirements for his ATP rating and I had the scheduling advantage of a fully qualified aircraft commander in the company turboprop. Our passengers, all company executives, began to enjoy the new form of travel and they also enjoyed flying with the father-son team in the cockpit.

During the summer of 1980 the company chairman decided to buy a Rockwell 500S (Shrike) Commander. It was a piston powered airplane but had good performance and was a delight to fly. The chairman put the airplane up for leaseback to the company and we began to operate it on the shorter trips as a corporate aircraft. It proved very useful, but it also made for some long weeks for Steve and me. We ended by hiring a third full time pilot to keep both airplanes operating up to demand. I also found myself back in the instruction business. The boss, once again failing to plan ahead or seek expert advice, found that he couldn't fly his own aircraft. The insurance company, because of the boss' age and experience, would not cover him unless he became instrument rated. Since I was an instrument instructor I agreed, with some reservations, to take on the job of getting him instrument rated. He had had some rudimentary instrument training as a naval aviator in WWII, but he was approaching 70 and the learning process was a slow one. He eventually qualified and had the good sense to not take on any serious weather without a qualified professional in the other seat. He was also generous in allowing us to use his airplane for our own purposes and we went on several week-end flying excursions as a family.

With my office in Valley Forge and the airplanes based at Coatesville, PA it became obligatory that we once again relocate. We chose a house about half way between Valley Forge and Coatesville with a Pottstown mailing address. Our friends had trouble believing that we were moving from Pittstown to Pottstown, but after moving more than 20 times since our marriage, and never having lived at any one place for more than four years, we were destined to reside in this house for the next 31.

No description of one of our moves would be complete, of course, without an accompanying shaggy dog story. We had left Tiki in a kennel for several weeks while we lived in a hotel and looked for a house. When we picked him up he let us know that he didn't like being stuck in kennels by refusing to have anything to do with us. But after a few square meals at his new Pottstown digs he tentatively forgave us and seemed to return to normal. Then the stray dog genes once again took over and Tiki decided to explore his new neighborhood. He somehow sneaked out through an open door, and having learned nothing from his high-risk stroll on the interstate in D.C., proceeded to wander down the centerline of route 100, the main north-south traffic artery in the area. Tiki was by now deaf as a stone and completely oblivious to the honking horns from cars traveling in either direction. Once again Tiki's handsome appearance saved his life. A school bus driver spotted a dog which she thought was far too handsome to be a stray, so she turned on the flashing red lights stopping traffic from both directions while she scooped up Tiki and took him home with her. Tiki was still wearing his New Jersey dog tags, so the school bus driver went to some considerable trouble, calling New Jersey authorities to find the dog's owner. She eventually delivered the dog to Marion who related Tiki's previous adventures over a cup of tea. That would have ended the story except that a reporter for the local newspaper, "The Pottstown Mercury", happened to be one of the motorists delayed by the bus driver's actions. He recorded the bus' number and later called the driver for an explanation, whereupon he got the full story of the stray from Laos. Now, stories about exotic places like Laos are pretty rare in Pottstown so the reporter called Marion to fill in the details and the next day the "Mercury's" front page bannered a human interest story, "Tiki, the wonder dog--nine lives and counting". Tiki, despite his penchant for living on the edge, had many more happy years, eventually passing on from natural causes. --and we all still miss him.

The family's experience with "exotic places" caused occasional problems with the human family members as well. Doug was assigned the task of writing a short composition for school describing some event in his life. He chose his evacuation from Laos. The teacher graded his paper down because fictional events like being confronted by hostile soldiers brandishing AK-47s and being flown across the Mekong by his Dad had no place in what was supposed to be a factual recitation. It took a phone call from Marion to re-establish Doug's credibility with a highly embarrassed teacher.

While the family, especially me, slowly absorbed the realization, after two years that we were and would remain civilians, my job at UGI continued to expand. Our two airplanes were busy all the time and my regular passengers began to wonder aloud why we couldn't get them to their destinations a little faster. They had hit on my favorite subject. With much of our energy business in Texas and with our people commonly traveling to the west coast, we, the flight department needed a jet! I had surprisingly little difficulty convincing the senior staff of this. The chief financial officer was firmly in my corner which helped considerably. I produced a study comparing the virtues of various corporate jets and eventually narrowed the search to the Lear 35 versus the Westwind. The Lear won the prize for low operating costs while the Westwind had better passenger comfort. I arranged for a demonstration flight to Texas with a full load of passengers in each aircraft. The passengers who went to Texas in the Lear switched to the Westwind for the return trip and vice versa. The consensus was overwhelming. Every passenger preferred the Westwind. When I showed them how much more the Westwind operating costs would be none of them changed his mind, nor did anyone express concern over the slightly longer flight time in the Westwind.

I found a good, used Westwind on the market and Steve, I, and our third pilot, Dave Spence were soon working on our "Type Ratings" with ground school and simulator time at the Flight Safety International training facility. The Westwind was a nice airplane to fly. Its heritage stemmed from the Rockwell Jet Commander series and, like all Commanders it was a bit stiff-legged on landing. This never caused any problem aside from an occasional bruised ego on the part of a careless pilot. Steve and Dave Spence were new to jet operations, but they both progressed rapidly. I was back in my element and was loving it! We had a piston aircraft, a turboprop and a jet and keeping current on all three was a challenge--and it was also great fun. We had a good flight department that was being properly used for profit generating business flying, and I think we were well thought of not only for operating safely but also for running a well-managed operation. I should have known that things were going too well to last.

In the summer of '83 I began to get worried over articles I read in the "Wall Street Journal" about impending trouble in the energy business. It so happened that the company president had scheduled a staff briefing by a group of "experts" on the subject of the world oil business. I was invited by the chairman to attend if I so desired.

I did attend and came out shaking my head. These guys apparently weren't reading the same newspapers as I was because they painted the rosiest of scenarios for the future of the energy business. I told the chairman that I thought they were nuts, but he only chuckled, probably thinking that I should stick to managing my flight department. I was happy to do so but it turned out, unfortunately, that I was right.

Oil prices began slipping and then went into free fall. Smaller energy companies began going out of business and the mood at our corporate headquarters looked to me like defeatism. My immediate boss, incidentally, was a nervous, chain smoking administrative vice president who wanted only to circle the wagons and try to survive. I thought that we should be flying people around more than ever to reassure our traditional customers and to find new ones in the competitive energy market. My boss who, in addition to his other endearing qualities, was deathly afraid of flying, reacted to the challenge by ordering a travel moratorium and grounding of the corporate fleet. His Maginot Line mentality won the day and the company announced its first layoff in its 100 year history. The strategy worked just as well for the company as it had for the French in 1940. It was evident to me that change was coming and I didn't have long to wait.

All departments were required to down size and the Flight Department wasn't spared. I was required to lay off one pilot and the part timer who tidied up the airplanes. I had been faced with many difficult personnel decisions, including firings and layoffs during my Air Force career, but this was the toughest. The fair solution was to keep the pilot who had been there the longest and had the most experience. This was clearly Steve and had he not been my son there would have been no discussion. But in real life there are other considerations. Steve was a bachelor, living at home with no serious responsibilities. Dave Spence, on the other hand, had a wife and family with a mortgage to worry about. After agonizing for several days I issued the pink slip to Steve, a decision that never would have stood up in a union shop. Steve, to his credit, agreed with my decision. While it certainly was not self-evident at the time, it turned out to be the best thing that could have happened to Steve. It got him out from under the old man's thumb once and for all. I was always super critical of Steve when we flew although I knew he was a top-notch professional pilot. In the back of my mind there was always the fear that I would fail to tell him of some technique or of some mistake I had made that could lead to his being in an accident. I actually knew that I was doing this, but like a compulsive drunk, I was unable to stop. Steve tolerated it very well--much better than I would have--but it was high time that he flew from the nest. His time at UGI had transformed him from a light plane flight instructor into a professional pilot qualified in light twins, turboprops, and jets. As a young man with a Westwind type rating in hand he had little difficulty finding a new job, initially in New Jersey and later in Columbus Ohio. The job in Columbus was interesting and it involved flying ex-President Ford and the former First Lady in the Westwind on a regular basis. He later got really lucky and married Caren, our wonderful daughter-in-law and produced our equally wonderful grandchildren, Nicholas and Jennay. Steve later began his present career with American Airlines flying 757s, and it all stems from his beginnings with UGI, an experience which at the time seemed to have ended very badly. Dave Spence, after the inevitable demise of the UGI flight department, also was hired very quickly by a company in Indiana which operated a Westwind, and I, too, landed on my feet.

The UGI flight department was a good one and it didn't die easily. A number of the top executives, including the new Chairman, had grown to like the airplanes and thought, as I did, that they paid their way by multiplying the time available to the company's decision makers who would otherwise be sitting around airport terminals. But the other faction, including our chain smoking administrator, who were petrified by the prospect of flying, especially in "little airplanes", won out. I could accept that decision as having been fairly arrived at, and even though I disagreed with it would have quietly faded away. Unfortunately, the process became unnecessarily ugly. When I saw the handwriting on the wall I met separately with my chain smoking boss and the outgoing chairman whom I had taught to fly instruments. I wanted some straight answers so I could shut down the flight department in a dignified, organized way and arrange for future employment of the pilots. But when I asked point blank whether the flight department was going to go out of business I was assured that it was not, and, in fact, was told by my boss that he "could not imagine UGI in the future without a flight department". That was quite simply a lie told most likely because he feared that I would not be available to sell the airplanes. He had nothing to fear since it never occurred to me not to finish what I had started. It did, however, cause me to turn down an interview for an excellent job on the west coast because I had been told we would continue to operate and I felt a sense of loyalty, a sense which obviously wasn't reciprocal.

While I never felt apprehensive about any of us getting jobs, I was depressed about leaving the company with a sense of betrayal. I was simply disappointed in people that I trusted failing to shoot straight with me over something that they had nothing to fear. Having spent my Air Force career with people who, no matter how vehemently they disagreed with me, could always be depended upon to act with honor and, very simply, to tell the truth. I had been employed by two civilian companies now since I retired from the Air Force five years earlier, and had felt a lack of concern with the concept of honor from top people in both cases. It seemed to me that they simply either didn't understand the concept or thought it irrelevant. My feeling of disappointment with my fellow man was profound and greatly influenced decisions regarding my future employment.

Those decisions were set in motion, ironically, by my early efforts to, first, reduce fixed operating costs by flying charter, and later to sell the Westwind, something I made conscientious efforts to do despite knowing by now that I had been deceived. I had established a very good relationship with the Fixed Base Operator at the airport where we based our aircraft and had begun to fly charter trips using their air carrier certificate. I enlisted their help in finding a buyer for the Westwind while continuing to operate it on charter. Flying on commercial charter flights, incidentally, had involved significant red tape and proving flights with the FAA.

The flight checks required by the FAA, were usually perfunctory and boring. But we, unintentionally, managed to make ours interesting. After completing most of the checks required we were about to fly our last leg, a short hop from Dulles to Coatesville late at night. I was glad to be finishing the square-filling ordeal because we had been harassed by an officious, young bureaucrat from the FAA who was determined to impress his superiors with his knowledge and tenacity. He had recently completed the Westwind training curriculum at Flight Safety International and was thus the FAA's "expert" on operating the aircraft. Since this was the final night of our flight check, most of the Westwind's seats were filled with a half-dozen or so FAA people expert in various fields such as maintenance, avionics, and so forth. All were eager to finish and go home. Their chief happened to be an old friend from my T-6 days at Marianna, Matt Elkan, who had joined the FAA after his Air Force years. Matt knew that I would not run an unsafe operation and he had been reasonably successful in keeping his young colleague off my back, knowing that my patience was wearing thin; I appreciated Matt's efforts, but, as insurance, I had asked Ray

Conway, Chief Pilot of the charter certificate holder, Chester County Aviation, to go along on the trip. Ray loved to talk and, observing that my mood was such that I might explode all over the young twerp, promised to do his best to keep him entertained.

We taxied out normally with Dave Spence in the left seat since it was his leg. Take off was normal until I called "Rotate". Dave responded normally pulling the nose into the black of a moonless night. As I reached for the landing gear handle I noticed the oil pressure on the left engine dropping rapidly. This was followed immediately by an oil pressure warning light and a sudden drop in RPM. It didn't take a power plant engineer to determine that we had just experienced total oil system failure which would be followed quickly and inevitably by total left engine failure. I immediately stop cocked the left engine and began cleaning up the items on the checklist for engine failure emergency. Things were happening so fast that Dave thought I had pulled back the power lever in order to simulate one more emergency at the behest of the FAA examiners. He finally realized that this was the real thing when I called Dulles Tower informing them that we had an emergency and were going to turn downwind for an immediate landing. Since I had not yet found time to inform the passengers of the problem, one of them asked Ray Conway what all the red lights were about. Ray replied that they were on to tell everyone that they weren't going home for a while.

I finally found time to tell the passengers of the emergency while we were on downwind, and I immediately regretted it. The twerp felt compelled to visit the cockpit to share with us his vast knowledge of single engine procedures. I told him as gently as I could through clenched teeth to sit down and shut up! Someone else, probably Matt, doubtless saw the hint of violence in my eyes and forced the young man into his seat belt. The rest of the pattern and landing went routinely and Ray called in a light twin to pick us up and take us home in the wee hours. The young bureaucrat later tried to force us into another flight since we had not completed the trip back to Coatesville but he was overridden. Since we had successfully coped with a real-life serious emergency the final leg was waived. The twerp was transferred soon thereafter and never bothered us again.

I understand he was later quietly let go and found a different line of work.

We continued our charter service after replacing the left engine even though we found it somewhat awkward to fly customers with a figurative "For Sale" sign on the airplane. By now, the disingenuous comments from upper management about continued life for the flight department had ceased and there were no longer any illusions about its operational future. At this point the imposing presence of Herb Lotman came upon the scene.

Herb is a business man, a very good business man. His business has been primarily to act as a major supplier of beef and chicken products for McDonald's. The primary instrument of his business was Keystone Foods Corporation, a private corporation which very few people have heard of but which measures sales in the billions, with a 'b'. Herb started in the food business with his father, selling meat from the back of a truck. If there is a stereotypical self made man it would be Herb Lotman.

Herb and his business would be the subject of another book, but my relationship with him stemmed from the fact that he believed strongly in the value of corporate aviation. He had been chartering aircraft from Chester County Aviation for years and as luck would have it, he was in the market for his own jet aircraft just as I happened to be selling one. Chester County had been flying Herb around the country mostly in Lear 35s. Ray Conway was sold on the Lear because of its superior performance and operating cost numbers. But again, as luck would have it, Chester County at the time had only one jet on its operating certificate, our Westwind. So we began flying Herb regularly. He had never before seen a Westwind and his reaction to it was exactly the same as we had seen with our UGI executives when I staged the fly-off between the Lear and the Westwind. He loved the Westwind! I explained to him the difference in operating costs but it was never a contest. Herb is a <u>big</u> man, tipping the scales at somewhere north of 300 pounds. The bigger cabin was in itself reason enough for him to make an offer on our airplane. I was neither asked nor did I offer to participate in the financial aspects of the sale. As a result, Herb was able to buy the airplane at an incredibly low price. When the price was posted, as happens in the aircraft sales business, the local Westwind salesman, a friend of mine, called me to ask if we had taken leave of our senses. I advised him of the fact that I had been nowhere in the loop on the sales price and offered my apologies for knocking the bottom out of the Westwind market. The only guy who was truly happy was Herb who was now the proud owner of an airplane that was made for someone his size and that he had purchased at a bargain price.

My prime focus now became putting food on the table for my family. I had already gone for several interviews and had been verbally offered a job as an instructor with Flight Safety International, a job which I did not particularly want. Herb solved my problem immediately by offering me the job of flying his airplane. I had been flying him around the country for several months and we got along well. We had also been in a few tight weather situations and I think Herb had developed a sense of confidence in my ability to get him from point A to point B in one piece. There remained the problem of the structure of my employment.

Herb had worked with Chester County Aviation for many years and wanted them to manage the day-to-day operation of the aircraft. I would have preferred to continue to manage it myself, but I liked Ray Conway and his partner, Al Sheves and I saw no reason why it wouldn't work. Herb asked me whether I would prefer to work for Keystone Foods or for Chester County Aviation. I opined that since they were to manage his airplane it might be cleaner if I worked for Chester County Aviation. My salary would ultimately be paid by Keystone Foods in either case. In truth, I had just finished an unpleasant experience working for a large company and I didn't want to repeat it with another large company. So, I began working for Chester County Aviation. I would be the primary pilot of the Westwind, but Ray Conway, who was an excellent pilot, would back me up as needed. I, in return, would be available to fly the various aircraft that CCA operated if the Westwind were down for maintenance. I, as always, was eager to fly different types of airplanes, so I was quite content with the arrangement. I thought it would work beautifully. In fact, it was a disaster.

The failure of the arrangement had nothing to do with my personal relationship with Ray and Al. Ray was the ultimate extrovert. He loved to tell stories and he told them well. He was fun to be around and we had many enjoyable trips together. He was also expert at working with or cajoling if necessary the FAA 's hard-nosed bureaucrats. His primary background was in light aircraft and I considered him the most knowledgeable person I ever knew on the subject of light twin engine aircraft. He also had excellent eye-hand coordination and had no difficulty in mastering the Westwind.

Al Sheves was the diametric opposite of Ray. Quiet and somewhat introverted, he was nevertheless highly intelligent and a self-educated man. I considered him a mechanical genius. He could literally fix anything, and the staff of experienced mechanics at the airport used him as their go-to guy whenever they were stumped by a mechanical problem. I once had a serious problem with the turboprop engine on our Turbo Commander. I was in touch with the highest level of engine experts at the factory who advised me not to allow anyone to employ their fix, which involved drilling through the engine casing itself, unless that person was the very best kind of machinist. Al picked up the phone and quickly convinced the factory experts that they had indeed run across a real gem in the machinist trade. I held my breath watching Al drill precision holes in my engine case, half convinced that the engine would never run again. But it ran perfectly and the factory experts were delighted with the workmanship. Al's reputation for this type of work was widespread, and all agreed that he was truly a mechanical genius. There was, however, one problem. Al liked being a pilot much more than being a mechanic. Unfortunately, his genius as a mechanic did not transfer into the cockpit. He left behind a long string of bent and bruised aircraft on which he had inflicted his piloting skills. He had the courage of a lion and would fly literally anything from a WWII fighter to a home built crate that had been assembled in some one's garage. Al's adventures and mishaps are worthy of another book, but one example, which I admit I did not personally witness but is part of the aviation lore in Chester County, needs to be re-told.

Al was flying a restored WWII Wildcat, a Navy fighter, in the Chester County air show. He was to make a low level high speed pass down the runway. Carried away with the moment, Al, who had no real training in acrobatics, decided to thrill the crowd with a roll. He made the same mistake that has killed many military pilots over the years in not raising the nose enough to compensate for loss of lift when the aircraft rolls. Fortunately, the terrain at the east end of the Chester County runway drops off precipitously for several hundred feet. The Wildcat disappeared below the horizon and slowly clawed its way back into view. The show's narrator captured the moment for the crowd, broadcasting over the loud speakers, "Here comes Al Sheves in that beautifully restored World War II Wildcat, and there he goes......HOLY S**T!!!" His ineloquent vocabulary upset some of the parents with children in attendance, but it perfectly expressed the feeling of pilots in the crowd who had just watched Al stare down the grim reaper yet again.

Despite such occasional irregularities, I thoroughly enjoyed my relationship with Ray and Al. They were honest businessmen, highly skilled in their respective specialties, and a pleasure to work with. After my two previous encounters with civilian business people, I had begun to believe the worst. Ray and Al changed my outlook.

Our eventual split was amicable and probably had as much to do with my perfectionism, identified by UGI's industrial psychiatrist years before, as anything else. I had learned to manage assets in the Air Force, and in some instances I had learned the hard way, by living through conspicuous blunders. I had also learned quite a lot during my three years on the ORI Team and as Third Air Force's Director of Safety. Watching other peoples' mistakes can be very educational. And, for better or for worse, it can also lead an otherwise perfectly normal human being into being a perfectionist. Chester County Aviation had learned to manage assets the hard way as well, but their methods of identifying problems and taking corrective action were different from mine and never seemed to meet my standards. I still considered the Westwind to be my responsibility and Herb felt the same way. This was a frustrating and ultimately intolerable situation for me since Herb held my feet to the fire for situations over which I had no control. The maintenance people, for example, didn't work for me and didn't respond to my complaints. In fact, they complained about my harassing them over things that were not my responsibility as a pilot. I was frustrated and I didn't like it.

I worked under these conditions for several years, enjoying the variety of the small airport charter business but greatly annoyed by my inability to get things done. I'm sure my time as a base commander influenced my state of mind. I was used to getting things done and having the power to make changes immediately if what was done didn't meet my standards.

Things came to a head in 1988 when the Westwind went to a large maintenance facility in New York for a routine inspection that Chester County Aviation couldn't fit into their maintenance schedule. The New York maintenance facility grounded the airplane for what they deemed to be egregious oversights in maintenance requirements. The requirements had been CCA's responsibility. This was a serious flight safety finding and the inspection facility, correctly, informed the owner, Herb, as well as CCA. Herb was furious as was I. He called me and let me know, in no uncertain terms, that he wanted changes made. I agreed with him and mapped out a plan. All of this happened to coincide with Herb's decision to replace the Westwind with a Hawker 700, a larger and more luxurious corporate jet. So, it was a good point in time to change management arrangements. Herb called me in for a formal interview in his office so we could discuss the new hierarchy. It basically meant that I would take over all responsibility for the airplane and that I would report directly to Herb as a Keystone employee. I was driving from the airport to Keystone's corporate headquarters through a driving snow storm when it occurred to me that Herb was now my boss, not the regular passenger I had been flying around the country. I had addressed him as Herb for years since that was how he had introduced himself to me. Maybe, I thought, I should start calling him Mr. Lotman in deference to his exalted position as CEO of the company. The matter was settled while I was waiting outside his office. As Herb stepped out of his office, the janitor happened to be working between him and me and Herb greeted him with a "Hi, John". John replied, "Hi, Herb, how's it going?" Informality, I learned, was the order of the day at Keystone. I was to discover later that there were some limitations on that policy, but that lay in the future. We then got down to discussing management arrangements for what was, after all, a very high priced company asset.

The current, failed arrangement was, I admitted to Herb, my responsibility. I had made a fundamental error at the outset by suggesting that I work for CCA rather than Keystone Foods. This had left his airplane without any one person empowered to make operational decisions and to supervise maintenance. Herb agreed to correct that immediately by calling Ray with the new arrangement making me a Keystone employee. Ray seemed somewhat miffed but voiced no great objection. He still had us as a customer for fuel sales, hangar rent and maintenance, so he was really losing nothing. For me, a great burden was off my back. I was now a customer rather than a pilot/employee, and things were going to be done with the Hawker my way, or else. My first act as a Keystone employee was to put my intentions in writing to Herb. The first document was a detailed budget, something that he had received in the past only on an informal basis. Next, I proposed two major changes to take place immediately. They were going to cost some money but I deemed them necessary to an operation that was not only safe, but professional in every respect.

First, I intended to put the maintenance program under the Computerized Aircraft Maintenance Program (CAMP) system. Virtually all aircraft maintenance programs are computerized today, but when I set up the Hawker's system it was a fairly new concept.

It was replacing a pencil-note-and-mechanic's-memory system that had caused the inspection failures in the Westwind. The new system worked well and we never had a problem with the Hawker in the years that we operated it.

Second was the copilot situation. The FAA requirements for co-pilot qualifications were minimal, and I frequently flew with someone in whom I had very little confidence. I simply was not convinced that some of these part-time jet pilots could take over if something happened to me. My grousing led the dispatcher to always attempt to schedule the jet with the same copilot, but the dispatcher's requirements came first. If my regular right seater were needed on another aircraft, I got whomever was available provided he met the minimum currency requirements.

This was a constant annoyance, but it wasn't always that way. On occasion I got lucky for a while and flew with some very good people. One was Andy O'Brien, a furloughed airline pilot who had been out of smaller airplanes for some time, but adjusted quickly and was a dependable professional. He was also good at keeping me entertained and humble. Once while rushing to make a pick up I had been inadvertently taxiing faster than Andy thought was safe. He quietly muttered "V1" and smiled when I looked over at him quizzically. But I got the message and slowed down. Unfortunately, Andy's tenure was brief as he was shortly re-hired by the airlines.

Another accidental find was Bruce Thompson. I had met Bruce during my early days running UGI's flight department. He had been a classmate of Steve's at Embry-Riddle and was departing for Air Force pilot training as a member of the Delaware Air National Guard. Later, after he had won his Air Force wings and I had lost the UGI flight department, we ended up as the Westwind crew for CCA. I liked Bruce on our first flight and I especially liked the discipline and professionalism engendered by his military training.

But after a short time Bruce too went on to better things, signing on with USAir. We've kept in touch with Bruce over the years and he's almost a part of the family. He and Steve were partners in several real estate ventures, and I've watched his military career with great interest and pride. Steve, Marion and I recently attended his retirement ceremony, having watched him progress through the ranks to become a brigadier general! Not bad for a part time Westwind copilot.

Although Bruce, Andy and a few others provided temporary relief, the copilot situation had to be fixed. I told Herb that I wanted a full time crewmember and that I wanted both of us to attend recurrency training, including simulator training, at least once a year. I suspect that Herb by now was worried that he had created a money eating Frankenstein monster, but he agreed to all of my requests. I decided that military experience would rank very high on my list of things to watch for on résumés. I had had enough of free spirits in the cockpit.

My recent string of good luck continued. It happened that Marty Quinlan, who had previously been chief pilot at CCA and more recently had been flying a Lear for a coal company, was between jobs. I had flown with Marty enough times to know that he was a very competent pilot, but perhaps more importantly, I had noticed that he was a leader. While chief pilot at Chester County he had been a no-nonsense guy with the group of young pilots in his charge, even though it often looked like he was herding cats. Marty was also ambitious, a trait that I found desirable because I wanted someone I would feel confident with as a stand-in and as an eventual replacement. I suspected I might have to rein him in occasionally because ambitious people often think they can do a better job than the boss. I found that a desirable trait as well because I had always thought that anybody who didn't think he was smarter than the boss probably didn't merit eventually becoming the boss. Marty was also retired from the Delaware Air National Guard where he had been a flight engineer for many years on C-130s. His military background was evident in his demeanor, and I looked forward to a long, productive association with him. I would also have ample opportunity to develop a Napoleonic complex since Marty measured in at six foot five while I could reach five foot nine only on a good hair day.

Herb had known Marty for many years and I had no difficulty in selling him on my choice. That choice turned out to be fortuitous for all concerned. During almost a dozen years Marty lived up to all my expectations. He was not content to be simply an airplane driver, and, as expected, I had to occasionally rein him in. But that was fine. He never hesitated to tell me if he thought I was wrong, and when he did tell me I made it a point to listen because he was, more often than not, correct. I realized early on that I had to find some way to channel his energy and give him the amount of responsibility that he was clearly capable of handling. The FAA unknowingly presented me with the answer.

We had operated our charter service, which was a common way for corporate jets to reduce fixed operating costs, using Chester County's air carrier certificate. We were getting very few requests from CCA, so we switched to a different certificate holder in hopes of generating more income. When results turned out to be no better we decided to get our own certificate, knowing that we could do no worse. The first step in the laborious bureaucratic process of securing an air carrier certificate was to write the operating manual. That seemed simple enough and I quickly produced what I thought was a pretty fair document that met all regulatory requirements. I stuck with the Air Force's principles of good writing which essentially said do it in as few words as possible. I proudly presented my manual, which I considered to be a model of brief, concise prose, at our first meeting with the FAA. Their representatives read not a word but unanimously pronounced it "too short". I asked them how many pounds were required, but they had no answer. They suggested that we look at a nearby commuter airline's manual which they breathlessly described as having "hundreds of pages". I saw the writing on the wall and suggested we adjourn to allow us time to work on our tome.

Out of this defeat I suddenly saw opportunity. Here I had been presented with a job that was absolutely essential to our operation and was tailor made for Marty's considerable skill, which he had shown over the years, for working with the FAA. He was to become my representative with the FAA, and his first project was the manual. I handed him my rejected 25 or 30 pages and said, "Make it big, Marty". Marty took it on as a personal challenge and in a week or two had produced a masterpiece. He pointed out to me that he did not change a word of my original 25 to 30 pages, but he had added a table of contents, a voluminous index, color illustrations of God-knows-what, and stuffed it all into a large, colorful official looking binder. The FAA was ecstatic! And Marty had passed his first test as an administrator. From that point on, Marty was my point man with the FAA. All but the most momentous matters concerning the FAA were Marty's responsibility, with the sole stipulation that he keep me informed.

Philadelphia Jet Service was born and became a large and reasonably successful part of our flight department.

Corporate Aviation and Final Flying Days

My chosen "second career" after leaving the Air Force was notable mostly for its lack of drama. That, of course, is the way it should be. Corporate aircraft are designed with safety in mind and the best adjective that can accompany the description of a business flight is "uneventful". Some of my die-hard fighter pilot friends look down their noses at those of us who chose business flying as a second career, saying it's like going from an Indianapolis race car to a Volvo station wagon. I've always been puzzled by that attitude since the alternative to corporate flying is usually something like working in a cubicle counting beans for a government or business bureaucracy.

I am amazed at how quickly the years went by during my corporate flying career. While I spent 26 years in the Air Force, I spent almost as long, 22 years, flying corporate aircraft. Of my 15,000 hours in the air, fully 10,000 were in business aircraft. Admittedly, most of my business flying was done with the autopilot engaged and the airplane flying straight and level. This hardly compares with hurling your body at the ground in a 45 degree dive in an F-100, but it wasn't all boredom. Emergencies like the engine failure on takeoff in the Westwind, which I described earlier were rare indeed, but approaches in weather at minimums were not at all rare and helped to keep life interesting.

One such incident took place in my favorite business aircraft, the Gulfstream. In 1994, Herb decided that a man of his size needed a bigger airplane. After much research we settled on a Gulfstream III. I fell in love with the airplane on my first flight in it, a trip from Long Beach, California to Savannah, Georgia. The airplane was a shell, all seats and interior décor having been stripped for refurbishment. But ugly as it was, it handled beautifully. I had always told people that corporate aircraft all performed like twin engined T-birds, and I think that was accurate for most business jets, including the Westwind and the Hawker we operated. But it was certainly not true of the GIII! This thing would leave the old T-bird in the dust. But like any airplane it occasionally had problems.

We were flying on a routine trip to the west coast with a passenger pickup in Jackson Hole, Wyoming, a spot noted for mountainous beauty and severe turbulence. As expected, we encountered severe chop on landing approach and on departure after picking up our passenger. But once above the mountains we were in smooth air and settled down for a routine trip at 43,000 feet. After a few minutes at altitude, however, I noticed that the cabin altitude was a little higher than normal and was slowly creeping even higher. We requested progressively lower altitudes until the cabin altitude stabilized with the aircraft at 31,000 feet. I suspected a leaking seal on the cabin or baggage compartment door but with everything stable we elected to proceed to our destination and did so, uneventfully.

Gulfstream III At Company Hangar, Philadelphia International. Not Exactly An F-100, But There Are Worse Ways To Earn A Living.

After unloading the passengers, I checked the door seals for damage while Marty did an exterior post-flight inspection. Finding nothing wrong with the door seals, I went outside and found Marty staring at the underside of the aft fuselage. He had discovered a gaping hole where an antenna had been and the antenna cable protruding from a silver dollar size hole in the aircraft pressure vessel. We had obviously solved the mystery of our loss of cabin pressure. Amazing to me was the ability of the Gulfstream to maintain acceptable cabin pressure with that large a hole in the pressure vessel.

Investigating further, we found the half dozen or so screw fasteners that held the antenna in place to be missing but the nut plates that held the screws were in place. A thick layer of sealant for the antenna assembly had been applied and was obviously the only thing that had held it in place--that is, until we encountered the severe turbulence at Jackson Hole.

The aircraft had just undergone a major inspection at Gulfstream's manufacturing plant at Savannah. We confirmed that re-sealing of that antenna had been part of the inspection and my irate phone call to Savannah was sufficient to bring an embarrassed repair crew to the ramp to repair the damage. There was no charge for the work! There had been many arguments at the time about the use of "sky marshals" on air liners with the danger of stray bullets possibly causing catastrophic decompression of the cabin. Our experience would seem to indicate that it would take quite a few bullet holes to cause such a problem.

Aside from our lost antenna problem we had very few flights that could be called anything but routine. The capabilities of the Gulfstream, however, did open new and interesting ports of call around the world for us to visit. We began, for example, to fly across the Atlantic on a regular basis and made a number of trips to South America. Herb, always conscious of the fact that we spent a lot of time away from our families, frequently invited our wives to go along on the more interesting trips. We enjoyed stays in Edinburgh, Paris, Rome and Cabo San Lucos among other vacation spots. Life was good!

One factor which made my life slightly less good, though, was the advent of flight attendants into my carefully ordered life. While I could spot a good pilot--or a bad one for that matter--a mile away, my ability to pick winners did not extend to the strange (to me) world of the female flight attendant. It didn't take long for me to realize that my world was going to change with the arrival of these creatures. Shortly after I had hired "Laura", based more on Herb's admiration of her large, fluttering, brown eyes than on my own gut feelings, we were scheduled to attend the annual company Christmas party. Now, this was not your average company holiday party. Herb, as with most of his endeavors, went all out on these affairs. They were lavish events looked forward to by all of the employees. They were held in the ballroom of a prominent hotel in downtown Philadelphia, and a good time was always had by all.

But on Monday morning following one year's holiday bash, my phone rang at the hangar. It was Herb, and he seemed upset. The conversation went like this: "Al, you've known me for a lot of years". "Yes, I replied, it's been quite some time, Herb". "Now, you know I'm a pretty informal guy, right? I mean, everybody calls me Herb, none of this Mr. Lotman stuff, right?" "Right", I answered, completely baffled. "Herb, what's going on?"

"Would you tell your flight attendant that she can call me Herb or she can call me Mr. Lotman, but my name is not Sweetie, dammit!"

Unable to suppress a chuckle, I said, "Herb, I've never, ever, been tempted to call you Sweetie, and I will definitely brief my flight attendant that you'd prefer that she not call you that either".

Herb then told me the rest of the story. It seems that he was in a conversation group that included his wife and all the senior executives along with their wives, when "Laura" breezed by, fluttering her big, brown eyes. She waved and said, "Hi, Sweetie!", as she glided by the group toward the bar.

Herb's wife was not amused.

Needless to say, I had a closed door session in my office with our new flight attendant where we discussed basic protocol.

Further incidents led to my suggesting eventually that "Laura" seek another line of work. Follow-on flight attendants worked out somewhat better, but I always had the feeling that they thought that I worked for them rather than the other way around.

Despite the occasional flight attendant flap, life went on in the Keystone Flight Department and we were, I think, well thought of by the passengers who used our service. We ran a professional operation and we were proud of it. Those of us who crewed the airplane were well trained and we worked hard to make the passengers feel that they were in good hands. Our mechanic, Bill Hetrick, was hard working and as competent as they come in the care and feeding of airplanes. Our dispatcher, French-Canadian Pierrette Craemer, was efficient, pleasant and well liked by all.

A very large part of the credit for our success went to the boss, Herb. Operating a jet aircraft like the Gulfstream is an expensive undertaking and not for the faint of heart. I supplied Herb with a print-out of expenses past and future each month. I think he knew that I would never b.s. him on the numbers and he never turned me down on a purchase that I thought was needed.

Perhaps more important was his willingness to step aside on operational matters. If weather was down to minimums he knew that we'd give it our best shot, but if it went below minimums, he never once questioned my judgment about aborting a landing approach. On matters of flight safety he deferred entirely to the flight crew. Smart man! Not all corporate flight crews have that level of enlightenment from the front office and some have made bad or dangerous decisions under pressure to make something happen when weather or field condition called for discretion.

While I was still enjoying my job, I looked in the mirror one morning and saw a 67 year old man looking back. I felt I was still on top of the game, and I had no problem passing the normal flight checks and physical exams, but I had been doing some self-evaluation recently and I didn't like the results. The simple fact that I was questioning my own performance was enough. I stepped back and said to the image in the mirror, "You're not as good as you used to be, pal" -- and with that I made the decision to retire.

Once I had made the decision things happened fast. There was no question that Marty was qualified to take over the flight department and Herb agreed immediately with my recommendation that he do so. I spent about a month going over the routine paperwork, mostly budgetary, of the day-to-day operation of the department with Marty who was a quick study, and I finally stepped aside.

Herb, generous to the end, threw a farewell party at George Perrier's restaurant in Philadelphia. George, the famous French chef, had been a passenger with us several times and I had always used the occasion to practice my French, which George seemed to enjoy. He prepared a memorable feast for my party and Herb topped off the occasion by presenting me with a farewell gift--a cruise for Marion and me to anywhere we chose!

Send Off From Keystone Flight Dept. Bill Hetrick, Marty Quinlan, Left

After some deliberation we chose a cruise to Alaska. It seemed appropriate to take advantage of the opportunity to return for the first time to the place where Marion and I began our lives together and where I had begun my career as a fighter pilot. It turned out to be a wonderful vacation. We had kept in touch over the years with

my old radar observer from Moody and Elmendorf days, Gene
Polhemus and his wife, Noel. When Marion called Noel to tell her
of our good fortune she and Gene decided to go along with us on
the cruise. Gene and Noel had been back to Anchorage previously
and warned us that drastic changes had taken place since we last
departed in 1956. They were certainly correct. When we were there
in the 50s there were just two paved roads through the center of
town and only one high-rise building. The town was now a modern
metropolis with super highways and sky scrapers all around.

We felt obligated to make a pilgrimage to Elmendorf as well to
assess the changes at the base. Remarkably, there was relatively little
in physical change that was obvious to us. The officers' housing
compound, called Cherry Hill, had been greatly improved and now
housed enlisted families

**With Gene Polhemus (on right) Museum Piece Crew With
Museum Piece F-89, Alaska Cruise**

Our trip to the flight line revealed even less change. The hangar that
was our workplace incredibly was not only still there, but was still
the workplace for an active squadron. The only thing that looked

different was the airplanes. Our old F-89s had been replaced by sleek F-15s. But someone had paid tribute to the past by creating an excellent outdoor museum displaying all the fighter aircraft that had flown from the base over the years. Gene and I had our picture taken in front of the mint-condition F-89 like those we had flown a half century earlier. I made one mistake on our nostalgic visit to the flight line. One of our group suggested that we call the current squadron and ask for a tour of the facility. Remembering how I used to be annoyed at retirees dropping in unannounced when I was a commander, I voted against it, explaining that these guys were busy and probably didn't need an uninvited group of old codgers interrupting their work. My logic won out, but I came to regret it in later months. I discovered that the squadron inhabiting my old hangar was none other than the 90th Tac Fighter Squadron, the Pair o' Dice squadron that was my unit during my Vietnam tour. I'm sure the young tigers manning the F-15s of the current squadron would have been delighted to show off their hot shot airplanes to an old, washed up war relic who could tell them about flying combat for the Dice Squadron in the museum piece F-100! -- an opportunity missed.

Once the Alaska party was over I had to face the reality that I was now really retired and that my days as a professional pilot were over. Well, almost over. Marty occasionally needed a pilot and I was usually available to fill in. But it was not the way I liked to fly. I often went weeks or even months without flying the Gulfstream, but I felt obligated to study systems and procedures weekly in case a trip came up on short notice. The problem was taken out of my hands when Herb decided to upgrade to a GIV for which I had no type rating. My logbook shows my last GIII flight on April 9th, 2004. I remember thinking on final approach to runway 27R at Philadelphia that this would probably be my last landing in a corporate jet and I wanted it to be a good one. I got lucky--made a smooth one wheel crosswind landing, lowered the other main and nose wheel gently and braked to make the first turnoff at taxiway November. "Good time to quit while I'm ahead," I thought. And that was it for my corporate aviation career.

I wasn't yet ready to give up flying completely, and I had made arrangements to join in an aircraft partnership with two professional pilot friends before I retired. One of the partners was Bruce Thompson, mentioned earlier, and the other was Dick Simons, like me, retired Air Force and soon-to-be retired Chief Pilot for a Philadelphia corporation. We bought a Piper Aztec, a six place twin which Bruce and I had flown extensively while working for Chester County Aviation. We had a good partnership and became close friends as well as partners. Marion and I made many trips to Ohio to visit Steve and the grandkids and enjoyed the Aztec immensely. Unfortunately, our venture that started so beautifully ended in tragedy.

The Aztec

I was at home on a Sunday afternoon when the phone rang. It was the airport calling to tell me that the Aztec had just had an accident and that Dick and his lovely wife, Phyllis did not survive. Marion and I were shattered by the news. Dick was the last person I would have picked to be involved in a fatal aircraft accident. I had flown with him many times, not only in the Aztec, but also in the corporate GIII that his company operated, He was, in short, as talented a pilot as I had ever flown with. He was an Air Force fighter pilot, having flown primarily the F-105. He had survived 100 combat missions over North Vietnam in the "Thud" and one successful ejection. For him to lose his life in a docile light twin like the Aztec was beyond ironic.

The NTSB ran a perfunctory investigation of the accident and issued a final report which I, with the years in the Air Force I had spent investigating accidents, found lacking. It determined, in generalized terms that fuel mismanagement was the cause of the accident--true perhaps but too much was left unsaid. The report produced one more statistic adding to the column that reads "Pilot error, fuel mismanagement", but little else. I decided to run my own informal investigation for peace of mind if nothing else. In fact, while I was incredibly presumptuous in trying to investigate an accident without access to the wreckage, I felt that beyond a doubt Dick had made a mistake that every Aztec pilot has made at one time or another. Switching fuel tanks on an Aztec involves reaching a floor mounted valve selector which is very difficult to see. Most pilots move the selector by feel, stopping at the detent for the outboard or inboard tank. Unfortunately, between the left and right detent is an "off" detent. It is distressingly easy to stop short of the desired detent thus selecting "off" instead of a tank containing fuel. Without going into the details of the investigation it appears to me that Dick did just that and because of a series of conditions found himself with a dead engine with gear and full flaps and not enough time to correct his error. The Aztec flies very well on one engine, but not with gear and full flaps down. My informal re-investigation filled my need for "closure" on the loss of the airplane, but did nothing to ease the loss we felt for our two good friends.

Bruce and I briefly discussed buying another airplane, but the memories of Dick and Phyliss were still too fresh. The prospect of shopping for a new aircraft, modifying it to our liking, coordinating color schemes --something Phyliss had been deeply involved in on the Aztec-- all these things we had enjoyed as a group, just didn't seem like fun right now. After a while, we stopped talking about it.

Months later I had another of my self-evaluation sessions. I looked at the calendar and was forced to recognize the fact that I was 73 years old. I was beginning to fall victim to some of the maladies associated with old age, and my tennis playing made it apparent that my eye-hand coordination wasn't what it had once been. I didn't want to ever become one of the old geezers hanging around the airport making occasional death-defying flights with survival as the sole objective. I had to quit sometime and I decided that the time was now. I closed my log book and with it my flying career.

Life after Flying

Life without airplanes doesn't come as a sudden, dramatic explosion in your life. Months and then years go by when you find yourself talking mostly to non-aviation people. You discover that many of them, even most of them, shockingly, couldn't care less about what is going on in the aviation world. At first you find it difficult to cope when your friends seem more interested in discussing politics or school taxes than the status of the Air Force's new F-22s. Your efforts to switch the subject toward aviation are met with yawns, and you finally decide to think about other ideas and are surprised to learn that some of them are actually interesting.

One of the sidelights that kept my life interesting introduces my promised sequel to the story of my friendship, while a young Aviation Cadet, with Pierre Fortin, my fellow cadet from the French Air Force. As I said earlier, Pierre and I lost contact after basic training in the T-6. We went to different bases and lost each other's address. We then proceeded to forget about each other for the next 57 years. My son Steve was instrumental in changing that. Steve began flying from JFK to Paris on his job with American Airlines. His layovers in the City of Light re-kindled his interest in the French language, which he had studied sporadically while still a schoolboy. He found a local Alliance Française chapter in his Columbus, Ohio hometown area and began improving his French language skills. The French group's leader was a native born French woman. During the course of conversation, she mentioned to Steve that her brother was also an airline pilot, now retired, and that he had learned to fly in the U.S. with the U.S. Air Force.

When Steve told me about this I immediately wondered if he might have known my friend, Pierre either in the Aviation Cadet Program or the French Air Force. He did not, but offered to try to track him down. He was successful in doing so through one of his friends whom I had also known in cadets. In a few weeks he presented me with Pierre's mailing address in France. I sat down and laboriously composed a letter in French, secretly hoping that that Pierre had retained or improved his English. He had not, but within a week I received a letter, in French, from a delighted and very surprised,

Pierre. We exchanged some family photos and some fading shots from our cadet days, and have kept in touch since then via email. I've mentioned the possibility of our getting together, but at our present age it probably won't work out. In any case, it was a real treat to be able to renew a friendship from so many years ago.

Our life style changed fairly dramatically in 2011 when we decided to leave Pottstown after 31 happy years and set up residence in the Willow Valley Retirement Community near Lancaster, PA. Our residence is quite spacious, something we insisted upon so our kids, grandkids, wives, and fiancés can all stay in our house when they

With F102 At Elmendorf Museum

visit. We've been very pleased with our decision to move into the continuing care community. Primarily, we like the security of the continuing care facilities which insure that our kids won't be stuck with huge bills or responsibilities should one or both of us fall victim to a debilitating disease. And I'll admit that having all maintenance work done for us is appealing. I find that I miss cutting grass and shoveling snow much less than I had anticipated. In fact, I miss it not at all. I spend much of my time playing various racquet sports and working out in the beautifully equipped fitness center.

I'm frequently asked if I miss flying. My response is usually equivocal. I certainly enjoyed flying the beautiful F-102 and all the other wonderful machines I've been privileged to take aloft. But I didn't like losing one of the best years of my life living on the Greenland ice cap away from my family in order to fly the "Deuce". As with all things in life, flying for a living involves tradeoffs. There are lots of ways to make a living without having to endure the rigors of military flying. But then, on the other hand, there are events that only people who choose to be professional aviators are privileged to see and experience. They are dramatic enough to be seared into memory and I would not have missed them for all the security in the world. They are to me the "images" of a lifetime in aviation.

Images

Why do people like to participate in this strange activity that makes inordinate demands on your mind and body? In my case, the drive to fly airplanes was even more puzzling because it was linked to flying fighters. My job in corporate aviation was great. It allowed me to make a good living while engaging in what some people would call a hobby. My corporate career was almost as long as my military career, 22 years versus 26. But when some one asks me what I did for a living, I invariably talk about being an Air Force officer and, not just a pilot, but a fighter pilot. This is not to denigrate other aviators, some of whom have tougher jobs than I had. Aerial refueling of a B-52, for example, strikes me as being pretty hard work. And the guy who landed his airliner in the Hudson, "Sully" Sullenberger, had a pretty tough day on the job, too. But my reflections about life as a pilot are shaped overwhelmingly by my time in the fighter cockpit as opposed to my many hours at the controls of other kinds of aircraft.

So, why then would a man suffer being cramped in a claustrophobic cockpit with a rubber mask strapped to his face and an inflatable "g" suit strangling his abdomen? Add to this the likelihood of a combat tour wherein you can be assured that every day when you get up in the morning to go to work you do so with the certain knowledge that there will be people trying to kill you while you're doing your job. To paraphrase one of the WWII fighter aces, there are among fighter pilots those who are going hunting and those who go fly with the certain knowledge that they will be hunted. I must have been a hunter because I never worried about it. But I knew of some who did worry. And they went anyway, which probably makes them more courageous than the rest of us. But back to the larger question of why men will do this and even fight for the opportunity to do it. They do it, in my opinion, because they love the peculiar, unique beauty of flight, especially flight in fighters. They are privileged to see things that most men never get to see. They see the "images" of flight. The best of those images, to me, are seen from the cramped confines of the fighter plane cockpit. Here are a few:

How many people have made a formation takeoff at night? I've made many, but only one has created the "image". The picture forever in my mind is a takeoff on a pitch-black night in an F-102 from Suffolk County Air Force Base in New York. I was the wingman and it was my first night formation takeoff in the "Deuce". The explosion of lead's afterburner was clearly audible in my cockpit despite the noise of my own burner igniting and the close fitting helmet covering my ears. But most impressive was the huge, blinding tail of fire behind lead's tailpipe that illuminated everything nearby. I felt that we were in command of a hellish storm of brute power that was barely contained! I was to make many more night formation takeoffs in F-100s and F-101s as well as the deuce. The same afterburning J-57 engines produced the same, always impressive, fiery display, but the original "image" is the one I reflect upon.

More commonplace is the image of a forced sunrise. Breaking out on top of an overcast into bright sunshine after being on the ground on a dreary day is, I think, one of the most uplifting experiences in aviation. I was a fully trained but not very experienced pilot when we were launched on an early morning scramble from Elmendorf Air Force Base, Alaska. The sun had not yet risen but the sodden overcast, which we entered just after wheels-up, was beginning to show just a touch of forbidding gray amidst the overwhelming blackness. Suddenly we broke out on top of a mattress of soft, billowy clouds, clouds that a moment earlier had been dark and forbidding, but were now a thing of sheer beauty. The sun, not yet risen for those below, had just begun to rise above the cottony bed of pure white, and produced small rainbows, adding to the spectacular display. I have since broken out above an overcast many times, and it never fails to thrill me with its awesome beauty. But that first time in an F-89 formed the lasting image that is imprinted on my memory.

One of my first missions in Vietnam provided my memory with the image of power. As the newest guy in the squadron I was flying number four in the four ship formation. We were each carrying four 750 pound bombs and I had never before seen that much explosive firepower in a group of airborne fighters. The sinister gray-green camouflage paint scheme of the F-100s made the formation look deadly but with a perverse sort of beauty. As we dove on the target the other F-100s looked tiny and insignificant when they pulled up from their dives, but the oily, black smoke from the bomb explosions bore testament to the awesome power they could unleash. The condensation trail "streamers" from the wingtips of each aircraft on its high "g" pull out completed the contrast. Oily, smoky, black explosions competing with the graceful white arcs of streamers, ugliness competing with beauty in another unforgotten image.

I'm tempted to describe some of the other images that fill my mind's eye whenever I think of the past:

-- *breaking out of a 200 foot ceiling, at night, in a snow storm*

-- *flying wing on a smooth pilot as he leads the flight through a graceful barrel roll*

-- *waiting your turn to re-fuel from a tanker when someone ahead of you is having trouble hooking up*

-- *and many, many more.*

But it's time to wrap this up. I said at the outset that I wasn't sure that I'd ever finish this autobiographic endeavor, and I'm a little surprised that I have. I'm surprised, too, that the recitation of events involved so little difficulty. The difficult part is the self-examination that writing down the events of your life entails. There are so many things that I should have probably done better or at least differently. Professionally, I was a pretty ordinary guy. I never set any records in aviation, never flew to the moon as did a few of my contemporaries. But there's not much that I had in my power to change, so there aren't too many regrets.

Marion, Still Smiling After More Than Half A Century Married To This Guy.

On the personal side, however, looking back makes me squirm a little in my writer's chair. I've touched on this before, but my number one job was to be a good husband and father, and I don't feel that I earned many bouquets for either job performance. I spent too much time in pursuit of the aviation career that I had planned out for myself and too little time with Marion and the three boys. My excuse stems from the Depression-era upbringing that I describe in the sketches of my family in the beginning of this journal. There is some truth to that. There's no doubt that security was a major part of the motivation for everything I did. But there's also the recognition that I could have made some other decisions that might have made things a lot easier for the most important thing in my life, my own family.

But, what's done is done. Marion, always having my back, disputes my mea culpa self-analysis. In her view my many absences, including the two years when I left her to cope with raising the boys on her own, were character-building exercises. She insists, correctly, that she was fully capable of guiding the domestic ship in my absence, and that the boys were afforded many opportunities they would not otherwise have had. They were able, for example, to get to know the core family at home, including all the cousins, aunts and uncles and the rest who would otherwise have remained anonymous to them. I'd very much like to believe that Marion's right. Maybe my blunders ended up being for the best, with the boys developing stronger characters and everything working out for the best. I think I'll assume that such is the case--we all like happy landings.

This began as a sort of historical record for the grandkids. Hopefully they or their kids and grandkids will find something of interest in this voice from the past. It's the portrait of one ordinary, but very lucky guy who was able to do exactly what he wanted to do with his life--that is, FLY.

It's one man's flight through life and it involved some turbulence and even a few lightning strikes. But occasional rough weather is part of the big flight plan, and all-in-all, it's been a helluva ride!

Index

47714053R00183

Made in the USA
Lexington, KY
12 December 2015